MIND OVER MATTER

WHY INTELLECTUAL CAPITAL IS THE CHIEF SOURCE OF WEALTH

RONALD J. BAKER

BICENTENNIAL
1807
WILEY
2007
BICENTENNIAL

JOHN WILEY & SONS, INC.

Library of Congress Cataloging-in-Publication Data:

ISBN-13: 978-0-470-053614

Printed in the United States of America.

10 9 8 7 6 5 4 3 2 1

To my TA,
Paul O'Byrne, an exceptional friend.
Why?
Parce que c'était lui, parce que c'était moi.

*Whatever your hand finds to do,
do it with all your might,
for in the grave, where you are going,
there is neither working
nor planning nor knowledge
nor wisdom.*
—*Ecclesiastes 9:10*

CONTENTS

Foreword   x
Preface   xiii
Acknowledgments   xix
About the Author   xxv
About this Book   xxvii

1   **Mind Over Materialism**   **1**
Do Trade Deficits Diminish Wealth?   6

2   **Mind Over Marxism**   **15**
Karl Marx, False Prophet   19
The Marginalist Revolution   22

3   **The Economy in Mind**   **29**
The Ash Heap of History   32
"Like a Chrysalis"   43

4   **A Flawed Theory—The Old Business Equation**   **47**
The Three Types of IC   49
Negative Intellectual Capital   51
"Analyzing" the Predominant Business Equation   52

5   **A Better Theory—The New Business Equation**   **59**
The New Theory   60
Cognitive Dissonance   63
Where Do Profits Come From?   69
Summary and Conclusions   72

6   **The Scarcest Resource of All**   **75**
Thomas Sowell and Friedrich Hayek on Knowledge   76
Information Wants to Be Free, Knowledge Isn't   80
Sapere Aude!   87

7 Ideas Have Consequences   **91**

New Growth Theory   93

8 The Characteristics of Intellectual Capital   **99**

Knowledge Is a Verb   100

Defining Intellectual Capital   104

9 Human Capitalism   **107**

The More Human the Capital, the Less We Can Measure It   112

We Know More Than We Can Tell   118

Karl Marx's Revenge   122

10 Knowledge Workers Are Volunteers   **125**

People Have Value, Not Jobs   130

Becoming a Lightning Rod for Talent   133

11 Developing and Inspiring Knowledge Workers   **139**

The Scientific Management Revolution   142

What, Exactly, is Productivity?   148

A Framework for Knowledge Worker Effectiveness   151

Far Fewer Knowledge Workers Than We Think?   156

Sample Knowledge Organizations   161

Personality Testing and Performance Appraisals   166

The Importance of Continuing Education   173

What about Work-Life Balance?   178

Negative Human Capital   182

Summary and Conclusions   184

12 Structural Capital: If Only We Knew What We Know   **187**

The Economics of Structural Capital   190

Leveraging IC and Creating the World's Second Largest Currency 199

Knowledge Lessons from the U.S. Army   202

Summary and Conclusions   211

13 Social Capital: No Man is an Island   **213**

Is There Any Accounting for Tastes?   218

Leveraging Social Capital   221

Customers   222

Reputation and Brands 224
Referral Sources and Networks 226
Suppliers and Vendors 228
Shareholders and Other External Stakeholders 229
Joint Venture Partners and Alliances 230
Industry Associations and Formal Affiliations 232
Alumni 233
Unions 234
Corporate Universities 236
Open Source—Mass Collaboration 244
Cultural, Moral, and Ethical Capital 251
Putting All Your Social Capital Together: The Concierge Service
   Model 254
Summary and Conclusions 258

14 Knowledge versus Beliefs **259**
Profits Come from Risk and Uncertainty 262
Debits Don't Equal Credits 268
Financial Model Reform 277
Summary and Conclusions 283

15 Purpose **285**
Vocation: What Is Calling You? 288
Continuously Develop Your Intellectual Capital 295
Adventure 296
Leaving a Legacy 300

Bibliography **303**
Suggested Reading **315**
Additional Resources **329**
Index **333**

FOREWORD

I first met Ron Baker in May 2006 at an Association of National Advertisers conference, where he was speaking to a group of CFOs and procurement managers from both advertisers and agencies. Ron was explaining in no uncertain terms how their business of creating and using advertising was being severely limited by the way they measure and account for their services and intellectual capital. You could hear a pin drop! You could see many of the CFOs, from both advertisers and agencies alike, squirming in their seats. Ron talked of value pricing, no time sheets, no detailed task oversight, and no examining each other's costs and profits. Many were probably questioning who this man was and wondering if perhaps he had landed in the wrong room.

But to me, his point of view, his approach, was refreshing. In the crowded room, it was as if he were speaking only to me, challenging the beliefs of the new world I had just joined. You see, I had just assumed the responsibility for agency compensation systems at the world's leading advertiser, Procter & Gamble. I had come into a world that was a bit of a mystery to me—the world of agency/client compensation and deep relationships. My career at P&G had started with learning about process systems and people in our manufacturing operation. I then moved to Finance, learning about budgets, accounting, and portfolio analysis; and then most recently I had led Human Resources for Finance & Accounting, focusing on how to develop new, breakthrough ways of attracting, developing, and training our men and women in Finance and Accounting.

So for me, hearing Ron's talk, only three months after taking this new role, gave me hope that there is a better way to manage the compensation between us and our agencies that truly unleashes the creativity of our agencies and our brand builders.

I devoured Ron's first book in the Intellectual Capitalism Series, *Pricing on Purpose*, and it became the oft-quoted resource in my discussions with our chief marketing officer and our agency leaders. Then his next work, *Measure What Matters to Customers*, hit at exactly the time that we started thinking about our way forward in the area of agency compensation. His latest work, *Mind Over Matter*, again comes at a time when it's most needed for me. In this latest work, Ron does a masterful job of weaving the key learning from his first two books in the Intellectual Capitalism Series, and builds upon them to explore the vitally important role of people, behaviors, and society in the business world.

I feel this latest book differs in some ways from his earlier works. Ron has come a long way since his days in the accounting practice of KPMG. In my opinion, this book showcases Ron in a role he has played for me, as an executive coach and mentor. *Mind Over Matter* does a wonderful job of helping the reader understand the essential side of our work to inspire and stimulate those in the knowledge worker environment in which we operate. He brings simple, compelling lines of reasoning to the issues we face today in terms of attracting, motivating, energizing, and empowering the people both inside and outside who touch our organizations.

I was struck by his discussion and research in the chapters "Human Capitalism" (Chapter 9), "Knowledge Workers Are Volunteers" (Chapter 10), and "Developing and Inspiring Knowledge Workers" (Chapter 11). Much of his research rings true for me and has reinforced my learning while working to develop and inspire our knowledge workers in Finance and Accounting at P&G.

However, the chapter that impacted me the greatest and caused me to challenge my thinking and work, is Chapter 13, "Social Capital." In many ways our agency partners are knowledge firms who help us develop and preserve the equity of our brands. One of his closing comments in this chapter conveys what we want to achieve with our partners, "... leverage this inexhaustible source of intellectual capital to create value for everyone who comes into its sphere of influence ... and improve the quality of its social, not to mention its financial life. ..."

Again, I feel that Ron is writing this book to me—personally—to coach me, inspire me, bolster and challenge me to continue our path to find a way to unleash the significant intellectual capital that exists in my company and in our agency partners to help us continue our journey of "Touching Lives, Improving Life" at P&G.

Read, enjoy, but be careful—you too might become one of Baker's disciples!

Richard C. DelCore
Director of Finance—Global Marketing
Procter & Gamble

PREFACE

A moment's insight is sometimes worth a life's experience.
—Oliver Wendell Holmes, The Professor
at the Breakfast Table, 1859

I gradually became aware of a chink in the armor of accounting in 1981, my sophomore year in college. I was studying to become a certified public accountant, believing it would allow me to do anything I wanted in the world of commerce since everyone kept telling me it was the language of business. I was being taught the importance of proper accounting in operating a successful enterprise, from the definition of profit to the necessity of cash flow. It was a body of knowledge, a tangible reality I could grasp, a prism in which the world of enterprise I so admired could be refracted so as to make sense to a naïve student who believed he knew more than he did.

One of the problems with education is the constant pursuit of practical knowledge at the expense of pursuing answers to profound questions. No doubt we all need practical knowledge to function in everyday life, earn a living, to just get by in the world. But I now realize people are not guided by what they *know*, but rather what they *believe*—their worldview, through which we all refract reality. And in August of 1981, my worldview was about to be punctured permanently, albeit quite gradually, indeed, imperceptibly at the time. Looking back, *Playboy* magazine may be most responsible.

No, not for the prurient reasons you are forgiven for immediately thinking of, but a far more banal explanation. As a barber, my father was an inveterate reader of *Playboy*'s interviews, which are excellent if you have ever bothered to read one with someone in whom you have an interest. The roster of interviewees is quite impressive—world leaders, politicians, writers, and so forth—some of whom, no doubt, are self conscious about appearing in such a publication. As a matter of fact, when devout Catholic William F. Buckley Jr. was asked why he would write for such a magazine, he wittily answered, "I write for *Playboy* because it is the fastest way to communicate with my 17-year-old son."

In any event, my father read the interview with George Gilder in that August 1981 issue, which impressed him. Gilder had written *Wealth and Poverty*, a book Ronald Reagan was photographed with, along with giving it to members of his cabinet. It is little remembered, but Reagan had a degree in economics from Eureka College, translating into a lifelong fascination with the writings of economic thinkers. For some reason, my father was impressed with the Gilder interview, explaining to me over lunch how this author had read over 200 books to write his, and was being hailed as the most articulate, albeit amateur, supply-side economist in the country. Needless to say, I was not too impressed, pompously explaining to my dad how there are many crackpots who write economics books, most of which are useless, wrong, or belong in the fiction section of bookstores. I was mired in the mentality that only academic credentials lend credence to anyone writing on economics. Sure, Gilder may have been a graduate of Harvard, but he was not a professional economist such as Milton Friedman, whose book *Free to Choose* I had read the year before, which made a lasting impression on my worldview.

Fortunately for me, my father persisted, purchasing a copy of Gilder's book, convincingly insisting I should read it. I did. In one sitting. It changed my life. It opened my eyes to an entire new worldview that is beyond my capacity to describe in so brief a space. Little did I understand, but that was the sound of the first chink in the armor. The next chink came in 1982, when I read Warren T. Brookes's book, *The Economy in Mind*, the title of which you will see mentioned again in Chapter 3, in a more historical setting.

Mind Over Matter brings me full circle to that first sitting of reading Gilder's penetrating insights. It is a journey I have partially written about in the Prefaces of the first two books in the Intellectual Capitalism Series, illuminating the opportunity cost of the accounting career I chose, which was the road not taken—that of the economist. I traded away, for the ability to capture and record the historical cost of everything, an understanding of the nature and origins of value, wealth, and poverty. It was not until later in my career, after I left the then–Big Eight accounting firm of KPMG that I understood this opportunity cost was increasingly becoming prohibitive.

I came to recognize I was ensconced in the accountant's worldview, a belief system and body of knowledge that cannot really explain how wealth is created—it can only record it after the fact. Accounting is not a theory, so it cannot help us peer into the future; it can only provide assurance on the past. It understands nothing but itself, since it is an identity equation. Worse, it leads businesspeople to believe they can only manage what they can measure, as if weighing ourselves more frequently will change our weight. It confuses cause and effect, and results with process. It can audit the drunk's bar bill, but cannot change or explain his behavior. Even more pernicious, it focuses businesspeople on solving problems and fretting over yesterday, rather than pursuing opportunities and creating our futures, resulting in a costly mediocrity.

I will always remember a conversation I was having over the audit of a genetic laboratory customer we had at KPMG, one that was working on a cure for AIDS. Of course, the losses in this start-up were as illustrious as the scientific credentials of its shareholders and board members. As we were poring over the balance sheet—bayoneting the wounded after the battle, as it were—I turned to my senior manager and said, "But you realize the most important assets of this company will never appear on its balance sheet, such as the intangibles of its employees and its entrepreneurial spirit." I didn't use the terms *intellectual* or *human capital* back then, since an accountant's world is divided neatly into tangible versus intangible. Nevertheless, the manager cocked his head, giving me one of those RCA Victrola dog looks, and said, "That's an excellent insight." I scored big points with that sagacity, impressing my superiors, but it was at the expense of my accounting worldview. Chink, crack. The armor was in scraps.

Thus began a passionate study of value, effectiveness, intellectual capital, along with the real source of profits, all represented in the new business equation that each book in the Intellectual Capitalism Series expounds upon. The philosopher Heraclitus wrote, "You cannot step in the same river twice, because by the second step it will already have changed." Thus began my crossing of the river to reach the other side, seeing the world from a different direction—one of value, opportunity, and risk taking, rather than history, costs, problem solving, and an increasingly irrelevant accounting equation. I must say, this side of the river is more wondrous and panoramic, allowing me to explain to myself with much greater clarity how the world really works. This is the only reason I write books—to help me explain the world I live in, while helping me think and constantly challenge my beliefs, subjecting them to the empirical test of reality.

It was not until the early 1990s that I began to fully comprehend that we had shifted from a service to a knowledge economy, comprised of knowledge workers who are different from industrial or service workers of a bygone era. They now comprise some 30 percent of the labor force (up from about 17 percent in 1950), but create the overwhelming majority of the value for most organizations. This is a lesson I am painfully reminded of every day, that my colleagues in professional knowledge firms have *still not learned*. They are walking around with an errant worldview, at a cost that is simply incalculable. If my books can challenge that worldview, even if only in an infinitesimal way relative to what Gilder's did to mine, they will have achieved their purpose.

To tie all these synchronous events together, bringing me full circle back to that first reading of Gilder's *Wealth and Poverty*, I was thunderstruck when I read the afterword to Gilder's book *Men and Marriage* in the early 1990s, titled "The Faith of Fathers." Gilder explains that he never knew his father, a bomber pilot who was killed in World War II. The day after Gilder received the first bound copies of his *Wealth and Poverty* manuscript, an uncle told him about a box he came across in his attic of some of his father's papers. Here is Gilder, explaining what he happened upon in those papers:

> I eagerly went through them; at the top was a 175-page manuscript on economics that he was working on when he died. One of its themes was the importance of what he called "intangible capital." It corresponded nearly perfectly with the key message of *Wealth and Poverty*: that the driving force of a free economy was not material resources or even physical capital, but the metaphysical capital of family and faith. In fact, my father's work, if it had been completed, could very well have been entitled *Wealth and Poverty* (Gilder 1986: 192–193).

Gilder goes on to explain the ultimate source of wealth, which is an outstanding inauguration to our journey together:

> Demand, whether avaricious or just, is impotent to impel growth without disciplined, creative, and essentially moral producers of new value. All effective demand ultimately derives from supply; a society's income cannot exceed its output. The output of valuable goods depends not on lechery, prurience, lust, and license but on thrift, sacrifice, altruism, creativity, discipline, trust, and faith (Gilder 1986: 196).
>
> Greed, in fact, impels people to seek first their own comfort and security. The truly self-interested man most often turns to government to give him the benefits he lacked the moral discipline to earn on his own by serving others. ... Any system that does not uphold the value of freedom of individuals, however lowly, will miss most of the greatest technical and economic breakthroughs (Gilder 1986: 197).

I suppose all sons, at one time or another, come to appreciate the wisdom of Mark Twain: "When I was a boy of fourteen, my father was so ignorant I could hardly stand to have the old man around. But when I got to be twenty-one, I was astonished at how much he had learned." Thanks, Dad.

Peter Drucker, another mentor, was once asked why business-people fall for fads and fail to use empirical evidence, to which he replied: "Thinking is very hard work. And management fashions are a wonderful substitute for thinking." By and large, people do not engage in an endless search for the truth; they are busy trying to maximize utility. My books are written not so that you will think *like* me, but *with* me. But think you must, subjecting everything I say to your own belief system, challenging and discarding what you think is wrong, while acknowledging what may be right. Think of this book as a conversation between us; but you, dear reader, have the last word.

Ronald J. Baker
Petaluma, California
April 24, 2007

ACKNOWLEDGMENTS

How infinitesimal is the importance of anything I do, but how
infinitely important it is that I do it.
—*Voltaire*

This book is the physical embodiment of structural capital—one
of the three types of intellectual capital it explores—but it is the
product of an astounding collection of human and social capital. Once again, I have stood on the shoulders of giants, who
have helped me see the world as it is and form my beliefs on
why intellectual capital is the chief source of wealth. Some of
these giants have been absent teachers, educating me through
their books. Most, though, I have had the great good fortune of
meeting and working with. All deserve mention, all the while
recognizing Reinhold Niebuhr's warning: "There is always some
truth in the errors of others and some error in my truth." I, as
always, accept the final responsibility for any and all errors that
remain.

Writing, as opposed to researching, a book is a very soli-
tary undertaking. One has no way of knowing if the topics and
expression will resonate with anyone, until you have a chance
to—borrowing from Winston Churchill—"fling it about to the
public." I have the luxury of first flinging it at my colleagues
and other thought leaders, who always provide cogent critiques
and improve the final product. This book was no exception.
Much thanks to Peter Byers, Rich DelCore, Reed Holden, Sheila
Kessler, Ed Kless, and Paul O'Byrne for reviewing the rather
chaotic manuscript and contributing your insights, wisdom, and
tacit knowledge.

Untold gratitude must go to George Gilder for conducting an interview with *Playboy* that a barber read and was so inspired by, he purchased your book for his stubborn son, changing the boy's life forever after. Gilder has taught me mind over matter, mind over materialism, and mind over Marxism, with eloquence and logic without equal. His book *Wealth and Poverty* created the desire in me to write my own. His teachings on the morality of capitalism—especially his May 1997 speech to the Vatican, "The Soul of Silicon"—should be required reading for anyone who doubts the morality of free minds operating in free markets. Gilder is the Adam Smith of the twentieth and twenty-first centuries.

Many other economists have contributed to my understanding of intellectual capital: Warren T. Brookes, a former economics columnist for the *Boston Herald-American* and author of *The Economy in Mind*, a book that got me in trouble for being read at my desk—in a supposed knowledge organization—and the inspiration for Chapter 3. Former President Ronald Reagan, who cited Brookes's book in his speech at Moscow State University, has also contributed to my worldview. Many people forget that Reagan graduated from Eureka College with a degree in economics and was an inveterate reader of economic thinkers, including calling on Milton Friedman for counsel and distributing Gilder's *Wealth and Poverty* to his cabinet. Friedrich Hayek, probably one of the most consequential economists and political philosophers of the twentieth century, was writing cogently about how markets capture, create, and disseminate knowledge in the most valuable manner long before anyone else. Hayek inspired Thomas Sowell, another economic genius, to write his seminal *Knowledge and Decisions*, which taught me why knowledge is critical to creating wealth. Milton Friedman, RIP, along with Gilder, was my first introduction to economics, leaving an indelible impression on a young mind devoted to liberty. Gary Becker, one of Friedman's students, has also taught me much about the importance of human and social capital through his writings. Michael Novak, another of my favorite authors, has advanced the ethical argument that business enterprises are serious moral undertakings.

Of course, Peter Drucker, who introduced the terms *knowledge worker* and *knowledge economy* into the business lexicon over 45 years ago, has been a constant source of inspiration, teaching me the essentials of business without the fads, jargon, and unnecessary complexity of most business writers. Drucker had the rare gift of being simple while not being simplistic.

Karl Erik Sveiby is a pioneer in the area of intellectual capital, and the creator of the framework used in this work—breaking out intellectual capital into human, structural, and social. Thomas A. Stewart, a former writer for *Fortune* and now editor of *Harvard Business Review*, also contributed to my thinking with his two fine books on the topic.

Even though I am not Jewish, I am proud to have my very own rabbi—Daniel Lapin. His grasp of human behavior is astounding, his book *Thou Shall Prosper* is profound, and he was the inspiration for Chapter 14. Thank you, Rabbi.

In *The Structure of Scientific Revolutions*, Thomas Kuhn puts the question succinctly: "Suppose some well-trained young persons working in a discipline have a big idea in the nighttime; they propose a new interpretation of a problem that heretofore has defied resolution. How are they able, what must they do, to convert the entire profession ... to their way of seeing science and the world?" This is the very question my colleagues at VeraSage Institute ask themselves every single day, and while we may not have a definitive answer, we do know that change comes from influencing people one at a time. To the thousands of our colleagues around the world—in all kinds of professional knowledge firms from accounting to technology—thank you for listening to us rant and rave against the present orthodoxies, then having the courage and tenacity to test, apply, prove, and falsify our theories, all of which lead to better theories.

The entire team at the California CPA Education Foundation continues to take risks by allowing us to create and teach innovative new educational courses, which is a laboratory to test and refine so much of our thinking. Thank you, John Dunleavy (now retired), Kurtis Docken, Laura Ritter, Kay Phelan, and the rest of the crew for being such strong supporters of our work. Also, thank you to Tom Hood and his team at the Maryland Association of CPAs, and the Business Learning Institute, for recognizing the accounting profession is sorely in need of new ideas and fresh approaches if it is to remain relevant in an intellectual capital economy.

Eric Mitchell, president of Professional Pricing Society, deserves special thanks for continuing to put the discipline of pricing on the organizational charts in businesses around the world and for continuously supporting our work.

I am proud to know and have as my mentor Reed Holden. He constantly challenges my thinking, being gracious and patient enough not to knock out his very junior sparring partner on those rare occasions when we disagree. The logician Hilary Putnam once proposed the following test for a philosophical classic that I believe describes my relationship with Reed: "The smarter you get, the smarter it gets." Reed was kind enough to send me a copy of his first book, *On Orion's Shoulder*, a story about his father, which is deeply moving, containing much wisdom. I will cherish it, as I do our friendship.

Another of my mentors is Sheila Kessler, who has been a constant source of insights and wisdom regarding organizational functionality and dysfunctionality. I always learn so much from our exchanges, while Sheila is always gracious with her time in providing feedback on my manuscripts.

Much gratitude to Rich DelCore, director of finance, Global Marketing, Procter & Gamble, for taking time out of his incredibly busy schedule to write the Foreword to this book, and for challenging Tim Williams and me on our LIVE Model, advancing immeasurably our thinking and presentation. Rich is a true thought leader who understands the value of cognitive dissonance and being challenged to the point of becoming "uncomfortable."

Many thanks to Ron Crone, Paul Dunn, Mark Koziel, Michael McCulloch, Bill Mees, Ed Miller, Shirley Nakawatase, and Ric and Kerry Payne, colleagues who engage me professionally and—since Cicero said your friends are a second self—whose camaraderie I am blessed with every day.

David Hume said "Truth springs from arguments amongst friends." My colleagues at VeraSage Institute prove this axiom every day as we battle in the marketplace of ideas. Though we may not agree on everything, we have joined together to further our common quest of recognizing that professional service firms are really professional knowledge firms that create and sell intellectual capital, while its employees are human capital, not cattle. Each and every one of these individuals is a thought leader, enormously creative, intelligent, and committed to bettering their respective profession for posterity. I'm grateful beyond words for having the privilege to associate with them, and wish to extend my heartfelt thanks to Scott Abbott, Justin Barnett, Peter Byers, Michelle Golden, Daryl Golemb, Brendon Harrex, Paul Kennedy, Ed Kless, Christopher Marston, Tim McKey, Dan Morris, Paul O'Byrne, Tim Williams, and Yan Zhu.

Special thanks to Michelle Golden, our latest Cassandra, who has spread our ideas around the world with her passion for ideaphoria and blogging. Ed Kless for continuing to improve the presentation of our ideas. Peter Byers for his warm friendship who continues, in his gentle way, to shake the world down under. Paul Kennedy, who in his own Promethean way has adopted many of these ideas into his firm's knowledge bank, not to mention with the consulting work he performs with his customers, constantly adding to our never-ending knowledge creep. Our newest senior fellow, Tim Williams, has transferred much tacit knowledge to me about the advertising world, especially with his inspired improvements to the revolutionary LIVE Model, which Tim has successfully implemented with his own customers.

Ralph Waldo Emerson wrote in *Character*: "A chief event of life is the day in which we have encountered a mind that startled us." This aptly describes my colleague, Dan Morris, whose mind is like a thunderbolt—you never know when it is going to strike genius. Thank you, Dan, for constantly challenging the conventional wisdom and even some of my fervent beliefs.

When British chemist Michael Faraday was asked after a lecture if he meant to imply that a hated academic rival was always wrong, he snarled, "He's not that consistent." I'm sure this is how my British trusted adviser, Paul O'Byrne, feels about some of my economic viewpoints. It was Paul's idea for me to write the Intellectual Capitalism Series, though I am sure he denounces the second word in its title. Even though I know he does not agree with everything in this *vade mecum*, there is no more appropriate work of mine to dedicate to him that expresses my great good fortune of being able to call Paul a dear friend.

Elbert Hubbard wrote in 1923 that the job of an editor is to "separate the wheat from the chaff, and to see that the chaff is printed," which is the exact opposite of the results the talented team at John Wiley & Sons, Inc. produces. Thank you, John DeRemigis, Judy Howarth, Natasha Wolfe, and Susan Cooper for giving birth to this third book in the Intellectual Capitalism Series, at the same time as I missed every one of my deadlines.

Ambrose Bierce once wrote in a book review "The covers of this book are too far apart," a reaction I know my brother, Ken Baker, would undoubtedly agree with. Nevertheless, he remains an indefatigable supporter of my work and the best brother I could ever have asked for.

Anytime I receive an introduction that is far too generous, I am reminded of what President Lyndon Johnson used to say on similar occasions: "My father would have enjoyed it and my mother would have believed it." Fortunately for me, this is still—undeservedly—true, since my parents have been a constant source of encouragement and faith in the future.

ABOUT THE AUTHOR

Ronald J. Baker started his career in 1984 with KPMG's Private Business Advisory Services in San Francisco. Today, he is the founder of VeraSage Institute, a think tank dedicated to educating businesspeople around the world.

As a frequent speaker, writer, and educator, his work takes him around the world. He has been an instructor with the California CPA Education Foundation since 1995 and has authored 13 courses for them: How to Build a Successful Practice with Total Quality Service; The Shift from Hourly Billing to Value Pricing; Value Pricing Graduate Seminar; You Are What You Charge For: Success in Today's Emerging Experience Economy (with Daniel Morris); Alternatives to the Federal Income Tax; Trashing the Timesheet: A Declaration of Independence; Everyday Economics; The Firm of the Future; Everyday Ethics: Doing Well by Doing Good (with Daniel Morris); The New Business Equation for Industry Executives; Specialists Make More Money (with Michelle Golden); When Debits Don't Equal Credits (with Daniel Morris); and Implementing the Risk Assessment Standards: Skills for the Engagement Team (with Daniel Morris).

He is the author of the best-selling marketing book ever written specifically for professional knowledge firms, *Professional's Guide to Value Pricing* (6th edition), published by CCH, Inc. He also wrote *Burying the Billable Hour*, *Trashing the Timesheet*, and *You Are Your Customer List*, published by the Association of Chartered Certified Accountants in the United Kingdom (available at www.verasage.com). His book *The Firm of the Future: A Guide for Accountants, Lawyers, and Other Professional Services*, co-authored with Paul Dunn, was published in April 2003 by John Wiley & Sons, Inc. His most recent books, the first and second, respectively, in the Intellectual Capitalism Series, *Pricing on Purpose: Creating and Capturing Value* was published in February 2006, and *Measure What Matters to Customers: Using Key Predictive Indicators* was published in September 2006, both by John Wiley & Sons, Inc.

Ron has toured the world, spreading his value-pricing message to over 80,000 businesspeople. He has been appointed to the American Institute of Certified Public Accountants' Group of One Hundred, a think tank of leaders to address the future of the profession; named on *Accounting Today's* 2001, 2002, 2003, 2004, 2005, and 2006 Top 100 Most Influential People in the profession; and received the 2003 Award for Instructor Excellence from the California CPA Education Foundation.

He graduated in 1984 from San Francisco State University, with a bachelor of science degree in accounting and a minor in economics. He is a graduate of Disney University and Cato University, and is a member of the Professional Pricing Society. He presently resides in Petaluma, California.

To contact Ron Baker:
VeraSage Institute
Phone: (707) 769-0965
E-mail: Ron@verasage.com
Web site: www.verasage.com and www.verasage.co.nz

ABOUT THIS BOOK

Mind Over Matter is the third book in the Intellectual Capitalism Series. The entire Series centers around the reality that we now live in a knowledge—or intellectual capital—economy. As such, the old business equation needs to be replaced with the new business equation, as follows:

$$\text{Profitability} = \text{Intellectual Capital} \times \text{Price} \times \text{Effectiveness}$$

The first book in the series, *Pricing on Purpose: Creating and Capturing Value*, explained the pricing component in the above equation. The second book in the series, *Measure What Matters to Customers: Using Key Predictive Indicators*, examined effectiveness and why it is far more important than efficiency in a knowledge economy. *Mind Over Matter* studies intellectual capital (IC) in great depth. Because all three works orbit around the same theory, there is some overlap in content.

Readers of either of the first two books may recognize Chapters 4 and 5 in this volume, and unless you need a quick review of the problems with the old equation, and the benefits of the new one, you can comfortably skip these two chapters (although the careful reader will notice some new content in each). For those who have read *Pricing on Purpose*, you will notice some duplicative material on the labor versus subjective theories of value in Chapters 1 and 2. Since these are such important theories from economics, especially in the context of value and wealth creation, I wanted to include them in this work as well, but analyzed in the context of intellectual capital rather than pricing for value.

For those who have read *Measure What Matters*, you will also note some duplicative material with respect to Frederick Taylor and Frank Gilbreth in Chapter 11. I felt it was necessary to reintroduce these two gentlemen, along with their theories, because I wanted to examine them through the lens of intellectual capital, not just from an efficiency versus effectiveness prospective.

For those who have not read any of the Series, but may have read *The Firm of the Future: A Guide for Accountants, Lawyers, and Other Professional Services*, coauthored with Paul Dunn, you will recognize not only the equations but also the three components of intellectual capital—human, structural, and social. However, much more new content has been added to each of these sections than the content I kept from that book. In addition, the Series is written for a more general business reader, not just those working in professional knowledge firms.

There is an extensive Bibliography included in this volume, as in all my prior books. Obviously, some books will be repeated. There are also books not cited in the text, but included in the Bibliography, because they were a vital part of my research.

A Suggested Reading list is included as well, alphabetized by author—since the citations in the text are also by author and year—and every book included in it is also listed in the Bibliography, to make it easier to locate for those who wish to find the original source.

I have also included a Resources section, which is organized by chapter, to present additional online resources I found valuable while researching and writing this book. There are additional online sources cited in the text as well.

1

MIND OVER MATERIALISM

The United States must overcome the materialist fallacy: the illusion
that resources and capital are essentially things, which can run out,
rather than products of human will and imagination which in freedom
are inexhaustible. This fallacy is one of the oldest of economic
delusions, from the period of empire when men believed that wealth
was land, to the period of mercantilism when they fantasized that it
was gold, to the contemporary period when they suppose it is oil; and
our citizens clutch at real estate and gold as well. But economists
make an only slightly lesser error when they add up capital in
quantities and assume that wealth consists mainly in machines and
factories. Throughout history, from Venice to Hong Kong, the fastest
growing countries have been the lands best endowed not with things
but with free minds and private rights to property. Two of the most
thriving of the world's economies lost nearly all their material capital
during World War II and surged back by emancipating entrepreneurs.
The materialist vision, by contrast, leads merely to newer versions of
the fate of Midas.

—*George Gilder, Wealth and Poverty, 1981*

There is no such thing as a natural resource, except for the mind of
man. For centuries, economists have been exposing the "physical
fallacy"—that is, the belief that wealth resides in tangible things,
such as gold, land, raw materials, and so forth—and it seems as if
we still do not understand this basic economic concept. We seem
to think that *matter* is more important than *minds*, while in fact it

1

is the exact opposite. Natural resource endowment cannot explain why Israel has a per capita gross domestic product of $17,220 compared to Saudi Arabia's $8,870. Taiwan, Hong Kong, and Singapore have no "natural resources," and yet they all have a higher standard of living than Russia and Indonesia, both rich in natural resources.

Even the conventional wisdom recited by every realtor—location, location, location—does not explain how it came to be that the 27,400 acres of Florida swampland purchased by Walt Disney in 1964, at an average price of $182 per acre, are now worth over $2 million per acre. No doubt no more land is being created, yet scarcity does not explain wealth. If it did, your children's drawings on your refrigerator would be worth at least a few months of mortgage payments.

Adam Smith (see Exhibit 1.1) brought this profound insight into his seminal book *An Inquiry into the Nature and Causes of the Wealth of Nations* (1776). He wanted to explain why some countries were wealthy, not why most countries were poor (notice the title wasn't *An Inquiry into the Nature and Causes of the Poverty of Nations*). Poverty needs no explanation, nor do we learn much from studying it, since it is the natural condition of man since he emerged from the cave. What would we do once we discovered the *root causes* of poverty? Create more of it? What needs to be explained is *wealth*, not poverty. Indeed, wealth is the only known antidote to poverty.

Smith exposed the mercantile system fallacy, commonly accepted from 1500 to 1750, that wealth consisted of money, gold, silver, and other physical representations of capital. Although mercantilism wasn't a unified economic theory of growth, it did hold sway over government officials and merchants, who were its leading advocates. The word itself comes from the Latin word *mercare*, which means "to run a trade." Not only did the mercantilists see hoarding bullion as the road to wealth, they also believed the global volume of trade is fixed. Hence, all trade becomes a zero-sum proposition—a gain in one country is a loss in the other. This led the mercantilists to believe another road to wealth was a positive balance of trade, whereby the exports of a country always exceed its imports overall. To achieve this surplus, a country was wise to impose tariffs on imports, or other protectionist policies to protect its domestic industries, in order to subsidize exports and discourage imports. The advent of double-entry bookkeeping assisted governments with accounting for this inflow and outflow of goods and services, an obsession that continues to this day.

No less a leader than Mohandas Gandhi subscribed to these views, symbolized by his proposed Indian flag with a 24-spoked blue *chakra* (wheel) in the center, representing economic self-sufficiency. Gandhi was certainly an inspiring leader, but he was a dreadful economist. The jack-of-all trades would lead a poor, nasty, brutal, and short life. Not only would he remain impecunious by attempting complete economic self-sufficiency—what economists call *autarky*—so would an entire country.

Adam Smith's work was largely a refutation of these suppositions, while also establishing a framework for how an economy creates wealth. In the introduction to his *Wealth of Nations*, Smith puts forth his definition of the real wealth in an economy:

> The annual labour of every nation is the fund which originally supplies it with all the necessaries and conveniences of life which it annually consumes, and which consist always either in the immediate produce of that labour, or in what is purchased with that produce from other nations (Smith 1998: xv).

In effect, the welfare of a nation depended on its output of production, and production itself is dependent on the specialization and division of labor. Smith intuitively understood that man was the only creature possessing the capacity to produce more of a good or service than he himself could consume to satisfy his own needs. After producing a surplus, he would then follow "a certain propensity in human nature to truck, barter, and exchange one thing for another," a trait "common to all men." This is one of

EXHIBIT 1.1   THE GRAVESITE OF ADAM SMITH (1723–1790), EDINBURGH,
SCOTLAND. "I LOVE YOUR COMPANY, GENTLEMEN, BUT
I BELIEVE I MUST LEAVE YOU TO GO TO ANOTHER WORLD"
(SMITH'S LAST WORDS TO HIS FRIENDS).

Source: Photo by Paul O'Byrne

many characteristics distinguishing humans from animals, since
"Nobody ever saw a dog make as fair and deliberate exchange
of one bone for another with another dog" (Cohen 2001: 21).

Smith demonstrated how his ideas of specialization and division of labor created these surpluses available for exchange. Specialization of labor is the idea of people or nations producing a
narrower range of goods and services than they consume, which
is why modern economies are dependent on a far wider range

of people to provide for their daily sustenance. The division of labor breaks down a production process into many small steps and performs those steps separately, with different workers doing different tasks, as on an assembly line. In Smith's view, while specialization makes us productive, division of labor is what makes us rich. He illustrated these principles with his famous example of the operation of a pin factory:

> One man draws out the wire, another straightens it, a third cuts it, a fourth points it, a fifth grinds it at the top for receiving the head; to make the head requires two or three distinct operations; to put it on is a peculiar business; to whiten it is another; it is even a trade by itself to put them into paper. ... I have seen a small manufactory of this kind where ten men only were employed and where some of them performed two or three distinct operations. But though they were very poor, and therefore but indifferently accommodated with the necessary machinery, they could, when they exerted themselves, make among them about twelve pounds of pins a day. There are in a pound upwards of four thousand pins of a middling size. Those ten persons, therefore, could make among them upwards of forty-eight thousand pins in a day....But if they had all wrought separately and independently...they certainly could not each of them make twenty...perhaps not one pin a day (Dougherty 2002: 53).

Similar to Smith's tour of the pin factory, Henry Ford had a similar epiphany when touring a Chicago meatpacking plant, where he saw animal carcasses hung on an overhead rail being moved from butcher to butcher. When Ford inquired how long they had been processing meat like this, the reply was something to the effect that, "This is how we have done it for years." A tradition in one industry became a quantum revolution in another.

Smith also refuted the mercantilist idea of bullion being the true wealth of nations, writing:

> To attempt to increase the wealth of any country, either by introducing or by detaining in it an unnecessary quantity of gold and silver, is as absurd as it would be to attempt to increase the good

cheer of private families, by obliging them to keep an unnecessary number of kitchen utensils (O'Rourke 2007: 205).

Money is not wealth per se, it is merely how members of a society move it around. Money simply facilitates transactions, eliminating the need for a "double coincidence of wants" necessary in a barter economy. With money, a doctor doesn't have to spend time searching for a hairstylist that needs medical services at the same time she needs a haircut.

Real wealth is represented by the goods and services money can buy. If it were otherwise, any country could achieve wealth simply by printing more pieces of paper money. Hoarding precious metals is not a substitute for real wealth in an economy; otherwise, India, which had the world's largest supply of gold in 2003, would be one of the richest nations; yet it is actually one of the poorest. Perhaps this is better understood if we think of Nathan Mayer Rothschild, one of the founders of the international Rothschild banking dynasty, probably the richest man in the world at the time of his premature death in 1836 at the age of 58 from an infected abscess. Despite having the best medical care money could buy, he didn't have access to antibiotics that today could be purchased from any pharmacy for a few dollars. Would you rather have Bill Gates's income in today's world—with its abundance of goods and services—or during the time of Rothschild? Another way of articulating this is that the wealth of nations resides in consumer well-being, not profits.

DO TRADE DEFICITS DIMINISH WEALTH?

What happens when one country's imports consistently exceed its exports, creating a deficit in the international balance of trade? There is probably no greater misunderstanding about the real nature of wealth than when a discussion turns to the balance-of-trade question. Henry Hazlitt, author of *Economics in One Lesson* explained this phenomenon when he wrote: ". . . the same people who can be clearheaded and sensible when the subject is one of domestic trade can be incredibly emotional and muddleheaded when it becomes one of foreign trade" (Hazlitt 1979: 86–87).

I recently taught an economics course to a group of learned certified public accountants, and this one topic was the most contentious. Most everyone seemed to have an inordinate fear of China, India, and other foreign nations accumulating more and more of America's debt. I asked the group a simple question: If China and India become wealthier, is that a threat to America? The general consensus seemed to be yes, illustrating how zero-sum thinking is endemic to this discussion. Adam Smith eloquently wrote about this in 1776:

> Each nation has been made to look with an invidious eye upon the prosperity of all the nations with which it trades, and to consider their gain as its own loss. Commerce, which ought naturally to be, among nations, as among individuals, a bond of union and friendship, has become the most fertile source of discord and animosity (O'Rourke 2007: 108).

One of the reasons the United States of America is such a relatively wealthy country is that it maintains a free trade zone among its 50 states. The Constitution prohibits the states from interfering with trade among their respective citizens; there are no tariffs or import, export, or other restrictions within the 50 states. No individual state worries if it is running a deficit with another. Economist Russell Roberts posed this challenging question in his delightful academic novel, *The Choice: A Fable of Free Trade and Protectionism*:

> Shouldn't Florida help out Minnesota by importing just as many oranges from Minnesota as Minnesota imports from Florida? Trade flows should be unequal. . . . if you pick any one state in the United States and look at its trade position with respect to other states, you'd see a lot of deficits and surpluses (Roberts 2001: 67).

Trade deficits and surpluses are merely accounting conventions with no explanatory relationship to the underlying reality of an economy, which is why accountants and economists have different worldviews. If a free trade zone works internally for the United States, why would it not work internationally among the countries of the world?

It helps to keep in mind that *countries* do not trade, *people* do. In any transaction, as Adam Smith pointed out, both parties must gain for it to take place at all—the antithesis to a zero-sum condition. You buy a Lexus only because you perceive it as being of higher value than the price you are paying. The government, for all practical purposes, has nothing to do with it. As individuals, we run trade surpluses and deficits all the time. I run a deficit with my local grocery store, importing more from them than I sell to them. You run a large surplus with your employer, who pays you more than you buy in products or services from them in return. So what? The resulting accounting deficits and surpluses simply do not reflect the economic reality behind these billions and billions of individual transactions around the world. This is what Adam Smith meant when he wrote, "Nothing can be more absurd than this whole doctrine of the balance of trade."

The gains from trade are what we import, not export. The purpose of production, in the final analysis, is consumption. The more imports we can acquire for fewer exports, the wealthier we are, either as individuals or as a country. Other countries face the same realities, and we are no more likely to obtain the goods and services we desire by trading pieces of green paper with other nations than we are to send letters to the North Pole and get gifts from Santa Claus. Being a creditor or debtor nation simply has no correlation with a country's standard of living. Thomas Sowell exposes this fallacious concept in *Basic Economics*:

> In general, international deficits and surpluses have had virtually no correlation with the performance of most nations' economies.

Germany and France have had international trade surpluses while their unemployment rates were in double digits. Japan's postwar rise to economic prominence on the world stage included years when it ran deficits, as well as years when it ran surpluses. The United States was the biggest debtor nation in the world during its rise to industrial supremacy, became a creditor as a result of lending money to its European allies during the First World War, and has been both a debtor and a creditor at various times since. Through it all, the American standard of living has remained the highest in the world, unaffected by whether it was a creditor or a debtor nation (Sowell 2000: 288).

No one revealed the specious reasoning behind balance-of-trade concerns better than the French economist, statesman, and author Frédéric Bastiat (1801–1850), whom the Austrian economist Joseph Schumpeter said was "the most brilliant economic journalist who ever lived." Bastiat used entertaining fables and carried the logic of the proponents of protectionism to their logical extreme, with biting wit. One of his most famous essays, "Petition of the Candlemakers," was a parody letter from the manufacturers of "candles, tapers, lanterns... and generally of everything connected with lighting," arguing against the unfair competition—since its price was zero—of the sun.

Bastiat understood that exports were merely the price we pay for imports, and having to work harder to pay for those imports did not lead to wealth. Using impeccable logic, Bastiat wondered if exports are good and imports are bad, would the best outcome be for the ships carrying goods between countries to sink at sea, hence creating exports with no imports?

In another of his famous parodies, "The Right Hand and the Left (a Report to the King)," he made this obvious in a most satirical and effective manner. It is such an important point, since it also debunks another famous economist's theory of value, it is worth quoting from at some length (see Sidebar).

Sire,

When we see the advocates of free trade boldly disseminating their doctrine, and maintaining that the right to buy and to sell is included in the right to own property..., we may quite properly feel serious concern about the fate of our domestic industry; for to what use will the French people put their hands and their minds when they live under a system of free trade?

The government that you have honored with your confidence has been obliged to concern itself with so grave a situation, and has sought in its wisdom to discover a means of protection that might be substituted for the present one, which seems endangered. They propose *that you forbid your loyal subjects to use their right hands.*

Sire, do not do us the injustice of thinking that we have lightly adopted a measure that at first sight may seem bizarre. Deep study of *the protectionist system* has revealed to us this syllogism, upon which the whole of it is based:

The more one works, the richer one is.

The more difficulties one has to overcome, the more one works.

Ergo, the more difficulties one has to overcome, the richer one is.

What, in fact, is *protection,* if not an ingenious application of this line of reasoning, so cogent and conclusive that it must resist even the subtlety of M. Billault himself?

Let us personify the country and view it as a collective being with thirty million mouths and, as a natural consequence, sixty million hands. It makes a clock that it intends to exchange in Belgium for ten quintals of iron.

But we tell it: "Make the iron yourself."

"I cannot," it replies; "it would take too long. I could not make more than five quintals in the time that I can make one clock."

"Utopian dreamer!" we reply; "that is precisely the reason why we are forbidding you to make the clock and ordering you to make the iron. Do you not see that we are providing employment for you?"

Sire, it could not have escaped your discernment that this is exactly the same as if we were to say to the country: *Work with your left hand, and not with your right*.

The old system of *restriction* was based on the idea of creating obstacles in order to multiply job opportunities. The new system of *restriction* that we are proposing to take its place is based on exactly the same idea. Sire, to make laws in this fashion is not to innovate; it is to carry on in the traditional way.

As for the efficacy of the measure, it is incontestable. It is difficult, much more difficult than people think, to do with the left hand what one is accustomed to doing with the right. You will be convinced of this, Sire, if you will deign to put our system to the test in performing some act that is familiar to you, such as, for instance, that of shuffling cards. We can, therefore, flatter ourselves on opening to labor an unlimited number of job opportunities.

Once the workers in every branch of industry are restricted to the use of their left hands alone, imagine, Sire, the immense number of people that will be needed to meet the present demand for consumers' goods, assuming that it remains constant, as we always do when we compare different systems of production. So prodigious a demand for manual labor cannot fail to bring about a considerable rise in wages, and pauperism will disappear from the country as if by magic.

But as soon as your new law is promulgated, as soon as all right hands are either cut off or tied down, things will change. Twenty times, thirty times as many embroiderers, pressers and ironers, seamstresses, dressmakers and shirtmakers, will not suffice to meet the national demand (shame to him who thinks ill of it), always assuming, as before, that it remains constant.

It is true that this assumption may be disputed by dispassionate theorists; for dresses will cost more, and so will shirts. The same could be said of the iron that we extract from our mines, as compared with what we could obtain *in exchange for the produce of our vineyards*. Hence, this argument is no more acceptable against *left-handedness* than against *protectionism*; for this high cost is itself at once the result and the sign of the superabundance of effort and labor that is precisely the basis on which, in the one case as in the other, we maintain that the prosperity of the working class is founded.

Yes, we may picture a touching scene of prosperity in the dressmaking business. Such bustling about! Such activity! Such animation! Each dress will busy a hundred fingers instead of ten. No young woman will any longer be idle, and we have no need, Sire, to indicate to your perspicacity the moral consequences of this great revolution. Not only will more young women be employed, but each of them will earn more, for all of them together will be unable to satisfy the demand; and if competition reappears, it will no longer be among the workers who make the dresses but among the fine ladies who wear them.

You see, Sire, our proposal is not only in accord with the economic traditions of the government, but is essentially moral and democratic as well.

In order to appreciate its consequences, let us assume that it has been put into effect, and, transporting ourselves in imagination into the future, let us imagine that the system has been in operation for twenty years. Idleness has been banished from the country; steady employ-ment has brought affluence, harmony, contentment, and morality to every household; poverty and prostitution are things of the past. The left hand being very clumsy to work with, jobs are superabundant, and the pay is satisfactory. Everything has been organized on this basis; consequently, the workshops are thronged. Is it not true, Sire, that if at such a time utopian dreamers were suddenly to appear, demanding freedom for the right hand, they would throw the country into a panic? Is it not true that this supposed reform would upset everyone's life? Hence, our system must be good, since it cannot be destroyed without causing suffering.

Nevertheless, we do not intend to conceal from Your Majesty that there is one respect in which our project is vulnerable. We may be told that in twenty years all left hands will be as skillful as right hands are now, and it will then no longer be possible to count on *left-handedness* to increase the number of jobs in the country.

Our reply to this is that, according to learned doctors, the left side of the human body has a natural weakness that is completely reassuring for the future of labor.

If, then, Your Majesty consents to sign the decree, a great principle will be established: *All wealth stems from the intensity of labor.* It will be easy for us to extend and vary its applications. We shall ordain, for example, that it shall no longer be permissible to work except with the foot. This is no more impossible (as we have seen) than to extract iron from the mud of the Seine. Men have even been known to write without using either hands or feet. You see, Sire, that we shall not be lacking in means of increasing the number of job opportunities in your realm. As a last resort, we should take recourse to the limitless possibilities of amputation.

Finally, Sire, if this report were not intended for publication, we should call your attention to the great influence that all measures of the kind we are proposing to you are likely to confer upon men in power. But this is a matter that we prefer to reserve for a private audience.

Bastiat 1996: 258–265.

Bastiat passed away two years after one of the most famous economists would write a slim volume—*The Communist Manifesto*—that would have an enormous impact on world events far into the future. This economist also posited his own theory of value and how wealth is created, and since it is still misunderstood to this day—much like materialism in Adam Smith's day—we will focus on his legacy next.

2

MIND OVER MARXISM

> The philosophers have only interpreted the world in various ways.
> The point however is to change it.
> —*Inscription, Karl Marx's tomb, Highgate Cemetery, London*

Although Karl Marx's tomb inscription (see Exhibit 2.1) appeals to young revolutionaries who set out to remake the world in their anointed image, the real work of economists and other students of human behavior is not to change the world, but to understand it. Until we understand why people behave as they do, guided by their beliefs more than what they know, there is little hope of changing their behavior.

Adam Smith certainly laid out an explanation of how humans behave, guided by the invisible hand of the free market. Smith argued that it was your *conscience* that made you do the right thing, not greed. We desire not only to gain the external praise of others, we desire to gain the internal respect and praise of *ourselves*. We ultimately want to be *worthy* of our praise. We desire to be *praiseworthy*. Smith proposed a self-regulating system, also known as the classical model of competition:

- *Freedom:* the right to produce and exchange products, labor, and capital.
- *Self-interest:* the right to pursue one's own business and to appeal to the self-interest of others.

EXHIBIT 2.1   KARL MARX'S TOMB, HIGHGATE CEMETERY, LONDON
Source: Photo by Paul O'Byrne

- *Competition:* the right to compete in the production and exchange of goods and services.

Smith further argued that these three conditions would lead to a "natural harmony" of interests between workers, landlords, and businesspeople. Smith spoke of an "Impartial Spectator" ("the great inmate of the breast")—that is, your internal conscience and sentiments to do the right thing—and competition as the external spectator to ensure you serve the interests of others (the "invisible hand").

Capitalism is based on trust, with the overwhelming majority of market transactions being guided not just by Smith's invisible hand, but also by an invisible handshake, harmonizing the interests of both buyer and seller, making them each better off than in the absence of mutual cooperation and exchange.

Ideas have consequences. As John Maynard Keynes wrote in the final passage of his 1937 magnum opus, *General Theory of Employment, Interest, and Money*:

> [T]he ideas of economists and political philosophers, both when they are right and when they are wrong, are more powerful than is commonly understood. Indeed, the world is ruled by little else. Practical men, who believe themselves to be quite exempt from any intellectual influences, are usually the slaves of some defunct economist. Madmen in authority, who hear voices in the air, are distilling their frenzy from some academic scribbler of a few years back.... But, soon or late, it is ideas, not vested interests which are dangerous for good or evil (Buchholz 1990: 219).

Marx's idea was that labor was the source of all value. This idea has a very long history as humans have always correlated labor with value, inputs with outputs. In medieval English, the word *acre* meant the amount of land a team of eight oxen could plow in a morning. Some scholars have suggested that the labor theory of value originated in the thirteenth century with St. Thomas Aquinas, while Aristotle explained that a good could obtain a price because there was a need for it. Yet each of these explanations leaves us devoid of a more precise theory of value.

Even Adam Smith himself equated value with labor, writing in *Wealth of Nations*:

> Labour alone, therefore, never varying in its own value, is alone the ultimate and real standard by which the value of all commodities can at all times and places be estimated and compared. It is their real price, money is their nominal price only (quoted in Cohen 2001: 40).
>
> If it usually costs twice the labour to kill a beaver as it does to kill a deer, says Smith, "one beaver should naturally exchange for or be worth two deer" (Cohen 2001: 40).

"[The] real price of everything, what every thing really costs. . .
is the toil and trouble of acquiring it." Or in Smith's terms, "Labour,
therefore, is the real measure of the exchangeable value of commodities" (Cohen 2001: 68).

The value of any commodity, therefore, to the person who possesses it, and who means not to use or consume it himself, but
to exchange it for other commodities, is equal to the quantity of
labour which it enables him to purchase or command. Labour,
therefore, is the real measure of the exchangeable value of all
commodities (Cohen 2001: 72).

Yet Smith understood there were factors other than labor that
went into the cost of producing commodities, such as the cost of
capital, equipment, rent, and the risk the entrepreneur was assuming. All these factors also had to be compensated in the price of
the final commodity, so Smith posited a "cost of production" theory of value, in effect "adding up" labor, profit, rent, and cost of
capital to determine price. Of course, this begs the question of
how a company could ever lose money by following this theory,
since even the most inept businessperson would be able to add
up all of these factors to derive a price that generates a profit.

One of the wealthiest economists to have ever lived, the British
economist David Ricardo (1772–1823), who developed the law of
diminishing returns, along with probably one of the most famous
economic laws ever—the law of comparative advantage that
explains why international trade makes countries better off—in
his 1817 treatise, *Principles of Political Economy and Taxation*,
explains his theory of value:

The value of a commodity, or the quantity of any other commodity
for which it will exchange, depends on the relative quantity of
labour which is necessary for its production (Keen 2002: 276).

Ricardo also adopted a cost of production theory of value,
claiming price was determined by costs, although he did note
some exceptions such as rare works of art, books, coins, and
wines:

There are some commodities, the value of which is determined by their scarcity alone. No labour can increase the quantity of such goods, and therefore their value cannot be lowered by an increased supply. Some rare statues and pictures, scarce books and coins, wines of a peculiar quality, which can be made only from grapes grown on a particular soil, of which there is a very limited quantity, are all of this description. Their value is wholly independent of the quantity of labour originally necessary to produce them, and varies with the varying wealth and inclinations of those who are desirous to possess them (Keen 2002: 272).

... [M]y proposition that with few exceptions the quantity of labour employed on commodities determines the rate of which they will exchange for each other ... is not rigidly true, but I say it is the nearest approximation to truth, as a rule for measuring relative value, of any I have ever heard (Skousen 2001: 107).

In fact, Ricardo struggled with the labor theory of value until the last days of his life. As Mark Skousen writes in his luminous book *The Making of Modern Economics*:

About a month before his death he wrote a fellow economist, "I cannot get over the difficulty of the wine which is kept in a cellar for 3 or 4 years, or that of the oak tree, which perhaps had not 2/- [pence] expended on it in the way of labour, and yet comes to be worth $100" (Skousen 2001: 108).

Here we have two eminent economists—although they were called moral philosophers in their day—who struggled to develop a unifying and credible theory of value. It was not until Karl Marx popularized his theory of value that the economics profession discovered a more accurate theory of value. But before we get to that more correct theory, let us first look at the flaws in Marx's theory.

KARL MARX, FALSE PROPHET

Perhaps Keynes was thinking of Karl Marx (1818–1883) when he wrote the passage cited earlier, for we know he could not stand Marx or the communist experiment, which he regarded as "an insult to our intelligence." At a dinner with friends in 1934, Keynes reportedly said that of all the "isms," Marxism was "the worst of all and founded on a silly mistake of old Mr. Ricardo's [labor theory of value]" (Skousen, 2001: 154).

Marx is far from dead. His flock might have perished, but his church lives on. In a poll of 3 million Germans, he ranked as the third "best German" of all time, behind Konrad Adenauer and Martin Luther. His labor theory of value still wields enormous influence over our present-day concept of value and price. Here is how Marx explained his theory in *Value, Price and Profit*, published in 1865:

> A commodity has *a value*, because it is a *crystallisation of social labour*. The *greatness* of its value, or its *relative* value, depends upon the greater or less amount of that social substance contained in it; that is to say, on the relative mass of labour necessary for its production. The *relative values of commodities* are, therefore, determined by the *respective quantities or amounts of labour, worked up, realised, fixed in them*. The *correlative* quantities of commodities which can be produced in the *same time of labour* are *equal* (Marx 1995: 31).

This sounds quite reasonable until you put this theory to the test of explaining how people spend their money in the marketplace.

Marx's theory cannot explain how land and natural resources have value, since there is no labor contained in them. Taken to its extreme, the labor theory of value would predict that those countries with the most labor hours—such as China or India—would have the highest standards of living. But this is demonstrably false, and what we witness instead in countries with *less* labor input and more entrepreneurship—and secure private property and other institutions conducive to economic growth—are vastly higher standards of living, including shorter hours for workers.

If Marx's theory was correct, a rock found next to a diamond in a mine would be of equal value, since each took the same amount of labor hours to locate and extract. Yet how many rocks do you see in the local mall's jewelry store? If you were to have pizza for lunch today, under Marx's theory, your tenth slice would be just as valuable as your first, since each took the same amount of labor hours to produce. One glaring flaw in Marx's theory was that it did not take into account the law of diminishing marginal utility, which states that the value to the customer declines with additional consumption of the good in question. Two friends, both adherents to this theory, emerging from a movie would have to have enjoyed it equally, since it took the same amount of labor hours to produce, and therefore each would value it the same.

This idea led Frédéric Bastiat, introduced in Chapter 1, to illustrate the absurd by being absurd, especially in his essay, "The Left Hand and the Right." Ludicrous? Absolutely. Yet an effective way to falsify a theory is to show where and how it will not work.

Marx attempted to avert these dilemmas, and even recognized that art and land could appreciate in value without further labor, but he dismissed these anomalies as being of minor importance to the fundamental issue of labor power. He also constructed a novel concept he coined "socially necessary labour," which is the only type that creates value:

> It might seem that if the value of a commodity is determined by the *quantity of labour bestowed upon its production*, the lazier a man, or the clumsier a man, the more valuable his commodity, because the greater the time of labour required for finishing the commodity. This, however, would be a sad mistake. You will recollect that I used the word "social labour," and many points are involved in this qualification of "social." In saying that the value of a commodity is determined by *the quantity of labour* worked up or crystallized in it, we mean *the quantity of labour necessary* for its production in a given state of society, under certain social average conditions of production, with a given social average intensity, and average skill of the labour employed.
>
> If then the quantity of socially necessary labour realised in commodities regulates their exchangeable values, every increase in the quantity of labour wanted for the production of a commodity must augment its value, as every diminution must lower it (Marx 1995: 33–34).

But how does one determine what is "socially necessary labour"? Marx's theory ignored the consumer, who ultimately determines value, bringing Marx from a circuitous route right back to the values of the free market he so vehemently abhorred. The very nature of a transaction between a willing buyer and seller is not based on an equality of labor but rather the *inequality* in the subjective value of the good bought and sold. This takes us back to one of Adam Smith's central insights, that both the buyer and seller must gain from an exchange, or it will not take place. Were this not so, we could simply exchange five-dollar bills with each other and achieve a Marxian utopia.

After surveying these three seminal thinkers—Smith, Ricardo, and Marx—we still lack a convincing theory of value. This was not because the theory did not exist, for it did. Unfortunately, it was mostly ignored. Some truths need resurrection, not discovery, and nowhere is this more true than with respect to the Austrian school of economics and its subjective theory of value.

THE MARGINALIST REVOLUTION

[Carl] Menger is the vanquisher of the Ricardian theory. ... Menger's theory of value, price, and distribution is the best we have up to now.
—*Joseph Schumpeter, Ten Great Economists from Marx to Keynes,*
1951

In the middle of the nineteenth century, economic theory was at a dead end. Although the Industrial Revolution was progressing, the theories of classical economists such as Smith, Ricardo, and John Stuart Mill, among others, still lacked a comprehensive theory of value and price. There are particular epochs that occur throughout history, when an assembly of people construct the events that cause a substantial advancement for human society. One such year was 1776, with the publication simultaneously of Smith's *Wealth of Nations* and the Declaration of Independence. Another was 1871–1874, when three economists ushered in the "neoclassical" marginalist revolution, which was the undoing of Marxian economics.

Three economists, from three different countries, developed the theory of marginalism and created a revolution similar to the Keynesian tsunami of the 1930s, although it took longer to diffuse into the economics profession, taking approximately 20 years to become generally accepted theory: William Stanley Jevons (1835–1882) from Great Britain, Leon Walras (1834–1910) from France, and Carl Menger (1840–1921) from Austria. There were forerunners to the marginal theory, such as Hermann Gossen from Germany, Samuel Longfield, Antoine Cournot, and Jules Dupuit, and the early Spanish philosophers. But it was not until these three came together that the theory was accepted as valid in the economics profession. "Swedish economist Knut Wicksell, who lived through the marginalist revolution, described it as a 'bolt from the blue'" (Skousen 2001: 169).

What made this new theory so revolutionary? As Menger explains in his book *Principles of Economics*, written in 1871 when he was 31 years old:

> Value is ... nothing inherent in goods, no property of them. Value is a judgment economizing men make about the importance of the goods at their disposal for the maintenance of their lives and well-being. Hence value does not exist outside the consciousness of men. ... [T]he value of goods ... is entirely subjective in nature (Ebenstein 2003: 23).
>
> The value of goods arises from their relationship to our needs, and is not inherent in the goods themselves. ... Objectification of the value of goods, which is entirely *subjective* in nature, has nevertheless contributed very greatly to confusion about the basic principles of our science. ... The importance that goods have for us and which we call value is merely imputed (Menger, 1976: 120–121, 139).

Value is like beauty—it is in the eye of the beholder. Menger further developed this theory with his *law of imputation*, wherein he labeled final consumer goods "lower order" and the necessary producer goods "higher order" (sometimes called producer goods, or capital goods). He then demonstrated that the demand for the higher-order goods—land, equipment, and other necessary inputs—"is derived from that of the corresponding goods of lower order."

Menger illustrated this concept with the example of tobacco. Suppose, for some reason, that tobacco is no longer desired by people and the demand for it disappears. Existing tobacco products' price would fall to zero, even though it was produced at a considerable cost. But what would happen to all of the necessary factors of production—land, tobacco plants, tools, machinery, and so forth—the higher-order goods? They, too, would drop in price significantly, since the demand for these products is derived from the consumers' demand for tobacco. Some of these goods might have a value, but only in *alternative* uses, not in the production of tobacco.

This was a refutation of the Ricardo-Marx labor theory of value. Menger wrote:

> The determining factor in the value of a good, then, is neither the quantity of labor or other goods necessary for its production nor the quantity necessary for its reproduction, but rather the magnitude of importance of those satisfactions with respect to which we are conscious of being dependent on command of the good. This principle of value determination is universally valid, and no exception to it can be found in human economy (Skousen 2001: 182).

Menger here articulates the concept of marginal utility and opportunity cost, although he did not use these terms. This theory has enormous explanatory and predictive capabilities, because it explains why people dive for pearls. Marx would say pearls have value because people dive for them (thus supplying labor). Menger would retort that people dive for pearls because other people value them.

Philip Wicksteed, a British clergyman, wrote the first scientific critique of the Marxian labor theory of value in 1884, where he explained:

> A coat is not worth eight times as much as a hat to the community because it takes eight times as long to make it. . . . The community is willing to devote eight times as long to the making of a coat because it will be worth eight times as much to it (Howey 1989: 157).

Marginalism and the subjective theory of value, when combined, allow economists to explain much human behavior, far more accurately than the labor theory of value or Smith's cost of production theory of value. If the customers change their preferences, needs, wants, or desires, the value of some goods will increase while others decrease.

When we changed from a horse-and-carriage economy to the automobile, all sorts of goods of a higher order lost their value—hay production dropped, and blacksmiths, among others who supplied the old industry, lost jobs. Prices reflect what we value today, not of the "frozen labour"—Marx's term—required to create what we valued yesterday.

Value depends entirely upon the *utility*—a measure of pleasure or satisfaction—the customer will receive. Where psychiatrists speak of *subjective well-being*, economists use the term *utility*. Both are conveying the same idea: you engage in activities you receive pleasure or satisfaction from, not because others have toiled. People do not smoke to make the tobacco companies rich and happy, but rather from the utility they derive from doing so.

The popularity of the Atkins Diet caused some workers in the companies that make pasta, doughnuts, chocolate, beer, and other high-carbohydrate products to lose their jobs. The reason labor unions cannot "save jobs" is that they cannot control what customers value, and it is what customers value that gives them the jobs in the first place. The Channel Tunnel between London and Paris cost billions to build, but the return-on-investment calculations and sunk costs do not matter to today's customers. They are concerned only with the relative price of taking the "Chunnel," flying, or taking the ferry.

New evidence alters beliefs, yet most scholars are born and die within the same paradigm. A few, like Einstein, Darwin, and the marginalist economists, create new ones. Whereas revolutionaries in the nineteenth century spent their time trying to overthrow capitalism, twentieth-century revolutionaries spent theirs attempting to defend the labor theory of value. I have had the misfortune of arguing the labor versus the subjective theory of value with Marxist professors, and have concluded that their beliefs are not based on the scientific method of positing, observation, and falsifiability of theories, but rather a sort of blind faith—what Marx himself might have labeled the opiate of the communist economists. As Thomas Sowell wrote in plain words in *Basic Economics*:

> By the late nineteenth century, however, economists had given up on the notion that it is primarily labor which determines the value of goods. ... This new understanding marked a revolution in the development of economics. It is also a sobering reminder of how long it can take for even highly intelligent people to get rid of a misconception whose fallacy then seems obvious in retrospect. It is not costs which create value; it is value which causes purchasers to be willing to repay the costs incurred in the production of what they want (Sowell 2004: 177).

Some critics of the subjective theory of value maintain that it is too simplistic to explain value. Most economic theories are relatively simple; it is the fallacies that get complicated. It is an unnecessary complication to believe that complex effects must have complex causes. The fact that the earth tilts on its axis is fairly straightforward, but this certainly causes complex reactions in plants, animals, people, ocean currents, and so forth.

As John Maynard Keynes said, "The difficulty lies, not in the new ideas, but in escaping from the old ones, which ramify, for those brought up as most of us have been, into every corner of our minds," to which philosopher Bertrand Russell added, "The resistance to a new idea increases as the square of its importance." Just as geologists fought for decades against plate tectonics theory to explain earthquakes, and germ theory remained on the fringes of medical science until the late nineteenth century, the subjective theory of value is not widely taught, or practiced, in businesses. Yet when people see this theory explained, they intuitively understand it, because it comports to human behavior. And isn't this what learning is all about—understanding something you have known all along, but in a new way?

Despite this lesson, the labor theory of value—like mercantilism and materialism before it—die hard, much like the Brezhnev Doctrine: *Once a Communist nation, always a Communist nation.* Luckily, science and modern civilization do not progress like this.

One person who steadfastly refused to believe in the tenets of Marxism-Leninism was Ronald Reagan. Echoing the teaching of Leonardo da Vinci that "Simplicity is the ultimate sophistication," Reagan had an uncomplicated idea about the Cold War: America wins, the Soviets lose. In the last year of his presidency, he had the opportunity to articulate his vision of the new economy to a group of Soviet students at the alma mater of Mikhail Gorbachev, in what was perhaps one of the most prescient of his presidential speeches.

3

THE ECONOMY IN MIND

We were among the last to understand that in the age of information science the most valuable asset is knowledge, springing from human imagination and creativity. We will be paying for our mistake for many years to come.

—*Mikhail Gorbachev*

In *The Wealth of Nations*, Adam Smith wrote of four stages in society:

1. An age of hunters
2. An age of shepherds
3. An agrarian age
4. An age of commerce

Alvin and Heidi Toffler write in *Revolutionary Wealth* of the world's three wealth systems: "If the First Wave wealth system was chiefly based on growing things, and the Second Wave on making things, the Third Wave wealth system is increasingly based on serving, thinking, knowing and experiencing" (Toffler and Toffler 2006: 23). Iconically, these ages are represented by the plow, the assembly line, and the computer.

The transition from the agrarian age to the Industrial Age is conventionally dated from the late eighteenth to the early nineteenth century. The French employed the term *la révolution industrielle* (the Industrial Revolution) as early as the 1820s; Marx used it in his writings in the mid-1800s, while historian Arnold Toynbee introduced the phrase to common parlance in the 1880s.

In the 1980s, it was popular to speak of the "Service Economy," given prominence by Karl Albrecht and Ron Zemke's book, *Service America!* In fact, the term *service worker* was coined around 1920, when fewer than half of all nonmanual workers were actually employed in service jobs—such as banking, insurance, restaurants, government, and so on. The terms *knowledge industries*, *knowledge work*, and *knowledge worker* are less than half a century old. They were coined around 1961, simultaneously but independently, the first by a Princeton economist, Fritz Machlup, the second and third by Peter Drucker.

Drucker later expanded on this new phenomenon in his 1968 book, *The Age of Discontinuity*. He posited it was the 1944 G.I. Bill of Rights—which made available higher education to millions of veterans and was certainly the largest single investment in human capital up to that time—that helped cause the shift to a knowledge society.

Perhaps the term we use to describe this new economy is not up to us, just as the Industrial Revolution was not labeled by the people who launched that era. Echoing economist Joan Robinson's insistence that "There is no advantage (and much error) in making definitions of words more precise than the subject matter they refer to," I remain uncomfortable with the terms *knowledge economy* and *knowledge workers*. The idea of a knowledge economy is a bit of an exaggeration since man cannot live on knowledge alone. Yet these definitions are distinguishing—and accurate—enough from prior ages that they will be used throughout this book.

Knowledge workers are not like workers from the Industrial Revolution, who were dependent on the employing organization's providing the means of production (factories and machines). Today, knowledge workers themselves *own* the firm's means of production in their heads. This is a seismic shift in our economy, the ramifications of which we are still trying to comprehend.

Any structural change in the economy is bound to cause severe dislocations as creative destruction undermines the existing industrial infrastructure. We witness the materialist fallacy rear its ugly head even today when politicians and pundits constantly ask if America can long sustain its present standard of living without a strong manufacturing base—the so-called "hamburger flipper" theory of low-paying service jobs. But this is precisely the wrong question. A better question would be to ask if a manufacturing base could long survive without a strong knowledge sector. In fact, the distinction between goods and services is an anachronism, mostly used by governmental agencies. General Electric manufactures jet engines but makes more money from servicing them, and General Motors Acceptance Corporation makes more profit financing the cars GM manufactures. Is an Apple iPod merely a product or a service experience—an escape from the mundane?

In an ironic twist on Karl Marx's idea of the proletarian revolution, in today's capitalist society, labor—what economists prefer to call human capital—trumps capital as the chief source of all wealth. British Prime Minister Tony Blair delivered a keynote speech at "Knowledge 2000: Conference on the Knowledge Driven Economy," where he stated:

> I strongly believe that the knowledge economy is our best route for success and prosperity. But we must be careful not to make a fundamental mistake. We mustn't think that because the knowledge economy is the future, it will happen only in the future. The new knowledge economy is here, and it is now (Harrison and Sullivan 2006: 149).

Twelve years prior to Blair's speech, another world leader stood before the icons of a materialist mind-set as an ambassador from the future, illuminating how the New Age economy, rooted in human creativity and imagination, would usher in a new era of prosperity for mankind.

THE ASH HEAP OF HISTORY

Not since Richard Nixon had a president of the United States stood east of the Berlin Wall and spoken directly to the Soviet Union. Ronald Reagan, notorious for his virulent anticommunism, was certainly an improbable personality to address the citizens of the country he once described as an "evil empire." In an address to members of the British Parliament at the Palace of Westminster on June 8, 1982, Reagan prophetically predicted:

> What I am describing now is a plan and a hope for the long term—the march of freedom and democracy which will leave Marxism-Leninism on the ash heap of history as it has left other tyrannies which stifle the freedom and muzzle the self-expression of the people (Reagan 1989: 118–119).

Less than a year later, in his famous "evil empire" speech—at the annual convention of the National Association of Evangelicals on March 8, 1983—Reagan again envisaged communism's imminent implosion:

> I believe that communism is another sad, bizarre chapter in human history whose last pages even now are being written. I believe this because the source of our strength in the quest for human freedom is not material, but spiritual. And because it knows no limitation, it must terrify and ultimately triumph over those who would enslave their fellow man (Reagan 1989: 180).

Despite this rhetoric, and given the friendship that had developed between Reagan and Mikhail Gorbachev, the 1988 Moscow Summit was an opportunity for Reagan to speak directly to the future of the Soviet Union. According to Joshua Gilder, one of the speechwriters for the Moscow State University address (see Exhibit 3.1), Reagan, "ever so nicely, explained that freedom and technology were going to leave the Soviets on the dust bin of history unless they changed their act—which of course they did, much sooner than we expected" (Gilder [undated]: 6).

Here is how Reagan explained this rare opportunity in his memoirs:

For more than thirty years, I'd been preaching about freedom and liberty. During my visit to Moscow, I was given a chance to do something I never dreamed I would do: Gorbachev let me lecture to some of the brightest young people of Moscow—among them some of the future leaders of the Soviet Union—about the blessings of democracy and individual freedom and free enterprise.

On what was for me an extraordinary day I never thought possible, I tried in a few minutes at Moscow State University to summarize a philosophy that had guided me most of my life (Reagan 1990: 713).

There will be bumps in the road. But after talking with these bright young people in Moscow and seeing what was happening in their country, I couldn't help but feel optimistic: We were at the threshold of a new era in the political and economic history of the world.

I can't wait to see where it will lead us (Reagan 1990: 716).

Before reproducing the speech in its entirety, here is how Reagan set the stage in his book, *Speaking My Mind*:

The trip to Moscow was one of the most intriguing experiences of my years in office. You can understand more about a place by just seeing it. One thing I noticed was that there is such a visible break in the history of the Russian people. It's right there in the architecture.

The architecture of Moscow State University is quite ominous. The university is housed in this threatening, yes, evil-looking, building erected by Stalin. But speaking to these students, I felt I could have been speaking to students anywhere. The coldness disappeared.

What a step forward it was just being there in that auditorium with the big bust of Lenin right behind me. I couldn't speak to the entire student body because the hall wasn't large enough, so the Soviets only let in students who were members of the Young Communist League. I didn't know that at the time, but it didn't seem to make any difference because I could feel that I was still getting a good reaction. I could see the students turn to each other and nod every once in a while, occasionally smile. I came away from there with a very good feeling (Reagan 1989: 373–374).

EXHIBIT 3.1   "THEY GAVE HIM A STANDING OVATION THAT BEATS AGAINST LENIN'S CARVED COLLOSUS LIKE WAVES OF AN IMMINENT STORM" (EDMUND MORRIS, *DUTCH: A MEMOIR OF RONALD REAGAN*, 1999: 635).

REMARKS AT MOSCOW STATE UNIVERSITY, MAY 31, 1988

Thank you, Rector Logunov, and I want to thank all of you very much for a very warm welcome. It's a great pleasure to be here at Moscow State University, and I want to thank you all for turning out. I know you must be very busy this week, studying and taking your final examinations. So, let me just say *zhelayu vam uspekha* [I wish you success]. Nancy couldn't make it today because she's visiting Leningrad, which she tells me is a very beautiful city, but she, too, says hello and wishes you all good luck.

Let me say it's also a great pleasure to once again have this opportunity to speak directly to the people of the Soviet Union. Before I left Washington, I received many heartfelt letters and telegrams asking me to carry here a simple message, perhaps, but also some of the most important business of this summit: It is a message of peace and good will and hope for a growing friendship and closeness between our two peoples.

As you know, I've come to Moscow to meet with one of your most distinguished graduates. In this, our fourth summit, General Secretary Gorbachev and I have spent many hours together, and I feel that we're getting to know each other well. Our discussions, of course, have been focused primarily on many of the important issues of the day, issues I want to touch on with you in a few moments. But first I want to take a little time to talk to you much as I would to any group of university students in the United States. I want to talk not just of the realities of today but of the possibilities of tomorrow.

Standing here before a mural of your revolution, I want to talk about a very different revolution that is taking place right now, quietly sweeping the globe without bloodshed or conflict. Its effects are peaceful, but they will fundamentally alter our world, shatter old assumptions, and reshape our lives. It's easy to underestimate because it's not accompanied by banners or fanfare. It's been called the technological or information revolution, and as its emblem, one might take the tiny silicon chip, no bigger than a fingerprint. One of these chips has more computing power than a roomful of old-style computers.

As part of an exchange program, we now have an exhibition touring your country that shows how information technology is transforming our lives—replacing manual labor with robots, forecasting weather for farmers, or mapping the genetic code of DNA for medical researchers. These microcomputers today aid the design of everything from houses to cars to spacecraft; they even design better and faster computers. They can translate English into Russian or enable the blind to read or help Michael Jackson produce on one synthesizer the sounds of a whole orchestra. Linked by a network of satellites and fiber-optic cables, one individual with a desktop computer and a telephone commands resources unavailable to the largest governments just a few years ago.

Like a chrysalis, we're emerging from the economy of the Industrial Revolution—an economy confined to and limited by the Earth's physical resources—into, as one economist titled his book, "the economy in mind," in which there are no bounds on human imagination and the freedom to create is the most precious natural resource. Think of that little computer chip. Its value isn't in the sand from which it is made but in the microscopic architecture designed into it by ingenious human minds. Or take the example of the satellite relaying this broadcast around the world, which replaces thousands of tons of copper mined from the Earth and molded into wire. In the new economy, human invention increasingly makes physical resources obsolete. We're breaking through the material conditions of existence to a world where man creates his own destiny. Even as we explore the most advanced reaches of science, we're returning to the age-old wisdom of our culture, a wisdom contained in the book of Genesis in the Bible: In the beginning was the spirit, and it was from this spirit that the material abundance of creation issued forth.

But progress is not foreordained. The key is freedom—freedom of thought, freedom of information, freedom of communication. The renowned scientist, scholar, and founding father of this university, Mikhail Lomonosov, knew that. "It is common knowledge," he said, "that the achievements of science are considerable and rapid, particularly once the yoke of slavery is cast off and replaced by the freedom of philosophy." You know, one of the first contacts between your country and mine took place between Russian and American explorers. The Americans were members of Cook's last voyage on an expedition searching for an Arctic passage; on the island of Unalaska, they came upon the Russians, who took them in, and together with the native inhabitants, held a prayer service on the ice.

The explorers of the modern era are the entrepreneurs, men with vision, with the courage to take risks and faith enough to brave the unknown. These entrepreneurs and their small enterprises are responsible for almost all the economic growth in the United States. They are the prime movers of the technological revolution. In fact, one of the largest personal computer firms in the United States was started by two college students, no older than you, in the garage behind their home. Some people, even in my own country, look at the riot of experiment that is the free market and see only waste. What of all the entrepreneurs that fail? Well, many do, particularly the successful ones; often several times. And if you ask them the secret of their success, they'll tell you it's all that they learned in their struggles along the way; yes, it's what they learned from failing. Like an athlete in competition or a scholar in pursuit of the truth, experience is the greatest teacher.

And that's why it's so hard for government planners, no matter how sophisticated, to ever substitute for millions of individuals working night and day to make their dreams come true. The fact is, bureaucracies are a problem around the world. There's an old story about a town—it could be anywhere—with a bureaucrat who is known to be a good-for-nothing, but he somehow had always hung on to power. So one day, in a town meeting, an old woman got up and said to him: "There is a folk legend here where I come from that when a baby is born, an angel comes down from heaven and kisses it on one part of its body. If the angel kisses him on his hand, he becomes a handyman. If he kisses him on his forehead, he becomes bright and clever. And I've been trying to figure out where the angel kissed you so that you should sit there for so long and do nothing." [*Laughter*]

We are seeing the power of economic freedom spreading around the world. Places such as the Republic of Korea, Singapore, Taiwan have vaulted into the technological era, barely pausing in the industrial age along the way. Low-tax agricultural policies in the subcontinent mean that in some years India is now a net exporter of food. Perhaps most exciting are the winds of change that are blowing over the People's Republic of China, where one-quarter of the world's population is now getting its first taste of economic freedom. At the same time, the growth of democracy has become one of the most powerful political movements of our age. In Latin America in the 1970s, only a third of the population lived under democratic government; today over 90 percent does. In the Philippines, in the Republic of Korea, free, contested, democratic elections are the order of the day. Throughout the world, free markets are the model for growth. Democracy is the standard by which governments are measured.

We Americans make no secret of our belief in freedom. In fact, it's something of a national pastime. Every 4 years the American people choose a new President, and 1988 is one of those years. At one point there were 13 major candidates running in the two major parties, not to mention all the others, including the Socialist and Libertarian candidates—all trying to get my job. About 1,000 local television stations, 8,500 radio stations, and 1,700 daily

newspapers—each one an independent, private enterprise, fiercely
independent of the Government—report on the candidates, grill
them in interviews, and bring them together for debates. In the
end, the people vote; they decide who will be the next President.
But freedom doesn't begin or end with elections.

Go to any American town, to take just an example, and you'll
see dozens of churches, representing many different beliefs—in
many places, synagogues and mosques—and you'll see families
of every conceivable nationality worshiping together. Go into any
schoolroom, and there you will see children being taught the Declaration of Independence, that they are endowed by their Creator
with certain unalienable rights—among them life, liberty, and the
pursuit of happiness—that no government can justly deny; the
guarantees in their Constitution for freedom of speech, freedom
of assembly, and freedom of religion. Go into any courtroom, and
there will preside an independent judge, beholden to no government power. There every defendant has the right to a trial by a
jury of his peers, usually 12 men and women—common citizens;
they are the ones, the only ones, who weigh the evidence and
decide on guilt or innocence. In that court, the accused is innocent
until proven guilty, and the word of a policeman or any official
has no greater legal standing than the word of the accused. Go to
any university campus, and there you'll find an open, sometimes
heated discussion of the problems in American society and what
can be done to correct them. Turn on the television, and you'll see
the legislature conducting the business of government right there
before the camera, debating and voting on the legislation that will
become the law of the land. March in any demonstration, and there
are many of them; the people's right of assembly is guaranteed in
the Constitution and protected by the police. Go into any union
hall, where the members know their right to strike is protected by
law. As a matter of fact, one of the many jobs I had before this
one was being president of a union, the Screen Actors Guild. I led
my union out on strike, and I'm proud to say we won.

But freedom is more even than this. Freedom is the right to
question and change the established way of doing things. It is the
continuing revolution of the marketplace. It is the understanding
that allows us to recognize shortcomings and seek solutions. It is
the right to put forth an idea, scoffed at by the experts, and watch

it catch fire among the people. It is the right to dream—to follow your dream or stick to your conscience, even if you're the only one in a sea of doubters. Freedom is the recognition that no single person, no single authority or government has a monopoly on the truth, but that every individual life is infinitely precious, that every one of us put on this world has been put there for a reason and has something to offer.

America is a nation made up of hundreds of nationalities. Our ties to you are more than ones of good feeling; they're ties of kinship. In America, you'll find Russians, Armenians, Ukrainians, peoples from Eastern Europe and Central Asia. They come from every part of this vast continent, from every continent, to live in harmony, seeking a place where each cultural heritage is respected, each is valued for its diverse strengths and beauties and the richness it brings to our lives. Recently, a few individuals and families have been allowed to visit relatives in the West. We can only hope that it won't be long before all are allowed to do so and Ukrainian-Americans, Baltic-Americans, Armenian-Americans can freely visit their homelands, just as this Irish-American visits his.

Freedom, it has been said, makes people selfish and materialistic, but Americans are one of the most religious peoples on Earth. Because they know that liberty, just as life itself, is not earned but a gift from God, they seek to share that gift with the world. "Reason and experience," said George Washington in his Farewell Address, "both forbid us to expect that national morality can prevail in exclusion of religious principle. And it is substantially true, that virtue or morality is a necessary spring of popular government." Democracy is less a system of government than it is a system to keep government limited, unintrusive; a system of constraints on power to keep politics and government secondary to the important things in life, the true sources of value found only in family and faith.

But I hope you know I go on about these things not simply to extol the virtues of my own country but to speak to the true greatness of the heart and soul of your land. Who, after all, needs to tell the land of Dostoyevski about the quest for truth, the home of Kandinski and Scriabin about imagination, the rich and noble culture of the Uzbek man of letters Alisher Navoi about beauty and heart? The great culture of your diverse land speaks with a glowing passion to all humanity. Let me cite one of the most eloquent contemporary passages on human freedom. It comes, not from the literature of America, but from this country, from one of the greatest writers of the 20th century, Boris Pasternak, in the novel *Dr. Zhivago*. He writes: "I think that if the beast who sleeps in man could be held down by threats—any kind of threat, whether of jail or of retribution after death—then the highest emblem of humanity would be the lion tamer in the circus with his whip, not the prophet who sacrificed himself. But this is just the point—what has for centuries raised man above the beast is not the cudgel, but an inward music—the irresistible power of unarmed truth."

The irresistible power of unarmed truth. Today the world looks expectantly to signs of change, steps toward greater freedom in the Soviet Union. We watch and we hope as we see positive changes taking place. There are some, I know, in your society who fear that change will bring only disruption and discontinuity, who fear to embrace the hope of the future—sometimes it takes faith. It's like that scene in the cowboy movie *Butch Cassidy and the Sundance Kid*, which some here in Moscow recently had a chance to see. The posse is closing in on the two outlaws, Butch and Sundance, who find themselves trapped on the edge of a cliff, with a sheer drop of hundreds of feet to the raging rapids below. Butch turns to Sundance and says their only hope is to jump into the river below, but Sundance refuses. He says he'd rather fight it out with the posse, even though they're hopelessly outnumbered. Butch says that's suicide and urges him to jump, but Sundance still refuses and finally admits, "I can't swim." Butch breaks up laughing and says, "You crazy fool, the fall will probably kill you." And, by the way, both Butch and Sundance made it, in case you didn't see the movie. I think what I've just been talking about is *perestroika* and what its goals are.

But change would not mean rejection of the past. Like a tree growing strong through the seasons, rooted in the Earth and drawing life from the Sun, so, too, positive change must be rooted in traditional values—in the land, in culture, in family and community—and it must take its life from the eternal things, from the source of all life, which is faith. Such change will lead to new understandings, new opportunities, to a broader future in which the tradition is not supplanted but finds its full flowering. That is the future beckoning to your generation.

At the same time, we should remember that reform that is not institutionalized will always be insecure. Such freedom will always be looking over its shoulder. A bird on a tether, no matter how long the rope, can always be pulled back. And that is why, in my conversation with General Secretary Gorbachev, I have spoken of how important it is to institutionalize change—to put guarantees on reform. And we've been talking together about one sad reminder of a divided world: the Berlin Wall. It's time to remove the barriers that keep people apart.

I'm proposing an increased exchange program of high school students between our countries. General Secretary Gorbachev mentioned on Sunday a wonderful phrase you have in Russian for this: "Better to see something once than to hear about it a hundred times." Mr. Gorbachev and I first began working on this in 1985. In our discussion today, we agreed on working up to several thousand exchanges a year from each country in the near future. But not everyone can travel across the continents and oceans. Words travel lighter, and that's why we'd like to make available to this country more of our 11,000 magazines and periodicals and our television and radio shows that can be beamed off a satellite in seconds. Nothing would please us more than for the Soviet people to get to know us better and to understand our way of life.

Just a few years ago, few would have imagined the progress our two nations have made together. The INF treaty, which General Secretary Gorbachev and I signed last December in Washington and whose instruments of ratification we will exchange tomorrow—the first true nuclear arms reduction treaty in history, calling for the elimination of an entire class of U.S. and Soviet nuclear missiles. And just 16 days ago, we saw the beginning of your withdrawal from Afghanistan, which gives us hope that soon the fighting may end and the healing may begin and that that suffering country may find self-determination, unity, and peace at long last.

It's my fervent hope that our constructive cooperation on these issues will be carried on to address the continuing destruction and conflicts in many regions of the globe and that the serious discussions that led to the Geneva accords on Afghanistan will

help lead to solutions in southern Africa, Ethiopia, Cambodia, the
Persian Gulf, and Central America. I have often said: Nations
do not distrust each other because they are armed; they are armed
because they distrust each other. If this globe is to live in peace and
prosper, if it is to embrace all the possibilities of the technological
revolution, then nations must renounce, once and for all, the right
to an expansionist foreign policy. Peace between nations must be
an enduring goal, not a tactical stage in a continuing conflict.

I've been told that there's a popular song in your country—
perhaps you know it—whose evocative refrain asks the question, "Do the Russians want a war?" In answer it says: "Go ask
that silence lingering in the air, above the birch and poplar there;
beneath those trees the soldiers lie. Go ask my mother, ask my
wife; then you will have to ask no more, 'Do the Russians want
a war?'" But what of your one-time allies? What of those who
embraced you on the Elbe? What if we were to ask the watery
graves of the Pacific or the European battlefields where America's fallen were buried far from home? What if we were to ask
their mothers, sisters, and sons, do Americans want war? Ask us,
too, and you'll find the same answer, the same longing in every
heart. People do not make wars; governments do. And no mother
would ever willingly sacrifice her sons for territorial gain, for economic advantage, for ideology. A people free to choose will always
choose peace.

Americans seek always to make friends of old antagonists. After
a colonial revolution with Britain, we have cemented for all ages
the ties of kinship between our nations. After a terrible Civil War
between North and South, we healed our wounds and found true
unity as a nation. We fought two world wars in my lifetime against
Germany and one with Japan, but now the Federal Republic of
Germany and Japan are two of our closest allies and friends.

Some people point to the trade disputes between us as a sign
of strain, but they're the frictions of all families, and the family
of free nations is a big and vital and sometimes boisterous one.
I can tell you that nothing would please my heart more than in
my lifetime to see American and Soviet diplomats grappling with
the problem of trade disputes between America and a growing,
exuberant, exporting Soviet Union that had opened up to economic
freedom and growth.

And as important as these official people-to-people exchanges are, nothing would please me more than for them to become unnecessary, to see travel between East and West become so routine that university students in the Soviet Union could take a month off in the summer and, just like students in the West do now, put packs on their backs and travel from country to country in Europe with barely a passport check in between. Nothing would please me more than to see the day that a concert promoter in, say, England could call up a Soviet rock group, without going through any government agency, and have them playing in Liverpool the next night. Is this just a dream? Perhaps, but it is a dream that is our responsibility to have come true.

Your generation is living in one of the most exciting, hopeful times in Soviet history. It is a time when the first breath of freedom stirs the air and the heart beats to the accelerated rhythm of hope, when the accumulated spiritual energies of a long silence yearn to break free. I am reminded of the famous passage near the end of Gogol's *Dead Souls*. Comparing his nation to a speeding troika, Gogol asks what will be its destination. But he writes, "There was no answer save the bell pouring forth marvelous sound."

We do not know what the conclusion will be of this journey, but we're hopeful that the promise of reform will be fulfilled. In this Moscow spring, this May 1988, we may be allowed that hope: that freedom, like the fresh green sapling planted over Tolstoy's grave, will blossom forth at last in the rich fertile soil of your people and culture. We may be allowed to hope that the marvelous sound of a new openness will keep rising through, ringing through, leading to a new world of reconciliation, friendship, and peace.

Thank you all very much, and *da blagoslovit vas gospod* —God bless you (Reagan 1989: 374–384).

"LIKE A CHRYSALIS"

There is perhaps no better living proof of Reagan's message than a Finnish-born fanatical computer programmer who at the age of 20 posted an e-mail on a Newsgroup, which began, ". . . I'm doing a (free) operating system . . ." In a twist of irony, this youngster's father, Nil Torvalds, was active in the Communist party since he was a student in college during the 1960s, of which he later admitted "his enthusiasm for communism may have been born of naiveté" (Torvalds and Diamond 2001: 15).

Nil's son, Linus Torvalds, developed the Linux operating system as a graduate student at the University of Helsinki, the largest collaborative project in the history of the world, made possible by the very revolution then taking place that Reagan had described in his speech. Today, approximately 40 percent of American companies use the Linux operating system, along with more than 160 governments. Both Linus and Bill Gates created enormous wealth, yet both required only a modicum of capital; while the latter used a corporation, the former did not. Both relied on intellectual capital, the source of all wealth.

Reagan used the metaphor of a chrysalis to describe how the world economy was shifting from the Industrial Revolution to the Information Era—what I am calling the knowledge or intellectual capital economy—even giving a nod to the subjective theory of value by describing how the value of a silicon chip lies not "in the sand from which it is made but in the microscopic architecture designed into it by ingenious human minds." Think of the wealth Intel has created since its beginnings in 1968, largely from products made by one of nature's most abundant resources—sand. As of 2005, Intel was the seventh largest American company measured by market capitalization, worth more than $180 billion, and ranked eighteenth in terms of profitability. If a farmer in Palo Alto, California, had been told in 1900 that in less than 100 years' time only 2 percent of the population would be farmers, as opposed to a majority of workers at that time, he would have thought the Valley to be a desert wasteland rather than the innovative and creative fount of technology it has become. Even Detroit now spends more on silicon chips than it does on steel for its automobiles—another illustration of the triumph of mind over matter.

The chrysalis metaphor sounds romantic, but the transformation is anything but romantic for the caterpillar, which loses its legs and its sight, and whose very body is torn apart until it emerges with its splendid wings. Likewise, when economies shift from one era into another, there are the inevitable dislocations, adjustments, and creative destruction that take place to the existing infrastructure.

This very process is still unfolding in the former Soviet Union. Many books have been published since Karl Marx's day on—what he believed—was the inexorable transition from capitalism to communism. Very few books have been written on the actual alteration from communism to capitalism taking place around the world.

Consider the predicament of Mikhail Gorbachev when he took over the former Soviet Union. Here was a man whose entire world paradigm of communism was literally swept onto the ash heap of history, as Reagan had stated. He immediately blamed his predecessors for all his problems. In fact, a running joke in the Soviet Union at the time went something like this:

> A new manager of a collective farm finds two letters from his predecessor, with instructions to open the first when difficulties begin. When the farm fails to meet its quotas, the manager opens the first letter, which says, "Blame me." He does. It buys some time. But the farm fails again and he comes under fresh criticism, so he opens the second letter. It says: "Prepare two letters" (Will 1992: 67).

It is time for leaders in the business community to stop emulating their predecessors blindly and instead embrace the opportunities of the intellectual capital economy. This transition will take an enormous amount of faith in the future, an unleashing of the human spirit, the recognition of the universal desire for freedom, and the creativity of the ordinary person to perform extraordinary acts of wealth creation and contribute to something larger than themselves. It requires a country, or a company, to forget about yesterday and begin creating tomorrow.

Throughout history, the "physical fallacy" was an idea that reigned supreme. Economists now have a far better understanding of how wealth is created from free minds operating in free markets. This can be seen by observing various developing economies escaping the shackles of poverty, creating wealth and a better standard of living for their populations. It is now clear that approximately 75 percent of the wealth-creating capacity of a country resides in human capital, and economists have proven this at the macro level of economic organization. What is needed now is to apply these same ideas at the micro level of the business entity by positing a new theory for the intellectual capital company of the future. Before we do, though, let us examine the old theory of the company so we can improve upon it.

4

A Flawed Theory—The Old Business Equation

> A theory that cannot be refuted is not scientific.
> —*Karl Popper*

The self-important barnyard rooster Chanticleer—in poet Geoffrey Chaucer's fable, "The Nun's Priest's Tale"—had a theory: When he crowed every morning the sun came up. One morning Chanticleer forgot to crow, and lo and behold the sun still arose. The rooster had to modify his theory.

Theories are powerful because they seek to do at least one of three things: explain, predict, or prescribe. Yet, when one reads a typical business book today, the author will usually begin by saying something to the effect that "this book is not based on some 'ivory tower' theoretical model, but based on practical, real-world experience and examples." Beware when you read such a qualifier, because as Dr. W. Edwards Deming used to say, "Without theory, experience has no meaning. No one has questions to ask. Hence without theory, there is no learning. Theory leads to prediction. Without prediction, experience and examples teach nothing" (Deming 1994: 103). In a business environment, whether we know it or not, we are guided to a large degree by theoretical constructs that have evolved to simplify—and thus explain, predict, or control—our various behaviors. As Immanuel

Kant said, "Concepts without perceptions are empty; perceptions without concepts are blind." Theories build buildings and bridges, fly airplanes, and put men on the moon.

Practical knowledge not guided by a theory is usually knowledge of only the most superficial kind. A fact not illuminated by a theory is not very enlightening; we might as well read the phone book. In a world where Google has a larger market value than Boeing and Airbus combined, and Detroit spends more money on silicon than steel, the old notions of efficiency, productivity, cost accounting—and how they measure wealth creation—no longer apply.

How did Microsoft, in a little more than one generation, exceed the value—in terms of market capitalization, and depending on the day of analysis—of behemoths such as General Motors, Ford, Boeing, Sears, Lockheed, Kellogg's, Safeway, Marriott (including Ritz-Carlton), Kodak, Caterpillar, Deere, USX, Weyerhaeuser, Union Pacific, and others *combined*? It leveraged intellectual capital (IC), the chief source of all wealth.

Our understanding of the role IC plays in generating wealth is not well recognized by accountants or, for that matter, accurately measured by them. Generally accepted accounting principles (GAAP) do a horrendous job of valuing IC, as most of the cost of creating IC is treated as a period expense for GAAP. This explains how Microsoft's GAAP assets, as reported on its balance sheet, account for less than 10 percent of its market capitalization. Contrary to what every accounting student is taught, in the real world, debits do not equal credits.

Today, intellectual capital is sometimes thought of as nothing more than another "buzzword." However, IC is not about the "new economy," the dotcom, or the dot-bomb. IC has *always* been the chief driver of wealth, as economists have argued since the term human capital was first coined in 1961, and as far back as the late eighteenth century when Adam Smith discredited the idea of mercantilism. Wealth doesn't reside in tangible assets or money—it resides in the IC that exists in the human spirit;

and since this is so hard to measure (how does one measure the ambition of Steve Jobs to "change the world"), we tend to ignore it until it becomes so obvious—as in the case of Microsoft and Google—that we have to acknowledge our old theories of wealth creation are no longer relevant.

THE THREE TYPES OF IC

The wealth-creating ability of intangible assets over physical assets is indisputable as we move from capital-based enterprises to knowledge-based enterprises. An excellent example of this is American Airlines' Sabre reservation and information system.

On October 11, 1996, AMR Corporation, the parent company of American Airlines, sold (an equity carve-out) 18 percent of its Sabre subsidiary in an initial public offering that valued Sabre at $3.3 billion. On the previous day, AMR had a total market value (including Sabre) of about $6.5 billion. Thus, a reservation system generating income from travel agents and other users of its services constituted half of the market value of AMR, equaling the value of the world's second largest airline, owning 650 airplanes (in 1996) and other physical and financial assets, including valuable landing rights. A $40 million research and development (R&D) investment in Sabre during the 1960s and 1970s mushroomed into a market value of $3.3 billion in the mid-1990s. By October 30, 1999, Sabre's share in the total market value of AMR had increased to 60 percent, demonstrating the value creation potential (scalability) of intangibles relative to that of intangibles (Lev 2001: 24).

While the airplanes American Airlines owns show up on its balance sheet, Sabre was nowhere to be found. A teacher once asked Yogi Berra, "Don't you know anything?" and he replied, "I don't even suspect anything." GAAP's deficiencies in measuring intellectual capital notwithstanding, for our purposes we are going to separate a company's IC into three categories, as originally proposed by Karl-Erik Sveiby, a leading thinker in knowledge theory, in 1989:

- Human capital
- Structural capital
- Social capital (customers, suppliers, networks, referral sources, alumni, joint venture, alliances, etc.)

We will explore each of these in greater detail. Meanwhile, the crucial point to understand now is that it is the *interplay* among the three types of IC above that generates wealth-creating opportunities for your company. Human capital, for example, can grow in two ways: when the business utilizes more of what each person knows, and when people know more things that are useful to the firm and/or its customers. And since knowledge is a "nonrival" good—meaning we can both possess it at the same time—knowledge shared is knowledge that is effectively *doubled* throughout the organization. That is why former Hewlett-Packard CEO Lew Platt said: "If HP knew what HP knows, we would be three times as profitable."

Since knowledge can be found almost anywhere, and it does not have to be newly created, it is critical we incorporate social capital into our company's IC, because defining our knowledge solely by our own human and structural capital is too inward looking. The boundaries of a business do not just keep knowledge in; they keep it out as well. Expanding our definition of IC to the social environment within which a company operates gives us many more opportunities to leverage other's knowledge. This is why BP (formerly British Petroleum) gives a "Thief of the Year" award to the person who has "stolen" the best ideas, and Texas Instruments has a "Not Invented Here, but I Did It Anyway" award for ideas taken inside or outside the company. Knowledge companies constantly celebrate learning, not just the application of knowledge to the services it offers its customers. Knowledge companies have to do much more than merely extract eight hours of work from their human capital; they have to leverage their minds as well. This requires a different level of thinking, and a totally different set of metrics to assess the effectiveness of organizational learning.

NEGATIVE INTELLECTUAL CAPITAL

Before we leave this brief introduction to IC, it is necessary to explain something that may, at first impression, not seem obvious. When IC is discussed, it is normally done in a very positive context, as most of the examples used are from successes in leveraging IC, such as Microsoft or with the Sabre reservation system. Naturally, not all R&D projects or new products are successful, and, in fact, the failure rate is astonishingly high. Most new drugs fail, as do most consumer products and books published. Investments in intangibles contain much higher levels of risk and more uncertainty than in tangible assets. If my software product fails, those costs are usually gone for good, unless I can somehow leverage the knowledge I acquired into another attempt. However, if I purchase an office building or a mall and it fails, I can at least recover a portion of my investment.

But that is not the main point to make here and now. What is important is that there is such a thing as *negative* human capital, *negative* structural capital, and *negative* social capital. Certainly, this sounds counterintuitive, but it is nonetheless true. Not everything we know is beneficial. Think of the IC a thief possesses; it is knowledge in the sense that he knows how to perform his craft, just as much as United Airlines knows how to fly planes and transport people around the world. But that does not make the knowledge valuable; and with respect to thieves, the social loss they impose is a societal negative.

Think of countries that dogmatically adhere to the principles of socialism or Marxism, even though both of these theories of social organization have been repudiated by empirical evidence. There has been enormous negative social capital built up over the past five decades in Castro's Cuba, just as there was in the former Soviet Union. As the latter struggles to make its transition to a free market economy, these negative legacies are being felt. Vital social institutions, such as secure private property rights, an effective system of jurisprudence to adjudicate disputes, an efficient banking and credit system, and other institutions necessary for economic growth are conspicuously absent. When President Ronald Reagan was asked what he thought of the Berlin Wall during a visit to Germany, he gestured at the Wall and said succinctly, "It's as ugly as the idea behind it" (Morris 1999: 461).

Examples of negative intellectual capital in an organization would include a rigid adherence to old methods that are hindering your people from achieving their potential, and subtracting from value creation. High on this list would include cost-plus pricing, Industrial Age efficiency metrics, focusing on activities and costs rather than results and value, and other forms of negative IC that have embedded themselves into the culture. These negative ideas have permeated each type of knowledge discussed herein—human, structural, and certainly social—and have become part of our tacit and explicit knowledge systems. One of the duties of this book is to point out how these legacy systems are indeed *negative* forms of IC and need to be replaced in the knowledge company of the future.

Indeed, the purpose of this chapter is to examine the negative IC ingrained in the old theory of the Industrial Age enterprise in order to construct a better theory for today's intellectual capital enterprise. In general, the theory that originally explained the Wright brothers' flying machine has been significantly enhanced by Boeing to keep its 787 in the air. This is how theories and knowledge progress—and they can have an enormous impact on our behavior.

"ANALYZING" THE PREDOMINANT BUSINESS EQUATION

In Greek language, *analyze* means "unloosen, separate into parts," which we will proceed to do with this theory before positing a better theory. When you think about the traditional theory of an enterprise, you would no doubt construct a model similar to this:

$$\text{Revenue} = \text{Capacity} \times \text{Efficiency} \times \text{Cost-Plus Price}$$

Since this model dominates the thinking of business leaders to this day, it is worth explaining the model in greater detail to understand both its strength and—as will be increasingly detailed—its fundamental weaknesses.

Consider a professional knowledge firm—such as accounting, legal, architecture, engineering, consulting, advertising, and so on—the archetypal pyramid firm model rested on the foundation of leveraging people power, in effect their "capacity." The theory is this: Since the two main drivers of profitability are leverage (number of team members per owner) and the hourly rate realization, if each partner could oversee a group of professionals, this would provide the firm with additional capacity to generate top-line revenue, and thus add to the profitability and size of the firm. If a firm wanted to add to its revenue base, it had two primary choices: It could work its people more hours, or it could hire more people. It is no secret which choice the average firm tends to choose, much to the chagrin of its already overworked team members. In most firms, the partners wait until demand is bursting at the seams before they add more professionals.

Now compare this practice with respect to capacity in other industries—this process of adding capacity *after* revenue is backward. If you think of any other industry or company—from Intel to General Electric, from FedEx to Microsoft—capacity is almost always added *before* revenue. Consider specifically FedEx: Before Fred Smith could deliver his first overnight package, he had to have trucks, drivers, airplanes, and facilities throughout the country, all at enormous fixed costs (indeed, those large fixed costs almost bankrupted FedEx in the early days). Most organizations operate with capacity to spare, which is vital to maintain flexibility in changing market conditions.

Next, let us look at the second element in the old theory—efficiency. Efficiency is a word that can be said with perfect impunity, since no one in their right mind would dispute the goal of operating efficiently. In fact, it is well known that in free market economies, efficiency is critical, as it ensures a society's resources are not going to waste. It is also well established that different levels of productivity largely explain differences in wages across countries. An American farmer will earn more plowing with a tractor than a Cuban farmer with an ox and hand plow; the American farmer is more productive, hence higher wages and more profits.

There is no doubt that increasing efficiency—or at least not sliding into inefficiency—is important. But the pendulum has swung too far in the direction of efficiency over everything else. It seems innovation, dynamism, customer service, investments in human capital, and effectiveness have all been sacrificed on the altar of efficiency. It is critical to bear in mind that a business does not exist to be efficient; rather, it exists to create value outside of itself. This value creation function can be thought of as the difference between the maximum price a customer would be willing to pay minus the opportunity costs of the activities necessary to bring to market the product or service.

Peter Drucker was fond of pointing out that the last buggy-whip manufacturers were models of efficiency. So what? What happens if you are efficient at doing the wrong things? That cannot be labeled progress. In fact, one indicator an industry is in the mature or decline stage of the product/service life cycle is when it is at the apogee of its theoretical level of efficiency.

The point is this: In industry after industry, the history of economic progress has not been to wring out the last 5 to 10 percent of efficiency, but rather to change the model to more effectively create wealth. From Walt Disney and Fred Smith to Bill Gates and Larry Ellison, these entrepreneurs did not get where they are by focusing on efficiency. All of these entrepreneurs created enormous wealth by delivering more effectively what customers were willing to pay for.

Next is cost-plus pricing, a direct cousin of the DuPont return-on-investment formula. But the real antecedent of cost-plus pricing is the Labor Theory of Value, posited by economists of the eighteenth century and Karl Marx in the middle nineteenth, and falsified by the 1871 Marginalist Revolution, as described in Chapter 2.

The offense of believing that internal costs have anything to do with value is serious. A business should be judged—and price based—on the results and wealth it creates for its customers. The cost-plus pricing paradigm is not worthy of businesses operating in an intellectual capital economy, and it is time we throw it on the ash heap of history. It is an idea from the day before yesterday. This topic is covered in depth in the first book of the Intellectual Capitalism Series, *Pricing on Purpose: Creating and Capturing Value* (Baker 2006).

Last, consider revenue. It is one thing to get *more* business, it is quite another to get *better* business. The "bigger is better" mentality is an empty promise for most companies. Acquiring more customers is not necessarily better. Growth simply for the sake of growth is the ideology of the cancer cell, not a strategy for a viable, profitable company. Eventually, the cancer kills its host. It is worth looking at the historical origins of this market share myth. In the late 1800s and early 1900s, market share theory was an excellent rationale for antitrust enforcements. You can certainly see it in the algebraic effect of greater revenue in the equation. Once fixed costs are covered, any marginal revenue will contribute to the bottom line. Of course, this implicitly implies that any customer is a good customer, which is certainly a debatable proposition.

One widely quoted study is that of Harvard Business School professor Robert D. Buzzell, who, in 1975, published an article in *Harvard Business Review,* "Market Share—A Key to Profitability." This article provided empirical evidence that companies that had dominant market share had higher profitability levels. Of course, if one is not grounded in theory, then it is easier to confuse cause and effect by merely observing the manifestations of a competitive advantage. Height and weight are closely associated but you won't grow taller by eating more. Market share is the *result* of a sustainable competitive advantage, not the *cause.*

If market share explained profitability, General Motors, United Airlines, Sears, and Philips should be the most profitable companies in their respective industries. Yet they have all turned in mediocre profitability records. Growth in profitability usually precedes market share, not vice versa. Wal-Mart, for example, was far more profitable than Sears long before it had a sizeable market share. It seems that profitability and market share grow in tandem with a viable value proposition customers are willing to pay for. The road to hell is paved with the pursuit of volume. Don't make this mistake. More often than not, less is more.

BMW has approximately 1 percent market share, while recording record profits in the automobile market. Other traditional marketing and sales leaders, such as Procter & Gamble, General Electric, and Southwest Airlines, began to switch their focus from top-line revenue growth and market share to increasing profitability. Southwest Airlines is a leader in the low-fare travel niche, and it has remained focused on that niche like a laser beam. As former CEO Herb Kelleher pointed out, "Market share has nothing to do with profitability. Market share says we just want to be big; we don't care if we make money doing it. That's what misled much of the airline industry for 15 years, after deregulation. In order to get an additional 5 percent of the market, some companies increased their costs by 25 percent. That's really incongruous if profitability is your purpose" (Freiberg and Freiberg, 1996: 49).

I have exposed some of the flaws of the traditional Industrial Era business equation. Although this discussion is not meant to be comprehensive, it nevertheless sets forth a compelling case against the old theory. Is there a better theory, one that takes into account the real wealth-producing capacity and other critical success factors of the business of the future? It is a valuable accomplishment in and of itself to point out defects in a theory—or falsify it entirely. As the eighteenth-century French cartographer Jean Baptiste Bourguignon d'Anville wrote: "To destroy false notions without even going any further is one of the ways to advance knowledge." Another way to advance knowledge is to construct a new theory, which we turn to next.

5

A BETTER THEORY—THE NEW BUSINESS EQUATION

> The mere formulation of a problem is far more often essential than its solution, which may be merely a matter of mathematical or experimental skill. To raise new questions, new possibilities, to regard old problems from a new angle requires creative imagination and marks real advances in science.
>
> —*Albert Einstein*

Only a theory can replace a theory. If we reject our old notions of the way the world works, we need a new place to go. Certainly, we can make incremental improvements to the old business equation presented in the last chapter. Indeed, business books are full of such ideas—Total Quality Management, Six Sigma, reengineering, benchmarking, and so on. But if we endeavor to make significant improvements in performance and effectiveness in today's intellectual capital economy, we have to move beyond tactics and techniques. We have to work on our theories. Doctors used to believe in leeches and bloodletting, and no matter how efficiently they executed the procedures based on those theories, they simply were not medically effective. There is no right way to do the wrong thing. As Peter Senge wrote in *The Dance of Change*: "It is not enough to change strategies, structures, and systems, unless the thinking that produced those strategies, structures, and systems also changes" (Coens and Jenkins 2000: 11).

The old canard that good ideas and knowledge are everywhere and it is really execution that matters would be relatively easy to overcome if only it were true. But it is not true; for if it were, we would have better movies (not remakes of *Bewitched* and *The Dukes of Hazzard*), books, and other products; more memorable experiences; and longer-lasting transformations from the companies we patronize. Both ideas and execution are important, yet ideas are the more valuable of the two, as we learned in our discussion of materialism in Chapter 2. There is no effective way to implement a bad idea, with history providing many lessons, from Napoleon invading Russia to countries attempting to implement socialism and communism. Were these bad ideas or simply a case of poor execution? The old adage applies: "It is a poor carpenter who blames his tools."

THE NEW THEORY

Buckminster Fuller (designer, cosmologist, philosopher, mathematician, and architect—he designed the geodesic dome) once said, "You can't change anything by fighting or resisting it. You change something by making it obsolete through superior methods." The correspondence principle is what scientists use when comparing two theories. The new theory should be able to replicate the successes of the old theory and explain where it fails, while offering new insights. It is time to replace the old business equation described in the previous chapter with this new model:

Profitability = Intellectual Capital × Price × Effectiveness

Let us explore each component of the above equation; then we will discuss why it is a better theory for explaining the success of companies operating in today's marketplace.

We start with profitability, rather than revenue, because we are not interested in growth merely for the sake of growth. As many companies around the world have learned—some the hard way, such as the airlines, retailers, and automobile manufacturers—market share is not the open sesame to more profitability. We are interested in finding the right customer, at the right price, consistent with our purpose and strategy, even if that means frequently turning away customers. I have coined a corollary to Gresham's law—bad money drives out good—from monetary economics, Baker's Law: *Bad customers drive out good customers*.

Adopting this belief means you need to become much more selective about whom you do business with, even though that marginal business may be "profitable" by conventional accounting standards. Very often, the most important costs—and benefits, for that matter—do not ever show up on a profit-and-loss statement. There is such a thing as good and bad profits. Accepting customers who are not a good fit for your company—either because of their personality or because they reject your purpose—has many deleterious effects, such as negatively affecting team member morale, and committing fixed capacity to customers who do not value your offerings. This is why the new equation focuses on profitability, not simply gross revenue. When it comes to customers, less is usually more.

As pointed out in Chapter 4, for our purposes in this book, intellectual capital is comprised of three primary components:

1. *Human capital (HC).* This comprises your team members and associates who work either for you or with you. As one industry leader said, this is the capital that leaves in the elevator at night. The important thing to remember about HC is that it cannot be owned, only contracted, since it is completely volitional. In fact, more and more, knowledge workers own the means of your company's production, and knowledge workers will invest their HC in those organizations that pay a decent return on investment, both economic and psychological. In the final analysis, your people are not assets (they deserve more respect than a copier machine and

a computer); they are not resources to be harvested from the land like coal when you run out; ultimately, they are *volunteers* and it is totally up to them whether or not they get back into the elevator the following morning.

2. *Structural capital.* This is everything that remains in your company once the HC has stepped into the elevator, such as databases, customer lists, systems, procedures, intranets, manuals, files, technology, and all of the explicit knowledge tools you utilize to produce results for your customers.

3. *Social capital.* This includes your customers, the main reason a business exists; but it also includes your suppliers, vendors, networks, referral sources, alumni, joint venture and alliance partners, reputation, and so on. Of the three types of IC, this is perhaps the least leveraged, and yet it is highly valued by customers.

In the business of the future, *effectiveness* takes precedence over efficiency. A business does not exist to be efficient, it exists to create wealth for its customers. An obsessive compulsion to increase efficiency (doing things right) reduces the firm's effectiveness at doing the right things. The pursuit of efficiency has hindered many companies' ability to pursue opportunities; hence, these organizations spend most of their time solving problems. One cannot grow a company and continuously cut costs and increase efficiency. Today's IC companies are composed of human beings who do not check their emotions at the door, and they are subject to fears, doubts, variable levels of self-esteem, uncertainty, anger, rage, and a whole range of other emotions that cannot be captured by traditional efficiency measurements. In other words, *humans are messy*. Focusing on effectiveness does not eliminate these issues, but it does take them into account far better than efficiency metrics, which can be desensitizing and inhumane at times.

This new equation comports with the realities of an IC economy, taking into account knowledge workers who use their hearts and minds, not their brawn and hands. This equation recognizes the importance of mind over matter, the price thereof, and the effectiveness of the workers who produce it, as well as the customers who purchase it. It may not yet be a perfect theory, but it is far superior to the alternative discussed in the prior chapter.

COGNITIVE DISSONANCE

I am going to rely on the reader's ability to hold two opposite thoughts in his or her head at the same time, while still functioning. I have a love/hate relationship with the above equation. On the one hand, it is a superior model for the business of the future because it recognizes the realities of the marketplace in which companies operate, and it focuses on leveraging the right things. It takes into account the importance of dynamism, innovation, and a whole host of other human activities that are simply not captured in the old equation. On the other hand, because it is nothing more than an algebraic equation, it is an incredible simplification of the components that comprise the typical organization. When we look at equations, we tend to think of each component comprising a separate part that can be individually manipulated and controlled, a very one-dimensional view of a business made up of human beings. What the equation does not explain is *how* to raise prices, or *how* to increase effectiveness and intellectual capital, nor does it explain the interconnections and interdependencies of the various components. Certainly, the equation can describe an abstract feature such as effectiveness, but it does not really enhance one's understanding of how change occurs in the firm as a whole. In other words, it can explain the *ends* (profitability), but not the *means* (how does one measure effectiveness?).

Any equation assumes a certain cause-and-effect relationship that tends to lead us to believe these patterns are sequential and linear and not subject to the perpetual feedback of prior causes. In the old equation, increase capacity and revenue grows; in the day-to-day realities of a company, trying to work your team members more hours is going to have a whole host of unintended consequences that will ultimately affect the goal of increasing profit. No equation can capture the richness of these interrelated means.

Another problem with the equation is that it presents the characteristics of a firm as nothing but the sum of the parts; if you change one aspect, you invariably change another by an equal amount. But in a living, breathing, system such as a firm, parts and wholes are not linked so linearly. Thus, a small change in one of the parts can have a profound and dramatic influence on everything else. Think of the effects of a toxic manager who belittles and intimidates his team members. He may achieve higher efficiency in one aspect of the equation, but so totally destroy morale and motivation that the ultimate outcome will be a reduction in firm effectiveness, customer service, and profitability.

Peter Drucker has left business executives a rich legacy in his writings, extensively detailing why traditional management science fails to perform. Executives who believe they can change one aspect of a company without affecting others are ignoring the reality of a firm's being an *interdependent* system. Drucker explained the phenomenon this way:

> There is one fundamental insight underlying all management science. It is that the business enterprise is a *system* of the highest order: a system whose parts are human beings contributing voluntarily of their knowledge, skill and dedication to a joint venture. And one thing characterizes all genuine systems, whether they be mechanical like the control of a missile, biological like a tree, or social like the business enterprise: it is interdependence. The whole of a system is not necessarily improved if one particular function or part is improved or made more efficient. In fact, the system may well be damaged thereby, or even destroyed. In some cases the best way to strengthen the system may be to weaken a part—to make it less precise or less efficient. For what matters in any system is the performance of the whole; this is the result of growth and of dynamic balance, adjustment, and integration, rather than of mere technical efficiency.

Primary emphasis on the efficiency of parts in management science is therefore bound to do damage. It is bound to optimize precision of the tool at the expense of the health and performance of the whole (Drucker 2004: 97).

Any equation is similar to the difference between a map and a territory—one is a two-dimensional explanation, and the other is full of complex and rich interconnections that could never be captured on paper. It has been said that studying a living entity on paper is like performing an autopsy on dolphins versus swimming with them. Certainly, both activities will give you a better understanding of dolphins, but which one will let you observe the rich and contextual feel of a living creature? Clinical pathologists implicitly understand this difference, as they instruct physicians to never treat a test result but, rather, treat the patient.

The careful reader—perhaps the reader with scientific or marketing training—will note that the equation doesn't answer the important question of why we are in business, as it appears to put profitability above all else. This is a serious omission. The fact that a business needs to make a profit is a tautology, and is in fact quite irrelevant. Most importantly, a business must create and retain customers and add wealth to their lives by providing them more in value than the price they are paying.

Peter Drucker indefatigably pointed out that "there is only one valid definition of business purpose: to create a customer" (Flaherty 1999: 131). This is known as the *marketing concept*. The purpose of any organization—from a governmental agency or nonprofit foundation to a corporation or a church—exists to create results *outside* of itself. The result of a school is an educated student, as is a cured patient for a hospital, or a saved soul for a church. A business exists to create wealth for its customers.

The only things that exist inside of a business are costs, activities, efforts, problems, mediocrity, friction, politics, and crises. In fact, Peter Drucker wrote, "One of the biggest mistakes I have made during my career was coining the term *profit center,* around 1945. I am thoroughly ashamed of it now, because inside a business there are no profit centers, just cost centers" (Drucker 2002: 49, 84). The only profit center is a customer's check that doesn't bounce. Customers are indifferent to the internal workings of your company in terms of costs, desired profits levels, and efforts. Nobody wants to hear about the labor pains—they want to see the baby. Value is only created when you have produced something the customer voluntarily, and willingly, pays for. What makes the marketing concept so breathtakingly brilliant is that the focus is always on the *outside* of the organization. It does not look inside and ask, "What do we want and need?" but, rather, it looks outside to the customer and asks, "What do you desire and value?"

In fact, what is routinely called *capitalism* is more accurately described as *consumerism*, wherein the customer is sovereign—those with the gold rule. While the marketing concept has existed for decades, it is regularly ignored as businesses routinely lose sight of the fact that the sole reason they exist is to serve customers outside of their four walls.

A company exists to serve real flesh-and-blood people, not some mass of demographics known as "the market." As Stanley Marcus (the son of one of the founders of Neiman-Marcus) used to love to point out, no market ever purchased anything in one of his stores, but a lot of customers came in and bought things and made him a rich man. In the final analysis, a business doesn't exist to be efficient, control costs, perform cost accounting, or give people fancy titles and power over the lives of others. It exists to create results and wealth *outside* of itself. This profound lesson from Drucker must not be forgotten.

Unfortunately, in many instances, this lesson has never been learned. The conventional wisdom in business is to buy low and sell high and measure the bottom line by the historical profit-and-loss statement, which any first-year accounting student can manipulate. Our 500-year-old accounting model is utterly inadequate at relating internal costs to external wealth created, and simply ignores the wealth-producing capacity of an organization. This is why we see market valuations many multiples of book value.

Rather than maximizing shareholder value, leaders should focus on the wealth-creating capacity of their organizations, which is, ultimately, the leading indicator for optimizing shareholder value. As Jack Welch pointed out, "One thing we've discovered with certainty is that anything we do that makes the customer more successful inevitably results in a financial return for us" (Khalsa 1999: 25).

Another reason we lose sight of the truth that firms exist to create wealth is that the language of business is drawn largely from war and sports analogies. In sports, a competition is usually zero-sum, meaning one competitor wins and the other loses. This is not at all relevant in a business setting. Just because your competitors flourish does not mean you lose. There is room for both FedEx and UPS, Airbus and Boeing, Pepsi and Coke, Ford and General Motors, and while their sparring might be mistaken by some as war, as John Kay points out "not in Pepsi's wildest fantasies does it imagine that the conflict will end in the second burning of Atlanta [Coca-Cola's head office]" (Koch 2001: 73). When Coca-Cola changed its recipe to New Coke, company spokesman Carlton Curtis stated, "You're talking about having some guts—and doing something that few managements would have the guts to do." If you find it amusing that grown men talk about *guts* and *recipes* in the same sentence, then it should be obvious that business has nothing to do with war.

Business is not about annihilating your competition; it is about adding more value to your customers. War destroys, commerce builds. Both sides to a transaction must profit or it would not take place, the exact point made in the 1700s by Adam Smith. Marketplaces are conversations, derived from the Greek marketplace, the *agora*. It is where buyers and sellers meet to discuss their wares and share visions of the future, where supply and demand intersect at the equilibrium point with a handshake. It is as far removed from war as capitalism is from communism, and perhaps this war analogy, too, needs to be tossed onto the ash heap of history.

One more criticism of this equation should be mentioned before we leave this analysis of cognitive dissonance. New realities require new words. The word *efficiency* has been deliberately replaced with *effectiveness*, bowing to the observation that a business does not exist to be efficient but, rather, effective. What happens if you are 100 percent efficient at doing the *wrong* thing? Effectiveness stresses the ability of getting the right things done. Still, this word, too, is not quite precise enough at describing the effect a modern firm, based on the intangibles of intellectual capital, is trying to create. I much prefer the word *efficacious*, meaning "having the power to produce a desired effect." This term is used to describe the miraculous power of many drugs, since it suggests possession of a special quality or virtue that makes it possible to achieve a result. In an IC economy, where wealth is created using the power of the mind—as opposed to the body—these characteristics better explain the value created by knowledge workers.

In any event, while one could point out other weaknesses in the new equation, in a book we must break things down into separate components to deal with them more effectively. We cannot do everything at once. This is the advantage of a theory, because while it will never capture the true essence of a living organization, it can be studied in its quantitative and qualitative parts, advancing our understanding of how those parts are interdependent. A theory need not be elegant (Einstein quipped, "Elegance is for tailors"), nor capture the entire essence of the phenomenon it is trying to explain; all it has to do to be effective is allow us to predict, explain, or prescribe the behavior we observe. It is similar to a camera, not a photograph, in that it is a tool that can be used well or badly, to capture reality, not depict it.

Another important element of theory building is to have a preference to shave with Occam's razor—that is, any hypothesis must not be developed beyond necessity. Unfortunately, most business books contain a paucity of theory, and when they do, the razor couldn't cut butter. To this end, the new equation is presented only as a model—a map—to help us capture a deeper understanding of how organizations can operate more effectively in an IC economy. No one would argue that you can get anywhere by looking at maps without venturing out to sea. But no one would suggest you would be very safe at sea without a map.

WHERE DO PROFITS COME FROM?

A ship in harbor is safe—but that is not what ships are for.
—*John A. Shedd (1859 to circa 1928)*

In seminars around the world, we have presented to participants the following factors of production in any economy, and the type of income derived therefrom:

Land = Rents
Labor = Salaries and Wages
Capital = Interest, Dividends, and Capital Gains

We then ask a deceptively simple question: Where do profits come from? The answers range from entrepreneurs and value to revenue minus expenses and customers. Nevertheless, the real answer is that profits come from *risk*. The word *entrepreneur* comes from the French word, *entreprendre*, meaning "to undertake." It is the basis for the English word *enterprise*. But not just entrepreneurs (or feminine, entrepreneuses) make profits; so do established enterprises.

When a business engages in innovation, it is taking a risk. In Italian, the word *risk* derives from *risicare*, which means "to dare," which implies a choice, not a fate, as Peter L. Bernstein points out in his outstanding study of risk, *Against the Odds*. In other words, risk is an economic positive. There are five responses when confronted with risk: avoid it, reduce it, transfer it, accept it, or increase it. In the final analysis, a business cannot eliminate risk, as that would eliminate profits. The goal is to take calculated risks and choose them wisely. The dilemma in many firms is that they are allocating a disproportionate share of their resources in perpetuating yesterday and today rather than creating tomorrow. By setting a nice, comfortable floor on their earnings (via the cost-plus pricing mechanism), they have placed an artificial ceiling over their heads as well. This is self-imposed, and it comes from the attempt to avoid risk and uncertainty (which is very costly in terms of lost opportunities).

Consider labor unions, the epitome of an institution attempting to avoid risk. Talk with union members and you quickly discover that they credit the union for their standard of living. Certainly, they are paid an above-market wage (Milton Friedman has proved this point), and receive good benefits, a healthy pension, and generous time off. But have you ever met a wealthy rank-and-file union member? The trade-off they made for their union compensation package is an artificial ceiling they can never rise above, at least not while employed in a union job, since seniority and other stultifying restrictions limit their potential. Risk avoidance is the antithesis to a successful enterprise, condemning it to mediocrity, perhaps even extinction. The goal should be to maximize wealth-creating opportunities rather than to minimize risk, as Peter Drucker pointed out:

> A business always saws off the limb on which it sits; it makes existing risks riskier or creates new ones. . . . Risk is of the essence, and risk making and risk taking constitute the basic function of enterprise. . . . This risk is something quite different from risk in the statistician's probability; it is risk of the unique event, the irreversible qualitative breaking of the pattern (Kehrer 1989: 53).

Drucker is explaining a basic economic theory known as Böhm-Bawerk's Law—named after the Austrian economist Eugen Böhm-Bawerk (1851–1926)—which states, "Existing means of production can yield greater economic performance only through greater uncertainty; through taking greater risk" (Kehrer 1989: 298). Businesses have very sophisticated means of measuring the costs and benefits of risks, *once they have been taken*. But the risk occurs only *before* the event, and cannot be accurately measured until *after* it has occurred. There is no theory—in economics or finance—that measures the cost of *not* taking a risk. Yet, it is precisely these losses that cost the business the most.

Risk and uncertainty are the twin banes of human existence. Consider what people will sacrifice to avoid them. Risk avoidance has created a $1.5 trillion worldwide insurance industry. It is why rental car companies make more from the collision damage waiver insurance they sell then they do renting cars. It is why buyers of appliances (e.g., microwaves, stereos, and other electronic goods) will spend large sums on extended warranties for products that could be replaced more cheaply. It is why criminals and prosecutors plea-bargain, each being uncertain as to what a jury is going to do.

Peter Drucker classified risk into three categories: the affordable, the nonaffordable, and the compulsory:

> First, there was the risk a business could afford to take. If it succeeded at the innovation, it would not achieve major results, and if it failed, it would not do great corporate damage. Second, there was the risk a business could not afford to take. This risk usually involved an innovation that the company lacked the knowledge to implement, and usually would end up building the competition's business. Third, there was the risk a business could not afford not to take. Failure to undertake this innovation meant there might not be a business several years hence (Flaherty 1999: 172).

Naturally, in this book, the third type of risk taking will be advocated, that is, taking those risks that will spur the firm to higher levels of effectiveness and profitability. Too often in organizations, risk taking is seen as a negative, a reckless use of resources better spent on other functions. Nothing could be further from the truth. Committing a portion of today's resources to future expectations certainly entails risk, but since that is the source of profits—not to mention innovation, dynamism, and economic growth—it is a process inherent in the function of business entities. Economy-wide, profits may constitute only 10 percent of what the American economy produces, but in terms of creating an incentive to effectively produce the other 90 percent, they are essential. And profits are derived from risk; complacency is not an option.

This, by the way, is another defect you may care to note about the new equation, because it makes it look as if profitability appears by effectively leveraging intellectual capital at the right price, but misses the importance of risk. We must always remember that profits, ultimately, are derived from risk taking, and no equation, no matter how complex and intricate, will ever be able to capture the essence of an entrepreneur, an effective executive, or a profit-making enterprise with a distinguished purpose.

SUMMARY AND CONCLUSIONS

This chapter has laid the groundwork for the remaining chapters and all of the books in the Intellectual Capitalism Series. We have covered a lot of material here and have presented some radical (from Latin for "root") ideas. I have argued that the old equation is not worthy of enterprises that, more and more, are composed of knowledge workers because it leverages the wrong things and does not explain the elements of success in an IC economy. The new equation is a worthy model for the noble calling of enterprise. And while there are still shortcomings in the equation, it is a starting point for understanding the drivers of success for the business of the future.

When I first publicly presented and contrasted the new equation with the old one at a seminar for a professional knowledge firm, an attendee explained to me at the break why she thought the new equation was so superior to the old. She said, and I'm paraphrasing here, "Your equation presents so many more factors that enable a firm to achieve its objectives than the old one did. It is like being freed from a cage that has restricted our firm for decades." It is my fervent hope this new paradigm has a similar effect on all who study it and will change their behavior as a result. The old paradigm is indeed far too restricting, and it doesn't represent the realities of the marketplace in which companies find themselves currently. As Peter Drucker said in a 1994 interview in *Harvard Business Review*, "The assumptions on which most businesses are being run no longer fit reality" (Edersheim 2007: 19). Ronald Reagan delivered the same message six years earlier to the students at Moscow State University. The enterprises of the future must lead the way by following a model worthy of a proud heritage of free minds operating in free markets being the catalyst for dynamism and growth.

Modern firms are knowledge organizations, and it is time for them to begin acting as if they understood this fact, rather than trying to constantly enhance efficiency by treating their human capital as if they had no mind of their own. Humans are not simply machines that exist to operate at peak efficiency, and the old equation keeps us mired in this mentality. I believe we can—indeed, must—do better than the opportunities presented by an antiquated model. Let us now explore the nature of knowledge, the dominant force of all wealth creation.

6

THE SCARCEST RESOURCE OF ALL

> After all, the caveman had the same natural resources at their
> disposal as we have today, and the difference between their standard
> of living and ours is a difference between the knowledge they could
> bring to bear on those resources and the knowledge used today.
> —*Thomas Sowell, Knowledge and Decisions, 1996*

The distinction between ideas and knowledge may be subtle, yet
is well illustrated by the following tale:

> A peasant discovers that many of his chickens are dying, so he
> seeks advice from a consultant. The consultant recommends that
> the peasant play music in the chicken coop, but the deaths continue.
> The consultant then recommends changing the lighting in the coop,
> but the deaths continue unabated. Pondering again, the consultant
> recommends repainting the chicken coop in bright colors. Finally,
> all the chickens die. "What a shame," the consultant tells the peas-
> ant, "I had so many more good ideas" (Wheelan 2002: 225).

In reality, specific knowledge is rare, despite all of the glib gen-
eralities of knowledge being everywhere. Data and information are
certainly everywhere, especially since the introduction of the Internet, but information is not knowledge. The cost of reproducing
information has dropped significantly, while the cost of replicat-
ing knowledge is a far more expensive process. Epistemologists
have spent centuries trying to comprehend what it means to know
something. *Epistemology* comes from the Greek word *episteme*,
which means "absolute certain truth." But how do we know

something for sure? For that matter, how much does the world know? Is it all worth knowing? What is the value of the world's stock of knowledge? How much of it is obsolete? David Hume, the Scottish philosopher, was convinced you can know nothing for sure, "But now I am going to light my pipe and go out for a meal."

THOMAS SOWELL AND FRIEDRICH HAYEK ON KNOWLEDGE

... [T]he most severe constraints facing human beings in all societies and throughout history—inadequate knowledge for making all the decisions that each individual and every organization nevertheless has to make, in order to perform the tasks that go with living and achieve the goals that go with being human.

—*Thomas Sowell, Knowledge and Decisions, 1996*

In his landmark work on knowledge, *Knowledge and Decisions*, Thomas Sowell delineates various kinds of ideas by their relationship to the authentication process:

> There are ideas systemically prepared for authentication ("theories"), ideas not derived from any systematic process ("visions"), ideas which could not survive any reasonable authentication process ("illusions"), ideas which exempt themselves from any authentication process ("myths"), ideas which have already passed authentication processes ("facts"), as well as ideas known to have failed—or certain to fail—such processes ("falsehoods"—both mistakes and lies) (Sowell 1996: 4–5).

Sowell points out the difference between "general expertise" and highly specific knowledge with this historical example:

> One of the classic disasters of government planning involved the British government's attempts to grow peanuts in colonial Rhodesia after World War II. Although this scheme turned out to be a costly failure, ordinary farmers around the world had been deciding for generations where and how to grow peanuts, each on his own particular land, whose individual characteristics were known

directly from personal experience. Why was this government plan to grow peanuts such an economic disaster, when poorly educated or even illiterate farmers have been able to do what highly educated experts were not able to do? The farmers had highly specific knowledge, which is often far more important than general "expertise" (Sowell 2000: 250).

In a business enterprise, two sources of profit are possible: an *economic* profit and an *epistemological* profit, the latter of which has the ability to advance specific knowledge. The free market, meaning the sovereign consumer, is the authentication process Sowell alludes to, at least as it relates to product and service offerings. Any offering not valued by consumers will be ruthlessly repudiated in a free market. Compare this authentication process with many of the ideas of academics, which either do not work or have not been authenticated by experience. The only test appears to be if your colleagues agree with what you are saying.

The interesting thing about the difference between an advanced civilization and a primitive one is not that each person has more knowledge but actually that he or she requires far less. Philosopher Alfred North Whitehead said, "Civilization advances by extending the number of operations we can perform without thinking about them." A primitive savage must be able to produce a wide range of goods and services for himself and his family, whereas an auto mechanic today can get by with just knowing his area of expertise, as he will rely on the specific knowledge of others to provide his wood, food, clothing, and medical services. A photographer during the Civil War had to have far more knowledge of the photographic process than today's digital camera user.

In an effort to feed a family, perform productive work, and make a contribution to society, individuals engage in enterprise to serve the needs of others. In reality, *Homo sapiens* is the only animal that coordinates elaborate task-sharing activities among unrelated members of the same species. Our ancestors 12,000 years ago, who wandered the plains in small bands in search of food worrying about opportunistic strangers inflicting warfare, murder, and thievery, would be in awe of our ability to step out our front door into a city of 10 million anonymous people, drive to a supermarket stocked with just the right amount of meat, produce, and other essentials for daily sustenance—all done with no central coordinating intelligence. The amount of knowledge required to get products and services delivered to a place convenient for customers is an enormous challenge in terms of the general expertise that exists among millions of people that has to be shared. Consider those bananas you purchased. How would any one of us get people in Costa Rica, some of whom may not even like Americans, to work hard, grow, harvest, and ship bananas? What do any of us know about truck- and shipbuilding, or navigation? This knowledge is widely dispersed, residing in the minds of millions of people. It is beyond the capacity of the world's supercomputers combined.

Friedrich A. Hayek, the 1974 Nobel Prize winner in economics, believed that "Civilization rests on the fact that we all benefit from knowledge which we do not possess." As Will Rogers said, "Everybody is ignorant, only in different subjects." Hayek classified knowledge into scientific knowledge (general rules) and knowledge of the particular circumstances of time and place. Hence, the economic quandary confronting any society is not just how to allocate resources but how to utilize knowledge not possessed by anyone in its totality. Hayek explains:

> The real central problem of economics as a social science ... is how the spontaneous interaction of a number of people, each possessing only bits of knowledge, brings about a state of affairs ... which could be brought about by deliberate direction only by somebody who possesses the combined knowledge of all these individuals (Hayek 1948: 79).

When Hayek addressed the American Economic Association in 1945 on the occasion of his retirement as its president, the title of his address was "The Use of Knowledge in Society," wherein he called attention to the important social role of prices as carriers of information and contrasted this knowledge with so-called scientific knowledge. I quote Hayek here at length because in this address he articulated the concept of "special knowledge of circumstances of the fleeting moment not known to others:"

Today it is almost heresy to suggest that scientific knowledge is not the sum of all knowledge. But a little reflection will show that there is beyond question a body of very important but unorganized knowledge which cannot possibly be called scientific in the sense of knowledge of general rules: the knowledge of the particular circumstances of time and place. It is with respect to this that practically every individual has some advantage over all others in that he possesses unique information of which beneficial use might be made, but of which use can be made only if the decisions depending on it are left to him or are made with his active cooperation. We need to remember only how much we have to learn in any occupation after we have completed our theoretical training, how big a part of our working life we spend learning particular jobs, and how valuable an asset in all walks of life is knowledge of people, of local conditions, and special circumstances. To know of and put to use a machine not fully employed, or somebody's skill which could be better utilized, or to be aware of a surplus stock which can be drawn upon during an interruption of supplies, is socially quite as useful as the knowledge of better alternative techniques. And the shipper who earns his living from using otherwise empty or half-filled journeys of tramp-steamers, or the estate agent whose whole knowledge is almost exclusively one of temporary opportunities, or the *arbitrageur* who gains from local differences of commodity prices, are all performing eminently useful functions based on special knowledge of circumstances of the fleeting moment not known to others.

It is a curious fact that this sort of knowledge should today be generally regarded with a kind of contempt, and that anyone who by such knowledge gains an advantage over somebody better equipped with theoretical or technical knowledge is thought to have acted almost disreputably. To gain an advantage from better knowledge of facilities of communication or transport is sometimes regarded as almost dishonest, although it is quite as important that society make use of the best opportunities in this respect as in using the latest scientific discoveries (Hayek 1945: 521–522).

This observation has far-reaching implications for the study of intellectual capital. The majority of the most important knowledge in any field of endeavor, be it sports, entertainment, or business, is *tacit* knowledge—that is, knowledge specific to time, place, and circumstances. This form of knowledge is extremely difficult to articulate and relatively expensive to transfer, often traveling only through apprenticeship and trial and error. Your local Starbucks' knowing exactly how you like your morning ritual, a barber's understanding exactly how his customer likes his hair cut, the local hotel operator's being aware of how the college football schedule influences the demand for rooms, travelers in unfamiliar cities befriending a local resident to discover good restaurants and sightseeing locations, and the advantage a golfer has who has played on the course many times and is said to have local knowledge—all point to the fluctuating value of location, location, location.

INFORMATION WANTS TO BE FREE, KNOWLEDGE ISN'T

In the late 1960s, journalist, publisher, and cultural entrepreneur Stewart Brand founded the countercultural *Whole Earth Catalog*. The central idea contained in the *Catalog* was that technology could be liberating rather than oppressive, as many had imagined thanks to George Orwell's classic novel *1984*. Brand uttered a statement that made its way into the age of the Internet, assuring us "Information wants to be free." Many people foretold of the information explosion, including Nobel Prize–winning economist Herbert Simon, who claimed, "A wealth of information creates a poverty of attention." He posited that people develop short-cuts to decipher all of the information that bombards them on a daily basis—known as *heuristics*—and allow us to make more effective choices. One of the ways in which we achieve this is to purchase brands, since they reduce the search costs of buying goods and services.

Another prophet of the potential of the information age was Norman Macrae, then editor of *The Economist*, who in a moment of rare prescience wrote in 1972:

> The prospect is, after all, that we are going to enter an age when any duffer sitting at a computer terminal in his laboratory or office or public library or home can delve through unimaginable increased mountains of information in mass-assembly data banks with mechanical powers of concentration and calculation that will be greater by a factor of tens of thousands than was ever available to the human brain of even an Einstein (Cialdini 2001: 237).

In his address to the students at Moscow State University, Ronald Reagan spoke of computers "Linked by a network of satellites and fiber-optic cables, one individual with a desktop computer and a telephone commands resources unavailable to the largest governments just a few years ago." These statements are undeniable when you are discussing data and information, but, as Sowell and Hayek make clear from the last section, not so if we are talking about knowledge. We need to draw a distinction between data, information, and knowledge:

Data.   Factual information (as measurements or statistics) used as a basis for reasoning, discussion, or calculation. There is no judgment, interpretation, context, or basis for action. It knows nothing of its own importance or irrelevance.

Information.   Root in Latin is *formare*, meaning "to shape." Peter Drucker said information is "data endowed with relevance and purpose." It has to have a sender and a receiver, and it is the receiver, not the sender, who decides if the message is information or not. "We add value to information in various ways: Contextualized; Categorized; Calculated; Corrected; Condensed" (Davenport and Prusak 1998: 3–4).

Knowledge.   The fact or condition of knowing something with familiarity gained through experience or association. To turn information into knowledge we need: "Comparison; Consequences; Connections; Conversation" (Davenport and Prusak 1998: 6).

Knowledge is information in context, combined with understanding. Information, in and of itself, is very inefficient for transferring knowledge, especially tacit knowledge, since it is the receiver who gives the message meaning. If he does not understand the message, or cannot act on the information, we can hardly call the situation an effective knowledge transfer. Another way of analyzing the difference between information and knowledge is to consider who pays for information? Usually, the suppliers of it, which is the exact opposite of what you would expect with a valuable resource. Since it requires time and shoe leather—what economists term *search costs*—to convert information into useful knowledge, and since we cannot know whether it was worth the costs until after we are done, an inordinate amount of information has a negative value. In a world of TiVo and other digital recording devices, viewers can now skip over ads, which they perceive to be minuses, not pluses. A person in a poor country can use a cellular telephone and even hook up to the Internet, both of which plug him into the information economy. But it is a far cry from being in a knowledge economy.

Knowledge by itself is static, but *knowing* is dynamic. Knowledge enables us to act, which is its ultimate purpose. Knowledge requires us to use theory, since without theory there is no way to filter all of the information that is required to take effective action. Knowledge by itself is not the goal, as Peter Drucker wrote: "Executives are not paid for knowing, but for *getting the right things done*" (Drucker and Maciariello, 2006: Foreword). If knowledge alone were enough, millions of children would not be dying annually of dehydration due to diarrhea. Another distinction is that data and information tell us conclusively only about the past. To peer into the future, we need a theory.

All ideas and knowledge are, ultimately, subjected to the authentication process Sowell discussed above. When Milton Friedman (1912–2006) taught his graduate seminar courses in economics at the University of Chicago, he used to ask what his students came to call his two terrifying questions:

1. How do you know?

2. So what?

In terms of constructing a theory, these questions are profound: the first making us observe the world, the second forcing us to say what the effect is. In order to answer the latter, we need theory—a statement of cause and effect. Philosophers of science, such as Karl Popper and Thomas Kuhn, have explained how to construct a theory, which is done in a cyclical pattern, as follows:

Observation

Categorization

Prediction

Confirmation

Karl Popper believed that if a theory could not be refuted, it was not scientific. This is why all scientifically valid theories are formulated in a manner exposing them to being disproved. Scientists always ask, "What would it take to admit your theory is wrong?" If you answer nothing, you are arguing an assertion—a matter of faith—not reason. If you cannot be wrong, you cannot be right either. This is why scientists are constantly looking for anomalies. Indeed, many scientific breakthroughs come from such anomalies, and scientists are given awards for falsifying the theories of others. This is what David Hume meant when he wrote, "Knowledge is only ignorance postponed."

Theories are not judged based on their complexity, but rather on their usefulness to predict, prescribe, or explain, or as China's former communist leader Deng Xiaoping used to say: "It doesn't matter if a cat is black or white, so long as it catches mice." Some of the best theories are relatively simple, which is fortunate since life is complex enough. Occam's razor applies—*Entia non sunt multiplicanda praeter necessitatem*—Latin for "Entities should not be multiplied unnecessarily." A theory is like a map—a mere way to capture the territory—and a life-size map would be useless (as comedian Steven Wright cracks: "How would you fold it?").

For example, a lot of consultants will espouse best practices, which is nothing but *mimicking* the actions of successful companies—also known as *benchmarking*. Even worse is benchmarking only in one's own industry, the equivalent of measuring a ruler with itself. Harvard Business School Professor Clayton Christensen humorously points out the flaws in this method in *The Innovator's Solution*:

> Consider, for illustration, the history of man's attempts to fly. Early researchers observed strong correlations between being able to fly and having feathers and wings. Possessing these attributes had a high *correlation* with the ability to fly, but when humans attempted to follow the "best practices" of the most successful flyers by strapping feathered wings onto their arms, jumping off cliffs, and flapping hard, they were not successful ... It was not until Bernoulli's study of fluid mechanics helped him articulate the mechanism through which airfoils create lift that human flight began to be *possible* (Christensen and Raynor 2003: 14).

Rather than mimicking what successful companies *do*, executives should contemplate how they *think*. Christensen goes on to level this charge against management research:

> Many writers, and many who think of themselves as serious academics, are so eager to prove the worth of their theories that they studiously avoid the discovery of anomalies. ... We need to do *anomaly-seeking* research, not anomaly-avoiding research.
>
> We have urged doctoral students who are seeking potentially productive research questions for their thesis research to simply ask when a "fad" theory won't work—for example, "When is process reengineering a bad idea?" (Christensen and Raynor 2003: 27).
>
> Unfortunately, many of those engaged in management research seem anxious not to spotlight instances their theory did not accurately predict. They engage in anomaly-avoiding, rather than anomaly-seeking, research and as a result contribute to the perpetuation of unpredictability. Hence, we lay much responsibility for the perceived unpredictability of business building at the feet of the very people whose business it is to study and write about these problems (Christensen and Raynor 2003: 28).

In their endless quest to provide practical, nontheoretical tools executives can use on Monday morning, consultants are doing a disservice to their customers by confusing information with knowledge. If we desire true insight and wisdom, we should follow the advice of physicist David Bohm and "hang our assumptions in front of us." Henry Mintzberg, professor of Management Studies at McGill University in Montreal, Canada, explains in his enlightening and provocative book, *Managers Not MBAs*, why theory is an essential part of education:

> Managers who are doing their job live practice every day. They hardly need the educational setting to get them more practical. Education is hands-*off*; otherwise it is not education. It has to provide something different—conceptual ideas that are quite literally *un*realistic and *im*practical, at least seemingly so in conventional terms. People learn when they *suspend their disbeliefs*, to entertain provocative ideas that can reshape their thinking. That is what education is all about.
>
> Certainly managers have to be "practical"—they have to get things done. But they also have to be thoughtful. The best of them think for themselves. ...The worst copy others—not learn from others, just copy them, mindlessly. They look for some external secret to managerial success, some formula or technique, without realizing that this itself is a formula for failure. Put differently, a central purpose of management education is to encourage the development of wisdom. This requires a thoughtful atmosphere in the classroom, where individuals can probe into their own experience, primed by interesting ideas, concepts, theories.
>
> *Theory* is a dirty word in some managerial quarters. That is rather curious, because all of us, managers especially, can no more get along without theories than libraries can get along without catalogs—and for the same reason: theories help us make sense of incoming information.
>
> It would be nice if we could carry reality around in our heads and use it to make our decisions. Unfortunately, no head is that big. So we carry around theories, or models, instead: conceptual frameworks that simplify the reality to help us understand it. Hence, these theories better be good! (Mintzberg 2004: 249).

Managers these days are inundated with prescriptions. These are the problem in management, not the solution, because situations vary so widely. Who would go to a drugstore that dispenses one kind of pill? So why do managers go to courses that prescribe one kind of technique, the solution for every company, whether strategic planning or shareholder value? What managers need is descriptive insight to help them choose or develop prescriptions for their own particular needs. The fact is that better description in the mind of the intelligent practitioner is the most powerful prescriptive tool we have, for no manager can be better than the conceptual frameworks he or she uses. That is the basis of wisdom (Mintzberg 2004: 252).

Another reason theories are subject to constant falsification is they can show *correlation* but not necessarily *causation*, as Christensen's example of man attempting to fly by attaching feathers and leaping off cliffs proves. In Britain, the number of ham radio operator licenses granted annually was highly correlated with the number of people certified insane, illustrating how statistically significant information can be insignificant, especially if not illuminated by a theory. Many people die in hospitals, but that does not prove that hospitals *cause* death. Wet streets do not cause rain.

One of the most cited anecdotes regarding correlation and causation, and how selection bias in the data we assemble can lead to false conclusions, is regarding statistician Abraham Wald, who assessed the vulnerability of airplanes to enemy fire during World War II. The data showed that certain parts of the plane were hit more than others, and the military concluded that these parts should be reinforced. Wald, however, came to the opposite conclusion, advising to protect the parts hit least often. He understood the *selection bias* inherent in the military's data, which was based on those planes that had returned safely to the air base. Wald figured planes hit in a critical spot would not be likely to return, whereas those that did were hit in noncritical areas. Thus, reinforcing parts on the returned planes would not increase their safety.

Alvin Toffler provides the answer to a relevant question: *Why* (rather than *what*) do people believe what they do? He maintains that humans use six criteria for validating our knowledge:

1. Consensus
2. Consistency (fits with other patterns)
3. Authority
4. Revelation
5. Durability
6. Science (Toffler and Toffler 2006: 123–126).

Of these six methods, science is the least relied upon, since only a small fraction of the decisions we make every day are based on it. The other five methods may not be as precise as a testable scientific hypothesis, but comprise the shortcuts economist Herbert Simon says we use to make better decisions. Just take one of the methods, consensus, to illustrate how dangerous it can be to make decisions because a majority of others think it is correct. Real science is not based on consensus, nor does it advance by majorities believing in certain theories. Real science progresses by dissent, constantly testing and falsifying theories to develop better ones. This has been the history of the scientific method, which ushered in the Enlightenment Period.

SAPERE AUDE!

Dare to know! The motto of the Enlightenment. The concepts of hypothesis, falsification, parsimony, and the experimental method are all components of the scientific method, one of the 14 meta-inventions Charles Murray documents in his fascinating and scholarly book, *Human Accomplishment*. Murray claims the scientific method has given us the world we inhabit today, and he dates its creation from 1589, with the publication of Galileo's *De Motu*, to 1687, with the publication of Newton's *Principia*. But he also points out that he could date the invention to 1200, and then writes: "That the basic ideas were in the air for so long without being developed suggests how complex and mind-stretching the change was" (Murray 2003: 237).

Mind-stretching indeed. The diffusion of a new theory or idea is the process whereby an innovation is communicated through certain channels over time among the members of a social system. The term *diffusion* originates from chemistry to explain, for example, how purple iodine placed in a glass of water will diffuse until the water is lavender. It is essentially a social process, and often takes a substantial amount of time before an idea becomes accepted by an overwhelming majority of a population. When one studies the history of diffusing new ideas into a population, the timeline can stretch from decades to centuries, contrasted with the diffusion of new technology—say, for instance, going from dial-up to broadband, or the next-generation computer chip—which usually takes only a few years to reach a critical mass, or tipping point, to use the title of Malcolm Gladwell's best-selling book.

Contemplate, as evidence, germ theory—the idea that diseases are transmitted by specific germs, or microorganisms, as has been proved for many infectious diseases. Scholars have traced this theory back to the sixteenth century, when it was generally ignored until Jacob Henle revived it in 1840. At least since 1847, we know that the German-Hungarian physician Ignaz Philipp Semmelweis (who discovered the cause of puerperal ["childbed"] fever and introduced antisepsis into medical practice) insisted that medical students at the Vienna General Hospital wash their hands between performing autopsies and examining pregnant women. (Semmelweis was later commemorated on an Austrian postage stamp.) Still, it remained on the fringes of medical science and was not accepted by Florence Nightingale, who believed diseases were spontaneously generated from dirty or unventilated rooms and hospital wards. Not until 1865 did germ theory reach a critical mass of acceptance, becoming conventional wisdom by 1914. It is one of the most significant theories that bettered the human condition. Prior to its acceptance—until the 1920s, in fact—a trip to the doctor, on average, didn't do much good, and sometimes did a net harm.

Ponder the fax machine, invented in 1843 by Alexander Bain, a Scottish clockmaker who called it a recording telegraph. In

1948, RCA introduced a fax machine that transmitted messages via radio waves, yet the fax machine did not diffuse into the general population until 1987—150 years to become an "overnight" success. History, science, economics, and other books are filled with similar stories.

Despite being over 400 years old, the scientific method has not been widely used by business thinkers or writers. This is one of the most glaring weaknesses in most business books and management ideas: they are all practice with no theory. Most do little else than propound platitudes and compose common sense into endless checklists and seven-step programs. The management consultant industry is replete with jargon, and a lot of it is even copyrighted, since legally one cannot copyright an idea. Any theory worth having can be used by others in the marketplace of ideas with impunity, so the consultants are left to protect their own verbiage.

The schism between management theory and the scientific method is profound, one reason being that the latter is relatively young compared to its older siblings in the hard sciences, which date back hundreds of years. In their piercing book *The Witch Doctors: What Management Gurus Are Saying and Why It Matters*, John Micklethwait and Adrian Wooldridge, two staff editors for *The Economist*, level this charge against the immature discipline of management theory:

> Management theory, according to the case against it, has four defects: it is constitutionally incapable of self-criticism; its terminology usually confuses rather than educates; it rarely rises above basic common sense; and it is faddish and bedeviled by contradictions that would not be allowed in more rigorous disciplines. The implication of all four charges is that management gurus are con artists, the witch doctors of our age, playing on business people's anxieties in order to sell snake oil. The gurus, many of whom have sprung suspiciously from the "great university of life" rather than any orthodox academic discipline, exist largely because people let them get away with it. Modern management theory is no more reliable than tribal medicine. Witch doctors, after all, often got it right—by luck, by instinct, or by trial and error (Micklethwait and Wooldridge 1996: 12).

All theories are subject to falsification, precisely how all science progresses. This is an interesting phenomenon, because it implies that most new theories—and especially management fads of the month—have to be wrong or irrelevant or else knowledge would proceed at lightning speed and advance by Newtonian or Einsteinian leaps every day. It does not. This makes it difficult for editors and publishers to admit that most of what they publish is trivial or just plain incorrect. In reality, knowledge progresses slowly, in a never-ending iterative process best characterized as *knowledge creep*. Fortunately, this schism is starting to narrow in the field of management research with thinkers such as Christensen and Mintzberg (cited earlier).

Theory, data, and information are obviously dependent upon each other, but clearly theory is the senior partner. A verifiable theory combined with information is impregnable and becomes knowledge, at least until it is falsified; data and information without a theory are statistical orphans. Psychologist John Meacham summed up the balance we must all strike concerning what we know: "I have concluded that the essence of wisdom is to hold the attitude that knowledge is fallible and to strive for a balance between knowing and doubting" (Pfeffer and Sutton 2006: 220).

British economist, political thinker, and philosopher of science John Stuart Mill was reputed to have been the last man to know everything there was to know. Yet, our knowledge is greatly exceeded by our ignorance, which is why the future is unknowable and unpredictable—we simply cannot now know what still remains to be known. Hayek believed the mind could not see its own advance, which is why we all need humility as we function in the IC economy, always bearing in mind Milton Friedman's questions: "How do you know?" and "So what?"

Now that we have explored what knowledge is, let us turn our attention to the antecedents of knowledge and economic growth—ideas and innovation.

7

IDEAS HAVE CONSEQUENCES

I am enough of an artist to draw freely upon my imagination.
Imagination is more important than knowledge. Knowledge is
limited. Imagination encircles the world.

—*Albert Einstein*

The distinction between ideas and knowledge may be subtle, but
perhaps management consultant Sid Caesar clarified it best when he
quipped: "The guy who invented the first wheel was an idiot. The
guy who invented the other three, he was a genius" (Stewart 2001:
90). As Thomas Sowell taught us in the last chapter, ideas need to
go through an authentication process to become knowledge or facts.
Since so much knowledge is tacit and specific to time and place, it
stands to reason that knowledge is far more scarce than ideas.

Another reason ideas are so abundant is that it may take hundreds
of them just to produce one good one. The dairy farmer's cows
do not just produce cream. Most new products, drugs, books published, and businesses launched fail. Capitalism is really based on
consumer sovereignty—it is a profit-and-loss system. We celebrate
the profits but tend to ignore the losses. Yet the creative destruction
is responsible for much of the dynamism inherent in the system.
Silicon Valley may be a fount of creativity, but only because it
rests atop a mass cemetery of bankrupted hypotheses falsified by
the sovereignty of the customer. Similar to the scientific method
described previously, this built-in falsification process is critical to

ensure the survival of only those firms that continue to add more value to society than the resources they consume.

Ideas are what economists describe as *nonrival* assets—meaning more than one person can use it at a time. Contrast this with traditional rival assets, such as a building or an airplane, which can only be used for one purpose at a time. If I give you the tie off my shirt, now you have it and I don't; but when I give you an idea, now we both have it, can expand upon it, test it, and make it more valuable. Ideas are subject to *increasing*, rather than diminishing, returns. Thomas Jefferson, in a letter to Isaac McPherson in 1813, understood this concept:

> If nature has made one thing less susceptible than all others of exclusive property, it is the action of the thinking power called an idea, which an individual may exclusively possess as long as he keeps it to himself; but the moment it is divulged, it forces itself into the possession of everyone.... Its peculiar character, too, is that no one possesses the less, because every other possesses the whole of it. He who receives an idea from me, receives instruction himself without lessening mine; as he who lights his taper at mine receives light without darkening me (Howkins 2001: 24).

Economists have always struggled with how to explain economic growth. Many of their models embody the physical fallacy, a world where traditional factors of production—land, labor, and capital—are rival resources, innovation and entrepreneurship are treated as unexplained luck, and ideas are ignored since they cannot be quantified. Even Adam Smith, who did so much to falsify the physical fallacy, thought that only industrial work could be "productive." The work of a service provider, in contrast, "adds to the value of nothing." This is the hamburger-flipper argument of the eighteenth century. As usual, Thomas Sowell explains the impact on a country's standard of living between generating ideas and the physical act of carrying them out:

> Many of the products that create a modern standard of living are only the physical incorporation of ideas—not only the ideas of an Edison or Ford but the ideas of innumerable anonymous people

who figure out the design of supermarkets, the location of gaso-
line stations, and the million mundane things on which our material
well-being depends. It is those ideas that are crucial, not the physical act of carrying them out. Societies which have more people
carrying out physical acts and fewer people supplying ideas do not
have higher standards of living. Quite the contrary. Yet the physical fallacy continues on, undaunted by this or any other evidence
(Sowell 1996: 71–72).

On October 30, 1996, 36-year-old University of Chicago
economist Paul Romer attempted to fill the void in the economics
profession's inability to explain growth, with a paper entitled
"Endogenous Technological Change." It may not sound like the
most exciting document to read, but it did present a framework
for explaining why some countries grow and others do not, and
became known in the literature as "new growth theory."

NEW GROWTH THEORY

Great advances have always sprung from ideas. They don't fall from
the sky, but come from people.

—Paul Romer

Prior to World War II, Japan was an insular economy, resistant
to new ideas from the rest of the world. After World War II, with
its economy and infrastructure decimated, Japan became receptive
to incorporating ideas from other countries, such as those of Dr.
W. Edwards Deming, Joseph Juran, and Peter Drucker, which put
it on a trajectory of what can only be described as an economic
miracle. Paul Romer explains the importance of ideas this way:

Economic growth occurs whenever people take resources and rearrange them in ways that are more valuable. A useful metaphor for
production in such an economy comes from the kitchen: To create
valuable final products, we mix inexpensive ingredients together
according to a recipe. . . . Human history teaches us, however, that
economic growth springs from better recipes, not just from more
cooking (Dougherty 2002: 128).

In other words, economic growth revolves around *the human mind* and its capacity for invention, discovery, and the transformation of physical objects and ideas into valuable goods and services. Animals, too, rearrange physical objects, often with incredible precision, with birds building nests and bees constructing hives. Yet ideas are cumulative since human beings have the infinite capacity to improve upon their circumstances. We all stand on the shoulders of those who came before us, as Nobel laureate Charles Townes, the inventor of the laser, illustrated when he noted in his Nobel acceptance speech: "It's like the beaver told the rabbit as they stared at the Hoover Dam. 'No, I didn't build it myself. But it's based on an idea of mine!'" Unlike animals, man creates wealth through his capacity to dream, imagine, experiment, think, and take risks. Capitalism creates wealth not just because of private property, free markets, and the profit motive, all of which existed in precapitalist times, including the biblical era. The main engine is its receptiveness to testing new ideas.

Prior to Romer's model, the conventional explanation for economic growth was embodied in the Solow model, named after Robert Solow, whose paper, "A Contribution to the Theory of Economic Growth," was published in the *Quarterly Journal of Economics* in 1956, just prior to the Soviet's *Sputnik* launch. Solow's model allowed the determinants of economic growth to be separated into increases in inputs (labor and capital) and technical progress. Solow calculated that approximately four-fifths of the growth of the U.S. economy is attributable to technological innovation. In another article, "Technical Change and the Aggregate Production Function," published in 1957, Solow reached a surprising conclusion, as told by David Warsh in *Knowledge and the Wealth of Nations*:

> When Solow applied his model data for U.S. gross national product in order to estimate the relative contributions of capital and technical change to growth from 1909 to 1949, out popped another surprising conclusion. Assuming each received its marginal product, increased inputs of capital and labor explained barely half of

the increased output. Once adjustments were made for increased population, additions to capital explained barely an eighth; fully 85 percent of the increase was unexplained by what was in the model. This was the Residual, the portion of growth that the model did not explain (Warsh 2006: 146–147).

You could say the Residual was a measure of economists' ignorance in explaining economic growth. Solow's model treated knowledge as an external input, whereas Romer treated it as both an input and an output of production. Rather than traditional constraining factors of production—land, labor, and capital—Romer distinguishes between rival and nonrival goods. Ideas and knowledge are nonrival because they can be used at the same time, and the larger the market the greater the wealth-creating capacity of knowledge. Thus, Romer replaced land, labor, and capital with people, ideas, and things, and he described the main engine of growth as invention driven by entrepreneurs. It is not just knowledge that makes countries rich or poor, but how that knowledge is used. Formal education is not enough. While it is no doubt easier to measure the amount of schooling a country's citizens have completed, it does not necessarily correlate to how ideas are used by entrepreneurs. Steve Jobs, Bill Gates, and Michael Dell were all college dropouts, yet they have all contributed to the wealth of nations. Cuba and Sri Lanka may invest heavily in formal education and have high literacy rates, yet they remain marginal players in the global production of technological progress.

Charles Murray, in *Human Accomplishment*, explores 14 of the world's most important meta-inventions that occurred after 800 BC until 1950, essentially cognitive (not physical) tools for improving the world around us:

- Artistic realism
- Linear perspective
- Artistic abstraction
- Polyphony
- Drama

- The novel
- Meditation
- Logic
- Ethics
- Arabic numerals
- The mathematical proof
- The calibration of uncertainty
- The secular observation of nature
- The scientific method (Murray 2003: 211).

All of the above are nonrival goods, meaning we can all utilize them at the same time without their being diminished—your use of the alphabet does not inhibit mine. These ideas changed the world, creating untold wealth. They were also the contributions of an incredibly small number of individuals—4,002 to be precise, according to Murray.

In the arena of business management, ideas have an enormous capacity to apply knowledge to knowledge, thereby increasing innovation and wealth. Management consultant and author Gary Hamel has identified 175 significant management ideas between 1900 and 2000. He applied three questions to each idea to create the most important advances: Was it a marked departure from previous management practices? Did it confer a competitive advantage on the pioneering company or companies? And could it be found in some form in organizations today? Think of the global impact the following dozen management innovations have had, which all met Hamel's criteria:

- Scientific management (time and motion studies)
- Cost accounting and variance analysis
- The commercial research laboratory (the industrialization of science)
- Return on investment (ROI) analysis and capital budgeting
- Brand management

- Large-scale project management
- Divisionalization
- Leadership development
- Industry consortia (multicompany collaborative structures)
- Radical decentralization (self-organization)
- Formalized strategic analysis
- Employee-driven problem solving (Hamel 2006: 80)

Paul Romer is right—innovation rests on individuals' ability to create and test ideas, thereby creating new knowledge and wealth. Even something as prosaic as a pill bottle can become the genesis of a new idea that creates value and even saves lives. Deborah Adler's grandmother mistakenly took her grandfather's prescription medication amoxicillin by accident. While Adler was working on her master of fine arts thesis, she came up with an idea for an easier-to-read, user-friendly pill bottle with color-coded rings and other safety features. Target was so impressed with her redesigned bottle, it bought the design from her. In the autumn of 2005, the bottle was displayed in the New York Museum of Modern Art.

Business is about people, ideas, and things, not land, labor, and capital. Yet ideas are not easily measured or quantifiable, so they are not given the resources they deserve by many organizations. Creativity and dreaming take time, which does not enhance conventional productivity statistics. But in an intellectual economy, creativity is what propels economic growth. Tim Delaney, vice president, executive designer, creative development with Disney says, "The success of the Walt Disney Company has centered on two basic fundamental concepts: our ability to be great storytellers, and the constant and the vigilant search for exciting new ideas" (The Imagineers 2003: 72).

Let us turn our attention to a framework that incorporates Paul Romer's new factors of production—people, ideas, and things—and explore the characteristics of what is known as intellectual capital.

8

THE CHARACTERISTICS OF INTELLECTUAL CAPITAL

We know that the source of wealth is something specifically human: knowledge. If we apply knowledge to tasks that we already know how to do, we call it productivity. If we apply knowledge to tasks that are new and different, we call it innovation. Only knowledge allows us to achieve these two goals.

—*Peter Drucker*

Former Federal Reserve Bank of the United States Chairman Alan Greenspan use to stump audiences with his question, "How much does the new economy weigh?" Considering that New York City alone is estimated to contain on the order of 10^{10} stock keeping units (SKUs), it would seem as if the answer is heavier than ever before. But the truth is, the economy weighs the same even though its output is five times greater than it was in 1950. The entire music collection of hundreds of yesterday's jukeboxes can now be carried on your iPod, not to mention that every newspaper in the country can be delivered to your home, not physically, but online. Increasingly, as Paul Romer posits, the economy is made up of ideas and knowledge, and while people may be getting heavier, the output of our economy is creating less of a planetary footprint.

We no longer have so many large smokestack factories belching pollution into the air and turning out tangible products. In a knowledge economy, it is as if we have thousands of invisible factories working on turning ideas into knowledge and knowledge into value for customers, saving us from the strenuous labor our ancestors endured while equalizing opportunity for the sexes. It has been estimated that 97 percent of the world's wealth has been created in just the last 0.01 percent of our history (Beinhocker 2006: 11). FedEx Chairman Fred Smith estimates that goods transported by sea account for 98 percent of all the tons moved in international trade, while FedEx moves only 1.5 to 2 percent of all goods, yet that small percentage accounts for 40 percent of the entire value, and if agricultural and petroleum were removed, probably over 50 percent.

Brains trump brawn. According to the *New York Times*, Merv Griffin has made "close to $70 million to $80 million" in royalties from the *Jeopardy!* theme song, which he wrote in less than a minute. One of Japan's largest export industries, reaching an astounding $80 billion in 2004, is animation. Not even two years old, with no profits, YouTube was purchased by Google for $1.65 billion. Disney's *Snow White* video release generated $800 million in revenue, $500 million to the bottom line, from a movie made in the 1930s. Compare these supposedly ephemeral products to the value of an automobile from the same decade, and you quickly realize how important knowledge is to wealth creation. The knowledge economy has been a gradual evolution, resting on the shoulders of those who came before us, a testimony to the importance of mind over matter, as well as a further refutation of the physical fallacy.

KNOWLEDGE IS A VERB

Knowledge has always been at the heart of economic development, recognized by economist Alfred Marshall (1842–1924), who wrote, "Knowledge is our most powerful engine of production; it enables us to subdue nature and force her to satisfy our wants" (Warsh 2006: 82). Even Adam Smith in *The Wealth of Nations* recognized the importance of knowledge, labeling it "the acquired and useful abilities of all the inhabitants or members of the society" (O'Rourke 2007: 74–75). Smith attributed the wealth of nations to the division and specialization of labor, but Austrian economist—and one of the founders of the Marginalist Revolution—Carl Menger believed Smith wasn't exactly correct. He thought knowledge was ultimately what made nations prosperous.

Peter Drucker certainly brought the importance of knowledge to the attention of business leaders when he coined the terms *knowledge economy* and *knowledge worker*. Edith Penrose, in her classic 1959 management book, *The Theory of the Growth of the Firm*, recognized knowledge as one of the two constraints in growing a business (the other being complexity).

Austrian economist Fritz Machlup, who independently from Peter Drucker also coined the term *knowledge worker*, distinguished among five types of knowledge in his extensive study, *The Production and Distribution of Knowledge*:

1. Practical knowledge
   a. Professional
   b. Business
   c. Workman's
   d. Political
   e. Household
   f. Other practical
2. Intellectual knowledge
3. Small-talk and pastime knowledge
4. Spiritual knowledge
5. Unwanted knowledge (Machlup 1962: 21–22).

Obviously, not all knowledge is encoded in language—music and body language is also a type of knowledge. Knowledge has no finite capacity, since it can be used simultaneously without diminishing. When knowledge is sold, the seller's inventory is not diminished, as with traditional physical goods, much like telling someone the time while retaining your watch. This is what economists mean by a *nonrival* asset. On the other side of the transaction, the buyer usually does not need to purchase knowledge several times, even if it is used over and over. The knowledge is also *cumulative* and *uncontrollable*, since the buyer can add to it, improve it, and create more of it. Thomas Jefferson explained this cumulative property: "The fact is that one new idea leads to another, that to a third, and so on through a course of time until someone, with whom no one of these ideas was original, combines it all together, and produces what is justly called a new invention" (Foray 2004: 94). Moreover, the buyer is unable to judge the value of knowledge until he or she has had a chance to use it, much like your purchasing this book without knowing how valuable it is going to be until you have read it. These three characteristics of knowledge—nonrivalry, uncontrollability, and cumulativeness—can be combined to create new value. This makes it quite difficult to simply sum up the individual properties of knowledge.

Though Alvin and Heidi Toffler attempt to do just that, when they define the characteristics of knowledge in their book *Revolutionary Wealth*:

1. Knowledge is inherently non-rival
2. Knowledge is intangible
3. Knowledge is non-linear
4. Knowledge is relational
5. Knowledge mates with other knowledge
6. Knowledge is more portable than any other product
7. Knowledge can be compressed into symbols or abstractions
8. Knowledge can be stored in smaller and smaller spaces
9. Knowledge can be explicit or implicit, expressed or not expressed, shared or tacit
10. Knowledge is hard to bottle up. It spreads (Toffler and Toffler 2006: 100–101).

Knowledge is like the dark matter of the cosmos—we know it is out there, but we cannot see, touch, or measure it. Much argument has taken place, especially in the accounting profession, surrounding the difference between tangible and intangible assets. The former, auditors can kick and tick—to use their parlance—but the latter can be recorded only on a historical cost basis. Intellectual property such as patents, copyrights, trademarks, databases, and the like, are recorded on a firm's financial statements at cost, which does not at all reflect their value-creating capacity. Baruch Lev, professor at New York University's Stern School of Business, estimates that intangibles comprise $6 trillion of the balance sheets of American companies, two-thirds of the total assets. Indeed, the U.S. stock of intangible assets began to exceed that of tangible capital—such as property, plant, and equipment—at the end of the 1960s, approximately a decade after Drucker identified the knowledge economy. By the mid-1980s, the contribution of knowledge industries to the gross domestic product of all Organization for Economic Co-operation and Development (OECD) countries topped the 50 percent mark.

The United States Patent Office defines intellectual property as: "Creations of the mind—creative works or ideas embodied in a form that can be shared or can enable others to recreate, emulate, or manufacture them." The U.S. Constitution, Article I, Section 8, provides for the protection of intellectual property: "To promote the Progress of Science and useful Arts, by securing for limited Times to Authors and Inventors the exclusive Right to their respective Writings and Discoveries." This is adequate for those assets that can be codified by law, but intellectual capital (IC) goes far beyond these types of assets, and reaches across and outside an entire organization.

While historical accounting cannot see, let alone measure, knowledge assets until there is a transaction, we need a framework that allows us to understand this vital capital. Ultimately, we want to incorporate intellectual property within the broader context of IC into a coherent framework, turning knowledge into an actionable verb that firms can use to create value. Consequently, IC needs to be expanded beyond the concepts of tangible versus intangible assets, and even the intellectual property rights recognized by common law. This is much more than just a semantic distinction, since IC is defined by the economic utility and behavior of the asset, not just its physical or legal form. Tangible assets remain the same, but IC is defined by its context. In addition, managing and leading IC is a much different task than that of traditional tangible assets.

DEFINING INTELLECTUAL CAPITAL

The Intellectual Capital Management Gathering Best Practices conference in 1995 defined intellectual capital as "knowledge that can be converted into profits," which is an adequate definition for our purposes since it considers knowledge as a verb (Lev 2001: 155). IC should not be equated with knowledge management, which is merely a process, whereas IC is an entity.

Another useful way to think about IC is by ownership. Human capital is owned by the knowledge worker; structural capital is owned by the firm; and social capital is owned by no one, though it can be leveraged, accruing benefits to the owners of the firm. Contemplate who owns the Coca-Cola brand. The company's leaders learned the hard way when it reformulated the soft drink into New Coke just who, ultimately, is in charge of value—the customers.

It is in the interplay of these three types of IC where valuable knowledge and technical know-how combine, providing the leverage necessary to create wealth for others. As Walt Disney explained when asked about the secret to his success: "There's really no secret about our approach. We keep moving forward—opening new doors and doing new things—because we are curious. And curiosity keeps leading us down new paths. We're always exploring and experimenting ... we call it *Imagineering* [a term Disney coined]—the blending of creative imagination and technical know-how" (Disney Institute 2001: 111).

Specific knowledge may be scarce, as Thomas Sowell has taught us, but within any firm there resides all sorts of specific, applicable knowledge. The goal is to leverage this knowledge and use it to create new knowledge that can be validated in the marketplace by customers. In turn, this becomes the firm's IC, the ultimate fulcrum for the IC company of the future.

Ultimately, whether we are discussing ideas or knowledge, it springs from the human mind. The essential drama in economics is acted out in the area of human capital, which we will turn to next.

9

HUMAN CAPITALISM

The most valuable of all capital is that invested in human beings.
—*Alfred Marshall, Principles of Economics, 1890*

We should really call our economy a "human capitalist economy," for
that is what it mainly is. While all forms of capital—physical capital,
such as machinery and plants, financial capital, and human capital—
are important, human capital is the most important. Indeed, in a
modern economy, human capital is by far the most important
form of capital in creating wealth and growth.
—*Gary Becker, 1992 Nobel Laureate*

The term *human capital* was first used by Nobel Prize–winning
economist Theodore W. Schultz in a 1961 article in *American
Economic Review*. During 1946, Schultz spent a term teaching
at Auburn University, where he interviewed farmers in a particular neighborhood. As retold by economics professor Deirdre
McCloskey:

> One day he interviewed an old and poor farm couple and was struck
> by how contented they seemed. Why are you so contended, he asked,
> though poor? They answered: You're wrong, Professor. We're not
> poor. We've used up our farm to educate four children through col-
> lege, remaking fertile land and well-stocked hog pens into knowl-
> edge of Law and Latin. You can see that we're rich. The parents
> had informed Schultz that the *physical* capital, which economists
> think they understand, is in some sense like the *human* capital of
> education. The sense is accounting (McCloskey 2000: 177).

Schultz went on to develop a theory of human capital, the basic thesis of which was that investments in human capital should be accounted for in the same manner as investments in plant and machinery. This was not exactly a new idea; even Adam Smith wrote in *The Wealth of Nations*: "Man educated at the expense of much labor and time ... may be compared to one of those expensive machines," but it did lead to an intersection of the economics and accounting profession, at least in theory. The economists were in essence saying that accountants should treat investments in people the same as they treat investments in things; but we accountants never learned the lesson, continuing to this day to treat employees as nothing but expenses.

The obvious challenge is that investments in tangible, physical assets can be counted and comprehended, but those in people cannot. It is as if accountants would value the average human being at $10 since that is the approximate worth of our various chemical components. While the traditional factors of production—land, labor, and capital—are stocks, human capital is a flow, the most significant factor in generating knowledge. Gary Becker, who has done pioneering work in the field, estimates that human capital comprises 75 percent of the United States' total wealth. In spite of this, human capital is nowhere near as visible as other representations of wealth, such as the capital markets. When the U.S. stock market plummeted by approximately 25 percent on October 19, 1987, Becker wrote a column in *BusinessWeek* explaining why this was not really a substantial loss of wealth—a counterintuitive conclusion to be sure, but a correct one given the theory of human capital:

> The 25% decline in share prices over the last two months lopped almost $1 trillion from the value of stocks. Although that's a huge number, the average person's total wealth took only a modest fall because most wealth is embodied in the skills and training that generate present and future earnings. Such "human wealth" constitutes 75% or more of the U.S.'s total wealth. The rest consists

of corporate capital, capital in unincorporated businesses, housing, consumer durables, government capital, and cash.

The Commerce Dept. estimates nonhuman wealth at about $13 trillion. Thus a $1 trillion fall in the value of stocks reduces this wealth by less than 8%—and total wealth by less than 2%. Such a decline would have a noticeable effect on spending and a major effect on the demand for luxury homes and cars. But the decline in spending from a 2% fall in wealth cannot cause a major depression (Becker and Becker 1997: 301).

This is why wealth is not simply how much money you have; rather it is what you have left after losing all your money. Perhaps this is what U.S. Steel entrepreneur Andrew Carnegie meant when he once stated, in total confidence, "Take away my people but leave my factories, and soon grass will grow on factory floors. Take away my factories but leave my people, and soon we will have a new and better factory." Carnegie certainly understood the importance of human capital, emboldened on his tombstone: "Here lies a man / Who knew how to enlist / In his service / Better men than himself." People do not contribute just work to the organizations that employ them, but also knowledge. If it were just physical exertion that mattered, we would expect to see younger workers earning the most since that is the point in life which physical strength is at its apogee. In reality, what we witness is that, as knowledge workers age, their incomes rise, and this is consistent with the theory of human capital postulated by Schultz, Becker, and other economists since. Rising income can be thought of as increasing *profits* from investments in human capital, even though we may term this income *wages* from an accounting sense. Human capital transcends mere accounting, as the following example from Thomas Sowell illustrates:

A failure to understand the importance of human capital contributed to the defeat of Germany and Japan in World War II. Experienced and battle-hardened fighter pilots represented a very large investment of human capital. Yet the Germans and the Japanese did not systematically take their experienced pilots out of combat

missions to safeguard their human capital and have them become
instructors who could spread some of their human capital to new
and inexperienced pilots being trained for combat. Both followed
policies described by the Germans as "fly till you die."

The net result was that, while German and Japanese fighter
pilots were very formidable opponents to the British and American
pilots who fought against them early in the war, the balance of
skills swung in favor of the British and American pilots later in
the war, after much of the German and Japanese human capital
in the air was lost when their top fighter pilots were eventually
shot down and replaced by inexperienced pilots who had to learn
everything the hard way in aerial combat, where small mistakes
can be fatal. Economic concepts apply even when no money is
changing hands. German and Japanese air forces were less efficient
at allocating scarce resources that had alternative uses.

Uneasy as some people may be with the idea of thinking of
human beings as capital, this is not a denigration but an enhance-
ment of the value of human life. In addition to the intrinsic value
of life to each individual, that individual's value to others is high-
lighted by the concept of human capital. The old military practice
of going to great efforts to save cannon in combat, while using
soldiers as if they were expendable, has since given way to using
very expensive high-tech weapons, as in the Gulf War of 1991,
in order to minimize casualties among one's own military personnel, who represent very valuable human capital (Sowell 2000:
341–342).

Even though the concept of human capital is uncontrover-
sial currently, it was treated with much hostility when first discussed in the 1950s and 1960s, with critics complaining that
economists were equating humans with machinery, and education
as an investment rather than moral development and a cultural
experience. Historically, this is perhaps understandable since people have felt uneasy about the buying and selling of labor, mostly
as a legacy of slavery (an institution that existed on every inhab-
ited continent at various times throughout history). The word *capital* first appeared in the thirteenth century in the trading cities of
northern Italy, which later developed double-entry bookkeeping.

It describes any asset that enables or enhances future economic activity. *Capital* comes from the Latin *caput*, meaning head. In other words, all capital springs from the human mind. Today, the majority of personal income is derived from salaries and wages; thus, thinking in terms of employees being human capital investors lends dignity and respect to the value of each person.

When the G.I. Bill of Rights was passed in 1944—making education available to some 2,332,000 veterans—it was the largest single investment in human capital up to that time, which convinced Peter Drucker we were shifting to a *knowledge society* full of *knowledge workers*, terms he coined in 1961 and later expanded on in his 1968 book, *The Age of Discontinuity*. As Drucker later explained in his book *The Ecological Vision*:

> A simple example is the emergence of the knowledge as a key resource. The event that alerted me to the fact that something was happening was the passage of the GI Bill of Rights in the United States after the Second World War. This law gave every returning war veteran the right to attend college, with the government paying the bill. It was a totally unprecedented development. These considerations led me to the question: "What impact does this have on expectations, on values, on social structure, on employment, and so on?" And once this question was asked—I first asked it in the late 1940s—it became clear that knowledge as a productive resource had attained a position in society as never before in human history. We were clearly on the threshold of a major change. Ten years later, by the mid-1950s, one could confidently talk of a "knowledge society," of "knowledge work" as the new center of the economy, and of the "knowledge worker" as the new, ascendant workforce (Drucker and Maciariello 2004: 367).

But not everyone agreed this was a prudent policy, with some of the most vociferous critics coming from the major universities:

> In the wartime year of 1944, shortly after the Normandy invasion, FDR signed the GI Bill of Rights, a multibillion-dollar commitment to provide free college education and low-cost housing loans to what ultimately amounted to thirteen million returning veterans.

> ... [Leaders of elite universities were appalled]. Harvard's president warned that academe would be overrun with "unqualified people, the most unqualified of this generation." The president of the University of Chicago envisioned waves of "educational hobos" riding the rails coast to coast and mooching on one campus after another (Feulner and Wilson 2006: 70–71).

Between 1946 and 1950, the number of college graduates doubled, directly contradicting the critics regarding the potential of the new students. The G.I. Bill of Rights, it has been argued, became one of the most successful models of social legislation. But formal education, although it can be precisely quantified in terms of years of schooling, money spent, and graduation rates, is not the sum total of human capital. There are many forms of life experience that comprise human capital that defy definitive measurement.

THE MORE HUMAN THE CAPITAL, THE LESS WE CAN MEASURE IT

The September 10, 2005, issue of *The Economist* contained a survey of higher education titled "The Brain Business," and contained the following facts regarding college:

- The proportion of adults with higher educational qualifications in the OECD countries almost doubled between 1975 and 2000, from 22 percent to 41 percent.
- Between 1985 and 1997 the contribution of knowledge-based industries to total value added increased from 51 percent to 59 percent in Germany and from 45 percent to 51 percent in Britain.
- The best companies are now devoting at least a third of their investments to knowledge-intensive intangibles such as research and development, licensing, and marketing.
- The World Bank calculates that global spending on higher education amounts to $300 billion a year, or 1 percent of global economic output.

- There are more than 80 million students worldwide, and 3.5 million people are employed to teach them or look after them.
- America spends more than twice as much per student as the OECD average (about $22,000 versus $10,000 in 2001).
- European countries spend only 1.1 percent of their gross domestic product (GDP) on higher education, compared with 2.7 percent in the United States (*The Economist* 2005: 3, 4, 6, 10).

Yet primary and secondary education is only a proxy for human capital, certainly not the only means for acquiring knowledge. Economist Fritz Machlup, in his study of knowledge, published in 1962, distinguished among eight types of education:

1. Education in the home
2. Education in school
3. Training on the job
4. Instruction in church
5. Training in the armed forces
6. Education over television
7. Self-education
8. Learning from experience (Machlup 1962: 51)

While in the first six methods, knowledge is "taught," the last two are acquired by reading and/or doing, either in solitude or in interactions with others (a form of social capital). Consider the knowledge transmitted from parents to children, which economists label voluntary labor. Alvin Toffler frequently demonstrated this point with what he terms the *potty test*, by asking corporate managers the following "indelicate question": "How productive would your workforce be if someone hadn't toilet-trained it?" (Toffler and Toffler 2006: 155). This form of homemade knowledge is vitally important, but it does not enter the national-product statistics cited above. A lot of knowledge is not guided solely by market mechanisms since it is provided free of charge. This makes it difficult for economists to determine which investments in human capital will pay the largest rewards.

Politicians and the special interest education lobby will always call for more investments in schooling; indeed, the European Union (EU) has recently made this very argument as a way to become the premier knowledge society of the future. Taking the advice of Winston Churchill that "the empires of the future will be empires of the mind," at an EU summit in Lisbon in March 2000, Europe's leaders announced the goal of transforming Europe into "the most competitive and dynamic knowledge-based economy in the world by 2010," referred to now as the Lisbon Agenda. Former deputy foreign minister of Poland, Radek Sikorski, expressed his doubts: "I hadn't laughed so hard and so much since the Communist Politburo used to announce totally unrealistic production targets. It was the same kind of thing." In 2004, Germany confessed this goal was "unrealistic" and a "big failure" (Toffler and Toffler 2006: 351). *The Economist* proclaimed the goal was "not likely."

The contradiction between the EU's objective and reality is easy to diagnose: it confuses formal education with knowledge and economic dynamism. The Industrial Revolution was launched by individuals with very little formal education, with such pioneers as Thomas Edison having only three months of formal schooling, disqualifying him today from becoming a licensed engineer. The inventors of the airplane, two bicycle mechanics who never attended college, the Wright Brothers would most likely be denied a leadership position at Boeing today. Even Frank Lloyd Wright and Mies van der Rohe would not qualify to sit for the architect's certifying examination under current educational requirements. More recently, the list of entrepreneurs who launched successful enterprises with no, or very little, college education reads like a *Who's Who* of the business press—Michael Dell, Bill Gates, Steve Jobs, and Steve Wozniak, among many others.

Far more important than formal education is an economy that allows for economic experimentation, trial and error, profit and loss, secured by the liberties and freedom Adam Smith so eloquently wrote about. Thomas Sowell explains the difference between formal education and economic development in his text-book *Basic Economics*:

> Education has of course also made major contributions to economic development. But this is not to say that all kinds of education have. From an economic standpoint, some education has great value, some has no value and some can even have a negative value.
>
> Large numbers of young people with schooling, but without economically meaningful skills, have produced much unemployment in Third World nations. Since the marketplace has little to offer such people that would be commensurate with their expectations, governments have created swollen bureaucracies to hire them, in order to neutralize their potential for political disaffection, civil unrest or insurrection. In turn, these bureaucracies and the voluminous and time-consuming red tape they generate can become obstacles to others who do have the skills and entrepreneurship needed to contribute to the country's economic advancement.
>
> Hostility to entrepreneurial minorities like the Chinese in Southeast Asia or the Lebanese in West Africa has been especially fierce among the newly educated indigenous people, who see their own diplomas and degrees bringing them much less economic reward than the earnings of minority business owners who may have less formal schooling than themselves.
>
> In short, more schooling is not automatically more human capital. It can in some cases reduce a country's ability to use the human capital that it already possesses (Sowell 2004: 192–194).

The spirit of enterprise is just as necessary if ideas and knowledge are to be turned into wealth-creating businesses, but how do we measure the passion of Steve Jobs to change the world one desktop at a time without the authentication process of the free market to verify the result of his output? We can measure the literacy of the population of Cuba, but how do we go about explaining the difference between Cuba's abject poverty and the wealth of the Cuban immigrant population in Miami, Florida? India has been exporting entrepreneurs who have launched successful enterprises in all parts of the world, especially Silicon Valley. According to *The Economist*, 20 million Indians live abroad, collectively generating an annual income that is 35 percent of India's GDP. How do we explain the fact that as of 1994, 36 million overseas Chinese had produced as much wealth as the population in China itself? Obviously, there is more to creating the knowledge economies of the future than merely subsidizing higher and higher levels of formal education. As George Gilder explained in his seminal work *Recapturing the Spirit of Enterprise*:

> Economists see the rise of wealth as incremental gains in productivity, slow accumulation of plant and machinery, and investments in human capital. But, in fact, all these sources of growth are dwarfed by the role of entrepreneurs launching new companies based on new concepts or technologies (Gilder 1992: 164).

There is one shining example of an EU country that has achieved tremendous progress on the road to becoming the most competitive and dynamic knowledge-based economy in the world by 2010—Ireland. Since the 1980s, the country has orchestrated an aggressive campaign of cutting taxes and reducing regulation to counteract its prior economic slide in the 1970s, earning it the nickname "Celtic Tiger." In 2003, it cut its corporate income tax rate to 12.5 percent, making it the lowest in the world to that point. When Ireland entered the EU in the 1970s, it was among the poorest members. As of 2003, Ireland's per capita GDP was $38,430, exceeding the United Kingdom ($30,280), France ($29,240), Germany ($29,130), Italy ($25,580), and the rest of the EU nations except Denmark ($39,330) and Luxembourg ($52,990).

Ireland runs advertisements in business publications with the slogan "Ireland, knowledge is in our nature™." The ad copy, under an artistic image of the musician Bono, goes on to tout the benefits of doing business in Ireland:

> The Irish. Creative. Imaginative. And flexible. Agile minds with a unique capacity to initiate, and innovate, without being directed. Always thinking on their feet. Adapting and improving. Generating new knowledge and new ideas. Working together to find new ways

of getting things done. Better and faster (advertisement in *The Economist;* www.idaireland.com).

Whether or not the rest of the EU can cast off yesterday and embrace the changes of an opportunity economy remains to be seen. Peter Drucker wrote that the reason he left Europe in 1935 to live in America was that "America was starkly different from Europe. In America, people were looking to tomorrow. In Europe they were trying to re-create yesterday" (Edersheim 2007: 86). Some commentators, such as novelist Tom Wolfe and *Megatrends* author John Naisbitt, believe that Europe, with its sclerotic welfare state and declining populations, will become nothing more than a historical theme park people will visit for its bucolic and architectural splendor. Time will tell. What is beyond doubt is that the competition for human capital will intensify, not only among nations but within countries' cities as well. As Ireland advertises the benefits of its economy, Singapore is doing the same through its Web site, www.sedb.com, and New Zealand's minister for research, science, and technology, Peter Hodgson, claims: "We no longer think of immigration as a gatekeeping function but as a talent-attraction function necessary for economic growth" (Florida 2005: 8). Like any capital investor, human capital will go where it can earn a decent economic return and is well treated.

In any event, human capital is more than just formal education. It is knowledge, experience, judgment, leadership, problem-solving ability, motivation, ability to adapt, and wisdom put to use to serve others, the essential expression of wealth. Whether it is embedded in gradual accumulations over time or in the testable hypothesis of launching a new enterprise that creates a whole new industry, human capital is ultimately owned by sentient human beings. To complicate matters, converting that brain power into useful intellectual capital that organizations can use and reuse requires us to understand the difference between tacit and explicit knowledge.

WE KNOW MORE THAN WE CAN TELL

A teacher tells one of his pupils to write a letter to his parents, but the student complains: "It is hard for me to write a letter." "Why! You are now a year older, and ought to be better able to do it." "Yes, but a year ago I could say everything I knew, but now I know more than I can say" (Gregory 1995: 59).

Albert Einstein's research assistant-turned-philosopher, Michael Polanyi, drew a distinction between tacit and explicit knowledge. To illustrate tacit knowledge, he said, try explaining how to ride a bike or swim. You know more than you tell. Tacit knowledge is "sticky," in that it is not easily articulated and exists in people's minds. It is complex and rich, whereas explicit knowledge tends to be thin and low-bandwidth, like the difference between looking at a map and taking a journey of a certain terrain. It is the difference between reading the employee manual and spending one hour chatting with a coworker about the true nature of the job and culture of the firm. The Web site www.vault.com transmits such tacit knowledge, allowing prospective employees to learn what it is really like to work for the company without the noise and spin of the human resources department. For tacit knowledge to become explicit knowledge—that is, stored somewhere where it can be viewed, reviewed, and used by others—it must first be converted from the mind to another medium (a database, white paper, report, manual, video, picture, etc.). Tacit knowledge tends to be dynamic, while explicit knowledge is static; both are required for innovation and leverage to take place.

Converting tacit knowledge to explicit knowledge is one of the major roles of a chief knowledge officer (CKO). John Peetz, former CKO for Ernst & Young, summed up his knowledge mission this way: "For us knowledge management is critical. It's one of our four core processes—sell work, do work, manage people, and manage knowledge." As Thomas Stewart further explained, "In his self-written job description, Peetz outlined three responsibilities for a CKO: evangelizing about the value of sharing knowledge; running and backing projects that find, publish, and distribute knowledge around the firm; and managing a staff of about 200 people, mostly in the firm's Center for Business Knowledge in Cleveland, and a firmwide infrastructure of Web sites" (Stewart 2001: 82).

I have serious reservations about "managing people," especially since we are talking about knowledge workers, whom I firmly believe cannot be "managed" in the traditional sense. Nonetheless, the essential role of a CKO is to capture the knowledge that exists within the minds of people. As Ikujiro Nonaka and Hirotaka Takeuchi point out in their book *The Knowledge-Creating Company: How Japanese Companies Create the Dynamics of Innovation*, "The individual is the 'creator' of knowledge and the organization is the 'amplifier' of knowledge" (Nonaka and Takeuchi 1995: 240).

Tacit from the Latin means "silent or secret." This is why it is so hard to explain how to ride a bike or swim. Try describing, in words, Marilyn Monroe's face to someone, an almost impossible task, yet you would be able to pick her out among photographs of hundreds of faces in a moment. You could read all of the explicit knowledge contained in books, for instance, on the subject of playing golf like Tiger Woods, but until you actually got out on the links your understanding would be severely limited. Compare reading books on how to golf like Tiger to playing 18 holes with him. This is not to say that tacit knowledge is always superior, since the two complement each other. Explicit is from the Latin meaning "to unfold"—to be open, to arrange, to explain. Germans say *Fingerspitzengefühl*, "a feeling in the fingertips," which is similar to tacit knowledge (Stewart 2001: 123). The French say *je ne sais quoi* ("I don't know what"), a pleasant way of describing tacit knowledge. It is usually a totally different experience to read an author's book than it is to have a chance to talk to her about it. The latter will give you a much richer, contextual feel for the explicit knowledge documented in the book, and in some cases may even be more valuable. Or consider the difference between reading a customer profile and talking with the customer in person. The highest levels of knowledge and competence are inherently tacit, being difficult and expensive to transmit, which is why the concept of master and journeyman still exist, albeit in different forms. For instance, to become a licensed London cab driver, one has to learn "the Knowledge," which is the location of all the streets in a 10-kilometer radius; it takes years of part-time study. If it were simply a matter of making tacit knowledge explicit, then novices could perform at the experienced cabbie level, so learning from one's colleagues is just as important as having a rich bank filled with explicit knowledge.

This type of knowledge transfer is a "social" process between individuals, and is especially important in knowledge organizations where so much of the IC is "sticky" tacit knowledge. Studies have shown that managers receive two-thirds of their information through face-to-face meetings and phone calls, and during the physical meetings, body language can convey up to three times as much meaning as the words spoken for some types of interactions. Nonaka and Takeuchi postulate four different modes of knowledge conversion:

1. From tacit knowledge to tacit knowledge, which we call socialization;
2. From tacit knowledge to explicit knowledge, or externalization;
3. From explicit knowledge to explicit knowledge, or combination; and
4. From explicit knowledge to tacit knowledge, or internalization (Nonaka and Takeuchi 1995: 62).

All four are important to capture in a company, but how much time does the average firm spend in documenting and sharing what it knows when its primary metric is how efficient you were last week? How often do firms take the time to mentor their colleagues on the importance of learning and sharing knowledge?

"He's learning me all his experience," as Yogi Berra said about Bill Dickey. No doubt this gets done in most firms, but it is on an ad hoc and as-needed basis, rather than as a systemized, assessed part of the performance criteria of team members. There is simply no mechanism in most firms to reward continuous learning, the sharing of tacit knowledge with peers, or externalizing tacit knowledge to explicit knowledge by conducting an After Action Review, a process borrowed from the U.S. Army, which will be discussed in further detail in Chapter 12. Because most companies are so caught up in day-to-day work and worrying about this quarter's profit-and-loss statement, they are not building their invisible balance sheet—and the primary asset is the knowledge that exists in the firm. Yet capturing this type of knowledge would be incredibly valuable to the firm in terms of leveraging, ability to delegate to less experienced team members, and as a way to increase the structural capital of the firm just in case certain human capital investors decide not to return to work.

Managing explicit knowledge is certainly easier than managing tacit knowledge, since the latter exists in the heads of knowledge workers who are difficult to manage, to say the least. Nor is it possible to capture 100 percent of the tacit knowledge that exists in each team member's head, but that's not the goal. The goal is to capture as much of it as we can and place it somewhere (e.g., a file, intranet, Web portal, or blog) where anyone else in the firm can get it when they need it. This way we are not constantly reinventing the wheel, but rather trying to figure out the most effective way to place the other three wheels so we can get to our destination. Thomas Stewart gives this artful advice for managing explicit knowledge:

> Assemble it; validate it; as much as possible, standardize and simplify it; keep it up to date; leverage it; make sure everyone who needs it knows that it exists, where to get it, and how to use it; automate and accelerate the processes of retrieving and applying it; add to it; sue any bastard who steals it (Stewart 2001: 124).

Consultant Stan Davis likes to make his clients think about creating "smart products," and to that end he poses a question: "What would a Coke machine like to know?" (Stewart 2001: 146). Some of the more obvious answers would be its inventory and the phone number of its distributor so it could restock when needed, its physical location, the repairman's phone number to call when it's broken or malfunctioning, and whether the money fed into it is real or counterfeit. Another important piece of knowledge—and Coca-Cola actually announced this policy in a press release, but then decided to repeal it after it got negative publicity—is the temperature outside so it could adjust the price of drinks on hot days. The point of the exercise is to try and turn tacit knowledge into explicit knowledge to create value. With some creative thinking, your company can do the same thing.

KARL MARX'S REVENGE

Human capital determines the performance capacity of any organization. Today's knowledge workers, unlike the factory workers of the Industrial Revolution, own the company's means of production. This is what Daniel Pink, author of *Free Agent Nation*, calls "Karl Marx's revenge." It is time for leaders to start treating their people with the respect and dignity worthy of serious moral enterprises, and to stop viewing employees as simply machines who can check their emotions at the door. People are not assets—and will not be replaced by computers no matter how far advanced artificial intelligence becomes—or inventory, or resources; they are individuals entitled to a sense of mission and purpose in their lives, who congregate in firms to make a difference in the lives of others. The universal need of every worker is to perform meaningful work, in a community with others of like mind, to make a difference in the world. The real aspiration of an organization is to make people *better*, not just make them *better off*.

Characteristics like passion, desire, obsession, motivation, innovation, creativity, and knowledge may not show up anywhere on a firm's financial statements, but they are the traits that will ultimately determine the fate of the firm. Knowledge work is nonlinear and not subject to the cadences and rhythms of an assembly line from the Industrial Revolution; rather it moves by iteration and reiteration. Thinking is invisible. We simply cannot treat people as if they were bags of cement that companies can move around to maximize efficiency. We must stop thinking in terms of command-and-control management and operational efficiency metrics. Knowledge workers need to focus on effectiveness and deserve better than these other outdated modes of thinking.

Rabbi Daniel Lapin asks the following provocative question in his book *Thou Shall Prosper:* "Why do people raise their food to their mouths instead of lowering their mouths to the plate?" Lapin provides the answer:

> The head represents a person's spiritually lofty component, while food is a material commodity. Seated at the dining table, either the material can be lifted to the spiritual or the spiritual can be lowered to the material. As unique and special beings, people prefer doing the former rather than resembling animals in doing the latter.
>
> Wealth creation is partially how people express their spirituality. Of course, it is an unnatural act—no animals in nature ever do it—but overcoming nature, all nature, especially human nature, is what Judaism sees people as obligated to do. If people are nothing more than the rational animals that Aristotle considered them to be, then business may well be exploitative. It is certainly unnatural because no other creature on earth engages in behavior even remotely similar to business (Lapin 2002: 46).

This is the advantage in recognizing knowledge workers as human capital investors, deserving of dignity. Wealth creation is inherently spiritual, not material, in the sense that it cannot simply be measured using any scientific device. The desire of a Fred Smith to launch FedEx cannot be captured by measurement alone.

My VeraSage Institute colleague Dan Morris flies his firm's flag over his office building (below the American flag, of course) with its name and logo in three colors. Recall that those who first called themselves *liberals*—in the classical definition of the word—had in mind three liberations (which explains why the appropriate liberal flag is always *tricolor*). They intended to (1) liberate humans from tyranny and torture; (2) liberate humans from poverty; and (3) liberate humans from censorship and other oppressions of conscience, intellect, and art. It is time we hoist a new flag over the knowledge firm of the future and usher in a new order of the ages, one that respects the dignity, and earns the rewards, of its human capital investors.

10

KNOWLEDGE WORKERS
ARE VOLUNTEERS

An investment in knowledge pays the best interest.
—*Benjamin Franklin, Poor Richard's Almanack*

The management of knowledge workers should be based on the assumption that the corporation needs them more than they need the corporation. They know they can leave. They have both mobility and self-confidence. This means they have to be treated and managed as volunteers, in the same way as volunteers who work for not-for-profit organizations.
—*Peter Drucker, A Functioning Society: Selections from Sixty-Five Years of Writing on Community, Society, and Polity, 2003*

Peruse a corporate annual report, and inevitably you will read that "people are our greatest asset" (or "resource"). Stalin used to say it as well. Thinking of workers as resources—from the Latin *resurgere*, "to rise again"—is equally demeaning, implying people are no different from, say, timber, to be harvested when you run out. Even Michael Eisner, former chairman and CEO of Disney, has been recorded as saying, "Our inventory goes home at night." There's a new twist—people are now inventory to be turned over. Perhaps one of the reasons for the use of these demeaning words is that managers do not understand the worth of their people because they cannot be measured as exactly as accountants record assets, inventory, and other tangible resources.

One consultant suggested that we should capitalize all salaries and wages on the balance sheet to reflect the fact that workers are part of a company's capital. I remain skeptical; knowing the average accountant, they would set up a depreciation reserve, and that view of people is no better. Humans deserve more respect than a phone system or computer. Assets are passive, bought and sold in the marketplace at the whim of their owners; conversely, knowledge workers have ultimate control over their careers. Why do we insist on perpetuating this belief that people are resources to be mined rather than human capital to be developed?

A Chinese proverb teaches that the beginning of wisdom is to call things by their right names. Your people are not assets, resources, or inventory, but human capital investors seeking a decent return on their investment. In fact, your people—and especially those who are knowledge workers—are actually volunteers, since whether they return to work on any given day is completely based on their volition. Consider for a moment how people decide which volunteer organizations to contribute some of their time and talent to. The choice is usually based on a desire to contribute to something larger than themselves. They work hard for these organizations—some would say harder than at their regular jobs—because they are dedicated to the purpose, and possess the passion, desire, and the dream to make a difference in the lives of others. All for zero monetary pay. Why? This is not just an economic decision; it is a psychological and emotional decision.

The nonprofit sector offers many lessons in retaining and attracting talent. For someone to volunteer his or her precious time and money, nonprofits have to have an inspiring purpose and high expectations of their people, and be held accountable for performance and results. This is not a cottage industry, as is thought by some in the business world. It is also destined to grow. There were about 22,000 private charitable foundations in the early 1980s, whereas today the number is over 65,000. Coupled with the growth in worldwide billionaires, from 423 in 1996 to

691 as this book is being written, this sector is destined to play an increasing role in the world economy. America's voluntary sector employs some 7 percent of the population, one that received, in 2004, a record $249 billion in donations, over 2 percent of America's gross domestic product (GDP). In 2001, nearly 84 million Americans volunteered approximately four hours per week at an average hourly wage that equates to $239 billion—more than was spent on single-family homes in the same year.

People volunteer not for the money, but for the sense of inner peace and accomplishing meaningful work that impacts the lives of others. Are workers in the private sector motivated any differently? Noting that volunteerism had grown so much, and that many more for-profit executives were spending a portion of their time off doing charity work, Peter Drucker asked them why. "Far too many give the same answer: 'Because in my job there isn't much challenge, not enough achievement, not enough responsibility; and there is no mission, only expediency" (Watson and Brown 2001: 45). This is a profoundly sad commentary on the state of the business world today (no wonder "Dilbert" is so popular, with his images of cynicism and disdain for everything corporate). Charitable organizations view themselves as real communities, whereas many companies are nothing more than payroll ledgers.

Man does not live by bread alone. No matter how well we pay our people, if we don't give them that sense of purpose, the vision of creating a better future, we will not capture their pride and their hearts. We may get some 2,000 hours out of people per year, but will we tap into their potential to achieve great things? One organization that does understand producing results is the Salvation Army. Peter Drucker said that it is the most effective organization in the United States. "No one," he says, "even comes close to [the Salvation Army] in respect to clarity of mission, ability to innovate, measurable results, dedication, and putting money to maximum use" (Watson and Brown 2001: 16). The Salvation Army began in the United States on March 10,

1880, 15 years after being founded in England by William Booth. Today, it has an annual budget exceeding $2 billion and a workforce (employees and volunteers) of 3.4 million; and that number understates the value of the extra contribution by Army staffers, which *Forbes* magazine estimates, if taken into account, would rank the Salvation Army among the biggest companies in the Forbes 500. Not bad, considering that, of the original firms listed on the 1896 Dow Jones Industrials, only General Electric is still in existence.

The Salvation Army provides a range of services, seeing needs as opportunities, and problems as future assets. It operates more than 1,200 thrift stores, provides more than 75,000 individuals a place to sleep every night; responds instantly to disasters, and offers relief; and delivers long-term drug and alcohol rehabilitation (at effectiveness rates that make governmental agencies blush). In addition, it also provides "state-contracted counseling for former prisoners on parole or probation; day care for children and seniors; community sports and recreation programs; medical services; job training and placement; missing person services; summer and day camps for kids; and visitations to people in institutions" (Watson and Brown 2001: 22). At least 83 cents of every dollar collected goes to these services, with only 17 cents going for overhead and administration (a number that would make any governmental agency a defendant in a fraud case).

How does this organization achieve these spectacular results, especially when you consider that the workforce's average pay is less than $400 per week (not including Army benefits of housing and transportation, and that is provided only after 10 years), and they are not micromanaged? As Robert Watson pointed out in his book on the Salvation Army, they "engage the spirit." People work hard, real hard, when they believe they are making a contribution beyond just the bottom line. Here is some of the wisdom from Watson's remarkable book *The Most Effective Organization in the U.S.: Leadership Secrets of the Salvation Army*:

Can a charity really teach leaders who have to operate in the "real world" of business? If we truly believe that we all aspire to achieve our best selves beyond mere material concerns and that the organizations we build are simply extensions of our aspirations, then the difference between for-profit organizations and nonprofit ones is about accounting policies, not about proficiency and effectiveness. The bottom line is this: An organization is an organization is an organization (Watson and Brown 2001: 14).

As individuals, Salvationists are as unremarkable as any other man or woman you pass on the street. Not smarter, not stronger, not possessed of greater resources. Two things distinguish us, and both are available to anyone: An openness to God's grace and a commitment to demonstrating it through service to others. Hoard our assets? We exhaust them in the effort to reach more and more people. Lower our expectations? We are out to save the world. Trust no one? Our best customers—and future partners—are drug addicts, prisoners, the enfeebled, and the desperately poor (Watson and Brown 2001: 33).

If we, as Salvation Army leaders, are confident we're in harmony with our spiritual mission, we can make just about every other decision by answering questions such as these: "What does this have to do with helping hurting people?" and "Is this the best use of our resources to help people we're pledged to serve?" If we can't define a policy or a proposal or even a long standing program on those terms, it has to go. Managers in other enterprises can generalize these test questions to this one: How is this decision going to affect the lives of our customers? That's it. If you can't demonstrate that what you propose is going to create value for people, it's probably the wrong choice (Watson and Brown 2001: 75–76).

This is sage advice. Samuel Goldwyn is credited with saying: "The key for an actor is sincerity, because if you can fake that, you can fake anything." But you cannot fake sincerity, or pride, or being loyal to a team, let alone a company. Former Secretary of Labor Robert B. Reich said he used a simple *pronoun test* when visiting a company:

I ask frontline workers a few general questions about the company. If the answers I get back describe the company in terms like "they" and "them," then I know it's one kind of company. If the answers are put in terms like "we" or "us," then I know it's a different kind of company (Prusak and Cohen 2001: 93).

Despite all this evidence of human behavior, many organizations still treat their people as if they will slack off if they are not held accountable for every six minutes of every day. Organizations spend an inordinate amount of time checking and rechecking to make sure people do what is expected. Is this any way to inspire people to be their best? Is this any way to instill a spirit of service and dedication to serving customers? Or is this nothing but antiquated thinking about the nature of man being lazy and slothful unless forced to work? Jim Casey, founder of UPS in 1907, said in 1947: "A man's worth to an organization can be measured by the amount of supervision he requires." By definition, knowledge workers know more about their areas of responsibility than anyone else; otherwise, they would be useless. This makes them very difficult to supervise, let alone "manage." It is also why they are the most valuable members of any organization.

PEOPLE HAVE VALUE, NOT JOBS

Although economic rewards play an important part in securing adherence to organizational goals and management authority, they are limited in their effectiveness. Organizations would be far less effective systems than they actually are if such rewards were the only means, or even principal means, of motivation available.

—*Herbert Simon, 1978 Nobel Laureate economist*

Another salutary effect of thinking in terms of knowledge workers as volunteers is a rather counterintuitive supposition: It is *people* who have value, not *jobs*. There is not a market for jobs, per se, but there is a market for people who can create value. Hence, the issue is one of valuing people, not jobs, correctly. As Bill Gates said: "If it weren't for 20 key people, Microsoft wouldn't be the company it is today" (Gandossy et al. 2006: 64). Job positions may appear to be fixed in most companies, but in reality they are not. Jobs in any dynamic economy are not zero-sum. Jobs are limited only to the extent of knowledge workers' imaginations, not a scarce commodity at all. It is individuals who perform above—or below—average, not jobs. It is individuals who leave jobs and decide to invest their intellectual capital (IC) elsewhere; jobs do not. The notion of a fixed *job* for a knowledge worker is becoming outdated.

If you were to study the myriad of surveys that have been conducted over the decades of why people select one company over another—and indeed, why over time they show loyalty to any one firm—you would find essentially four factors that are taken into consideration (subject yourself to these categories, especially as to why you chose your first job, and perhaps why you left it, to see if they make sense):

1. *Intrinsic rewards.* These are the awards that are inherent in the work itself, factors such as the challenge of the work; the level of commitment to the organization's purpose and values; an environment that encourages creativity, fun (yes, fun), and innovation; and the social culture of the firm. These factors are precisely why people give their hearts, bodies, and minds to the volunteer organizations they work for. The satisfaction comes from a job well done and making a difference in the world.

2. *Opportunity to grow.* How is the firm going to help the person develop his IC? Is it going to offer room for growth and improvement? Will it invest an appropriate level of resources into educating the person to enhance his IC? How will the relationship with the firm not only enhance the worker's skills, but help him become better personally as well?

3. *Recognize accomplishments.* How does the firm recognize outstanding performance, including promotion and involvement in the strategy and direction of the company? How does it spread the recognition to other team members? Does the firm have "storytellers," those individuals who pass on

the legends and lessons of the past so they can inspire future workers to greatness? Does the firm have a culture of celebrating success, or does it spend most of its time solving problems and mitigating crises?

4. *Economic rewards.* This is the composition of wages, benefits, and other extrinsic aspects the worker receives. Is there a strong correlation between the effectiveness of the worker, his value to the organization, and his compensation?

Think back over your career and try to remember a *boss*—I do not like that word, let's substitute *executive*—that you truly respected, one you looked up to and admired; perhaps he was even a mentor. The relationship with the executive may be the most important factor in determining whether someone stays or leaves a firm. As an instructor at the Disney University pointed out, "People don't leave companies. They leave leaders in those companies." Dale Dauten wrote a splendid little book, *The Gifted Boss: How to Find, Create and Keep Great Employees*, with this advice:

> The old school is to hire someone you need by offering twenty percent more money. Well, try offering a hundred percent more freedom or a hundred percent more excitement ... gifted bosses and great employees want the same things from a workplace:
>
> - Freedom from ... management, mediocrity, and morons.
> - A change.
> - A chance. (Dauten 1999: Preface, 74).

Perhaps part of the problem, once again, is the words we use to describe the relationship between employer and employee. Terms such as *boss* and *manager* do not really describe the relationship knowledge workers have with the organizations that employ them. Even Peter Drucker became increasingly uncomfortable with the word *manager:*

> And while we're on the subject of words, I'm not comfortable with the word *manager* any more, because it implies subordinates. I find myself using *executive* more, because it implies responsibility for an area, not necessarily dominion over people (Drucker, 2003: 32).

Drucker also believed rather than bosses and subordinates, knowledge firms would be comprised of seniors and juniors. It is interesting to note the origin of the word manager:

> *Manager* is derived from the old Italian and French words *maneggio* and *manege*, meaning the training, handling and riding of a horse. It is strange to think that the whole spirit of *management* is derived from the image of getting on the back of a beast, digging your knees in, and heading it in a certain direction. The word *manager* conjures images of domination, command, and ultimate control, and the taming of a potentially wild energy. It also implies a basic unwillingness on the part of the people to be managed, a force to be corralled and reined in. All appropriate things if you wish to ride a horse, but most people don't respond very passionately or very creatively to being ridden, and the words *giddy up there* only go so far in creating the kind of responsive participation we now look for. Sometime over the next fifty years or so, the word manager will disappear from our understanding of leadership, and thankfully so. Another word will emerge, more alive with possibility, more helpful, hopefully not decided upon by a committee, which will describe the new role of leadership now emerging. An image of leadership which embraces the attentive, open-minded, conversationally based, people-minded person who has not given up on her intellect and can still act and act quickly when needed (Whyte 2001: 240–241).

Let us start to create an environment worthy of people's investment. In fact, my favorite one-dimensional test for creating a culture that is worthy of the respect and dignity of the people you are trying to attract is simply this: Would you want your son or daughter to work in your firm?

BECOMING A LIGHTNING ROD FOR TALENT

Getting the right people in the right jobs is a lot more important than developing a strategy.
—*Jack Welch*

Why is it easier to get into Harvard or Princeton than to be hired by Southwest Airlines, which accepts only 4 percent of its 90,000 applicants each year? Here is how Herb Kelleher explained it to the American Compensation Association back in 1995 when he was CEO at Southwest:

> Well, first of all, it starts with hiring. We are zealous about hiring. We are looking for a particular type of person, regardless of which job category it is. We are looking for attitudes that are positive and for people who can lend themselves to causes. We want folks who have a good sense of humor and people who are interested in performing as a team and take joy in team results instead of individual accomplishments (Prusak and Cohen 2001: 93).

Southwest does not hire for skills—it will teach people what they need to know—but for attitude, which is very difficult to teach, or change. Kelleher got it precisely right when he observed: "We hire attitude, we teach functionality."

Attracting good people and hiring are two of the most important jobs to which everyone in the organization can contribute input and ideas. Executives spend more of their time—or at least they should—making people decisions than any other. No other decisions have as many repercussions throughout the firm, or have lasting significant effects than hiring choices. The Heritage Foundation, a think tank in Washington, D.C., has this axiom as it relates to new presidential administrations making personnel choices: "People are policy." You would expect to find a high level of commitment and energy devoted to this task, but in the average company you do not. Typically, the average firm is batting 0.333 on its hiring decisions; that is, one-third turn out to be good decisions, one-third are minimally effective, and one-third are abject failures. This may be an exceptional average for baseball players, but it is rare in any other area that executives would accept this level of performance.

IC organizations are *people* companies, and dealing with people is always going to be full of challenges. When you hire someone, you do not just get his hands and labor; you get his emotions, desires, dreams, aspirations, expectations, and heart—if you do it right. The issue of attracting human capital investors is a *marketing* issue, which a lot of companies do not seem to understand. As in all marketing, the marketing function does not look *inward* and ask, "What do *we* want and need?" On the contrary, it looks *outward* and asks, "What do *you* want and need?" There is an enormous difference between these two approaches. This latter changes the mind-set from one of *allocating* resources to *attracting* investors. Silicon Valley works on the operating principle of attracting rather than allocating resources. If an idea has enough merit, it will attract capital and resources, in the form of venture capital or an entrepreneurial leap of faith. Think tanks also work on this principle. They gather ideas from anywhere, not just those they themselves generate, and put them out in the arena of ideas to do battle. In effect, firms have to do the same to win over people as they do to gain a new customer: show them why the company is their best competitive alternative. Google's founders, Sergey Brin and Larry Page, lay out a compelling "Top 10 Reasons to Work at Google." Compare how it focuses more on intrinsic rather than extrinsic rewards:

1. *Lend a helping hand.* With millions of visitors every month, Google has become an essential part of everyday life—like a good friend—connecting people with the information they need to live great lives.

2. *Life is beautiful.* Being a part of something that matters and working on products in which you can believe is remarkably fulfilling.

3. *Appreciation is the best motivation,* so we've created a fun and inspiring workspace you'll be glad to be a part of, including on-site doctor and dentist; massage and yoga; professional development opportunities; on-site day care; shoreline running trails; and plenty of snacks to get you through the day.

4. *Work and play are not mutually exclusive.* It is possible to code and pass the puck at the same time.

5. *We love our employees, and we want them to know it.* Google offers a variety of benefits, including a choice of medical

programs, company-matched 401(k), stock options, maternity and paternity leave, and much more.

6. *Innovation is our bloodline.* Even the best technology can be improved. We see endless opportunity to create even more relevant, more useful, and faster products for our users. Google is the technology leader in organizing the world's information.

7. *Good company everywhere you look.* Googlers range from former neurosurgeons, CEOs, and U.S. puzzle champions to alligator wrestlers and former Marines. No matter what their backgrounds, Googlers make for interesting cube mates.

8. *Uniting the world, one user at a time.* People in every country and every language use our products. As such we think, act, and work globally—just our little contribution to making the world a better place.

9. *Boldly go where no one has gone before.* There are hundreds of challenges yet to solve. Your creative ideas matter here and are worth exploring. You'll have the opportunity to develop innovative new products that millions of people will find useful.

10. *There is such a thing as a free lunch, after all.* In fact we have them every day: healthy, yummy, and made with love (www. google.com/jobs/reasons.html, accessed February 8, 2007).

Because knowledge workers are investing their IC with firms that will pay a fair return, rather than asking, "How much is this person worth to the firm?" the real question should be: "How much is the firm worth to this knowledge worker? How can the firm add to this person's IC and develop it even further?" These are the important questions to answer to create lasting success. Even with all the talk of a so-called free-agent workforce, and the boom in self-employment, people still need organizations to produce the goods and services customers will demand.

Viewing new hires as IC investors is a much better paradigm for making the best hiring decisions. While a lot of companies lament the fact that "you can't find good people," the simple fact is that you are not always going to be able to hire the best people. Statistically, this is impossible, as the labor pool is not composed of 100 percent top talent. Chief scientist Bill Joy of Sun Microsystems has come up with this law: "Most of the smartest people are never in your own company." Usually, when people talk about their companies, they mention how good its people are. This is a natural, and even healthy, viewpoint. But the important question that flows from that is, "Good for what?"

In the final analysis, your competitive advantage lies not necessarily in attracting the best talent, but rather in a superior ability to develop and inspire those you do hire, the subject of the next chapter.

11

DEVELOPING AND INSPIRING KNOWLEDGE WORKERS

> Increasingly, performance in these new knowledge-based industries will come to depend on running the institution so as to attract, hold, and motivate knowledge workers. When this can no longer be done by satisfying knowledge workers' greed, as we are now trying to do, it will have to be done by satisfying their values, and by giving them social recognition and social power. It will have to be done by turning them from subordinates into fellow executives, and from employees, however well paid, into partners.
> —*Peter Drucker (Florida 2002: 87)*

Organizations throughout history have always made attracting talent a priority. The East India Company, founded in 1600, utilized examinations to recruit brainpower, with impressive results. Among the company's employees were James and John Stuart Mill—two of Britain's leading intellectuals. Yet attracting talent is only one part of the challenge. Organizations also have to engage today's knowledge workers, a daunting task since these workers have more options than at any other time in the history of commerce.

There is much talk regarding "retaining" talent. But who wants to be retained? This is more of the human cattle mind-set. Knowledge workers want to be engaged, challenged, and valued. No matter how well we pay our people, if we don't give them that sense of purpose, the vision of achieving a better future, we will not capture their pride and their hearts. Once again we can learn from the nonprofit sector the importance of tapping into the soul of our workers, as explained by Robert Watson of the Salvation Army:

> You have to make the most of the link between pride and performance by continually clearing away the stuff that interferes with people connecting what they do in the organization with how it's received on the outside. That's why we keep sending out desk-bound officers and employees to experience programs and to talk to beneficiaries firsthand. Here's the important thing about that kind of pride. You can't "instill" it in an organization, as we so often hear. Pride is earned. It grows from performance in line with expectations everybody agrees on. And you risk losing the bonus pride affords an organization when you let your practices slip out of alignment with your purpose, no matter how compellingly you advertise your intentions. The first to notice the misalignment, even before customers, will be employees (Watson and Brown 2001: 101).
>
> [Explaining the grueling schedule of the average Salvation Army couple, Watson says]: For all this labor, which often starts early and finishes late each day and which provides precious little time off, this couple may draw less than $400 per week (not including Army benefits of housing and transportation). That's after 10 years as officers and includes allowances for two young children, whose concerns also have to be taken into consideration. ... This kind of exhausting schedule, with its simultaneous demands for broad skills and narrow focus, seems made to order for management burnout. There's always too much to do and too little time and resources. Yet our officers sign on for life and work happily and productively well into their retirement. How could you possibly compensate people for this kind of effort if you couldn't offer access to soul-deep satisfaction that was intrinsic to the job? (Watson and Brown 2001: 211).

FedEx's internal value statement is the ultimate expression of these concepts: "People-Service-Profit." Excellent companies have learned that when they put their people first—yes, even before customers—they will take care of its customers with excellent service, which ultimately drives profits. There is a strong correlation between employee relations and customer relations. How an organization treats its people internally will mirror very closely how its people treat external customers. Employees who are not engaged and loyal are not likely to create customers who are.

As James C. Wetherbe explained in his book *The World on Time: The 11 Management Principles that Made FedEx an Overnight Sensation*: "The rights and value of a single human life," begins the FedEx manager's training guide, "have become the central focus of social evolution in the industrialized world. ... FedEx, from its inception, has put its people first both because it is right to do so and because it is good business as well" (Wetherbe 1996: 15). And FedEx employees have responded in kind. At the end of one pay period in the difficult early days of the company, employees received a memo along with their paychecks (all of which contained this message on the envelope: "A Satisfied Customer Made This Possible"). The memo, from founder Fred Smith, stated that they were welcome to cash their checks, but, he suggested, it sure would be helpful if some of them waited just a few days. To this day, some of those checks remain uncashed. Their owners display them proudly, as a badge of honor, in frames on their FedEx office walls. Do your employees feel a similar sense of loyalty to your company?

Twenty-two year FedEx veteran Madan Birla, who worked closely with Fred Smith, explains that FedEx taps its team members' discretionary effort, which it defines as the difference between mere compliance with the job requirements and commitment. He notes that everything within FedEx is constantly challenged to improve the customer experience, except for how it treats people. This engages its team members to not only do the job, but to improve *how* the job is done (Birla 2005: 56–57, 78, 81).

Despite all of the empirical evidence that exists on the importance of treating employees well, too many organizations still do not trust their people to do the right thing. There is nothing more demeaning to knowledge workers than to feel that they are not trusted. Far too many organizations still believe they can "manage" knowledge workers, treating them like machines they can manipulate and mechanize to achieve maximum efficiency. These theories of command-and-control management are redolent of the techniques and attitudes pioneered by the father of the Scientific Management Revolution.

THE SCIENTIFIC MANAGEMENT REVOLUTION

The most famous preacher of the efficiency gospel was Frederick Winslow Taylor (see Exhibit 11.1), who observed endless ways to make laborers' work more rational, quantifiable, and scientific, writing about the "science of shoveling" and the "law of heavy laboring," topics that today would most likely make for lackluster book sales, but in Taylor's time ushered in a new era of management thinking. Taylor was born on March 20, 1856, into a prominent Quaker family in an upper-middle-class suburb of Philadelphia. As a teenager he became obsessed with cricket, which, like baseball, is a game where the statistics and batting averages are more exciting than the game itself. Allegedly, he never smoked or drank alcohol, tea, or coffee. And when he attended dances, he drew up charts classifying all the girls in attendance as attractive or ugly and precisely calculated his time so he spent one-half in conversation with each.

Taylor became an industrial engineer, testing his time-and-motion theories on the factory floor among his coworkers at the Midvale Steel Company in Philadelphia. He took all the romance out of work, and instead of a "noble skill" it was subdivided into a series of simple motions, much as the pin workers Adam Smith observed. All of the other aspects of human beings—creativity, initiative, imagination—were to be done somewhere else in the organization, usually the province of upper-management, who did the "thinking" while the workers did the "doing." This did not

EXHIBIT 11.1   FREDERICK WINSLOW TAYLOR (1856–1915)

foster an environment of trustworthiness in the factories where Taylor's ideas were implemented, but it did yield increased productivity, which also increased the wages of the common worker. It was Taylor, after all, who replaced the phrase *working harder* with *working smarter*.

Taylor's ideas were not implemented without friction, however. He viewed both managers and workers as "dumb oxen," and trade union opposition was on the increase. In 1915, Congress passed legislation, which stayed on the books until 1949, banning Taylor's beloved stopwatches from government factories.

Peter Drucker credits Taylor with coining the terms *management* and *consultant*, as well as being the world's very first knowledge worker. Taylor's calling card identified him as a "Consultant to Management," and he charged the princely sum of $35 a day—approximately $720 today—for his standard two-hour lecture.

Even Russian communist leader Vladimir Ilyich Lenin came under Taylor's spell: "We must introduce in Russia the study and teaching of the new Taylor System and its systematic trial and adaptation" (in Skousen 2001: 252). On the eve of the Bolshevik Revolution, Lenin declared that "accounting and control" were the key factors in running an enterprise and that capitalism had already "reduced" management to "extraordinarily simple operations" that "any literate person can perform"—that is, "supervising and recording, knowledge of the four rules of arithmetic, and issuing appropriate receipts." Such "exceedingly simple operations of registration, filing and checking" could, according to Lenin, "easily be performed" by people receiving ordinary workmen's wages (from Lenin's *The State and Revolution*, in Sowell 2000: 111).

Taylor wrote all of his theories down throughout the years, circulating them privately in 1911 in *The Principles of Scientific Management*. Taylor's theories have been credited with tripling output during World War II and making Mussolini's trains run on time in Italy, German precision engineering, Lenin's Five Year Plans, consumerism, Hitler's gas chambers, and the death of communism—all with a simple stopwatch. No doubt, Taylor contributed to most of these, some more than others, earning him the nickname "Speedy Taylor."

Some of Taylor's principles set forth in *The Principles of Scientific Management* are worth noting to compare them to what is needed to increase the effectiveness of today's knowledge workers (discussed later):

> In the past the man has been first; in the future the system must be first (Taylor 1967: 7).
> ...[T]he workman who is best suited to actually doing the work is incapable of fully understanding this science, without the guidance and help of those who are working with him or over him, either through lack of education or through insufficient mental capacity (Taylor 1967: 26).
> ...[A]lmost every act of the workman should be preceded by one or more preparatory acts of the management which enable him

to do his work better and quicker than he otherwise could (Taylor 1967: 26).

Perhaps the most prominent single element in modern scientific management is the task idea. The work of every workman is fully planned out by the management at least one day in advance, and each man receives in most cases complete written instructions, describing in detail the task which he is to accomplish, as well as the means to be used in doing the work (Taylor 1967: 39).

The first illustration is that of handling pig iron. This work is so crude and elementary in its nature that the writer firmly believes that it would be possible to train an intelligent gorilla so as to become a more efficient pig-iron handler than any man can be (Taylor 1967: 40).

The average boy would go very slowly if, instead of being given a task, he were told to do as much as he could. All of us are grown-up children, and it is equally true that the average workman will work with the greatest satisfaction, both to himself and to his employer, when he is given each day a definite task which he is to perform in a given time, and which constitutes a proper day's work for a good workman. This furnishes the workman with a clear-cut standard, by which he can throughout the day measure his own progress, and the accomplishment of which affords him the greatest satisfaction (Taylor 1967: 120–121).

This advice seems crude and unenlightened for today's knowledge economy, and organized labor viewed Taylorism as nothing more than a method to extract more sweat from labor, turning workers into impersonal slaves. One writer described it thusly: "Scientific management was degrading. ... In standing over you with a stopwatch, peering at you, measuring you, rating you, it treated you like a side of beef. You weren't supposed to think. Whatever workmanly pride you might once have possessed must be sacrificed on the altar of efficiency" (Skousen 2001: 252–253).

Henry Ford wrote in his autobiography *My Life and Work*: "Factory organization is not a device to prevent the expansion of ability, but a device to reduce the waste and losses due to mediocrity. It is not a device to hinder the ambitious, clear-headed man from doing his best, but a device to prevent the don't-care sort of individual from doing his worst" (Ford, 1922: 270). Not exactly an enlightened view of industrial organization, but it is also difficult to argue with Ford's ability to put the automobile within reach of the common man. There is no doubt that we owe a large portion of our present standard of living to Taylor and his methods of increasing the productivity of manual workers.

In defense of Taylor, he certainly did not view his methods as a way to extract more labor from each worker. One must consider how truly revolutionary these ideas were in Taylor's day, and his motivation for proposing them. His objective was not cost reduction, but rather to increase productivity to benefit the worker, not the owner, enabling capital and labor to enjoy a harmonious relationship. In fact, Taylor considered himself to be the "Great Harmonizer." He was one of the first to recognize the need to apply knowledge to work, even though he may have believed this to be the task primarily of management rather than the workers themselves. He agreed with Adam Smith's vision of universal opulence, and wrote: "The luxuries of one generation [will become] the necessities of the next [and] the working people of our country will live as well and have the same luxuries, the same opportunities for leisure, for culture, and for education, as are now possessed by the average business man" (Skousen 2001: 253).

Not only would increases in productivity be good for owners and workers, it would be a positive boon for customers as well. Andrew Carnegie ruthlessly focused on output per man-hour and unit costs, in order to slash prices, arguing that since steel was essential for a modern economy, reducing its price would lower the prices of virtually everything, thereby raising living standards. Carnegie was able to get the price of steel rails, which cost $160 a ton in 1875, down to $17 a ton by 1898, all the while paying his managers the highest wages in U.S. industry.

In 1907, Taylor met a bricklayer, Frank Gilbreth (see Exhibit 11.2), who had done his own time-and-motion analysis on laying bricks, which enabled his output to increase from

EXHIBIT 11.2 FRANK GILBRETH (1868–1924)

1,000 to 2,700 per day. Apparently, Gilbreth was more obsessed with his stopwatch than was Taylor, and 2 of his 12 children later wrote a portrait of him titled *Cheaper by the Dozen*, later made into a Hollywood movie with Clifton Webb as Gilbreth.

Frank Gilbreth went on to eventually repudiate the validity of time-and-motion studies as unethical and "absolutely worthless." In the meantime, Taylor pressed on, espousing his theories until his final day. In the winter of 1914, hospitalized with pneumonia, every morning Taylor arose out of bed to wind his precious watch. One morning, March 21, 1915, a nurse saw him winding it uncharacteristically early, 4:30 A.M. When she returned a half hour later, Taylor was dead; it was one day after his fifty-ninth birthday. Many of the so-called efficiency experts met an early death—which makes you wonder what, exactly, were they saving all that time *for*?

During the 1920s, when economists began to recognize a large and growing sector of the labor force known as *service workers*, they used metrics similar to Taylor's and Gilbreth's to measure their productivity—from the number of transactions a bank teller processed and tables a waiter or waitress turned in a shift to the number of cases closed by an insurance claims adjuster. These metrics were sufficient, as far as they went, to measure the productivity of manual and service workers; but when knowledge workers started to become a significant portion of the labor force—not to mention a disproportionate share of the value creation in the economy—Taylor and Gilbreth's measurements hit the proverbial brick wall. Time-and-motion studies require observation and precise measurement of physical actions, but knowledge work is invisible since it takes place in one's mind. How do we measure, and increase, the productivity of knowledge workers? To make progress on this ambition, we need to begin with a lesson from Plato: "The beginning of wisdom is the definition of terms."

WHAT, EXACTLY, IS PRODUCTIVITY?

The single greatest challenge facing managers in the developed countries of the world is to raise the productivity of knowledge and service workers. This challenge, which will dominate the management agenda for the next several decades, will ultimately determine the competitive performance of companies. Even more important, it will determine the very fabric of society and the quality of life in every industrialized nation.

—*Peter Drucker, Profession of Management, 2003*

Productivity is always a ratio, expressed as the amount of output per unit of input. Mathematically, it seems straightforward, as if there were one widely agreed-on definition of the components of the numerator and denominator. In an intellectual capital (IC) economy, however, it is a conundrum. One of the most common measurements is output per man-hour, which in the United States has increased at an annual average rate of 3 percent since 1996. But this measures only labor productivity. Economists also measure multifactor productivity (or total factor productivity), which is an attempt to capture inputs beyond labor, such as capital. Yet, it is much easier to tally up hours worked than the value of capital, especially human capital.

The government measures most outputs by the cost of the inputs; hence, it misses the prodigious growth of technology and other gains in knowledge, especially since the price of technology is constantly declining. This is exactly the quandary that led Nobel Laureate Robert Solow to utter in 1987, "We see the computer age everywhere except in the productivity statistics." It would appear that "productivity" is not the only measurement in a knowledge organization, as the following examples will illustrate.

What would you conclude regarding the productivity of a particular laser beam that wasted 60 to 90 percent of the electric power received at its back end before projecting an intense, blinding beam out the front?

It doesn't sound very efficient, does it? Yet that is exactly the productivity of the laser beam used for cataract surgery to restore eyesight. It is not at all efficient. So what? It is highly effective. In this case, the waste of energy is clearly a virtue, not a vice. You would never draw this conclusion studying the ratio of output to input, however, as the math misses the miracle of restoring the joy of human sight. If you were the patient, inefficiency is clearly superior to ineffectiveness.

If we are making wine, we could count the grapes, the bottles, corks, and so on. But none of those would help us define—let alone value—the final product. As they say, it is much easier to count the bottles than describe the wine.

If we were attempting to measure Rembrandt's productivity, we could sum up the costs of paint, canvas, brushes, and even the amount of labor hours spent plying his craft. Would there be any relationship to the final value of the output? Would counting the number of paintings produced over a given time period help? Companies have learned that costs are easier to compute than benefits, so they cut the costs in the denominator to improve the efficiency. This is the equivalent of Walt Disney's cutting out three of the dwarfs in *Snow White and the Seven Dwarfs* to reduce the inputs, making the resulting ratio look better. Since *Snow White* contained over 2 million painstakingly crafted drawings, this reduction would have been quite efficient—but hardly effective. More companies fail not due to being inefficient but rather from being ineffective—producing things nobody wants.

Measurable inputs do not correlate with output, since we have observed differences in factory productivity as high as 50 percent between, and even within, companies with similar equipment and equivalent size labor forces that are paid the same. The difference comes down to those intangibles that are not easily calculable in input/output tables—leadership, purpose, motivation, commitment, spirit—for both companies and individuals.

This, in a nutshell, is the problem with the way we attempt to measure the "productivity" of knowledge workers. The metrics we are using are redolent of the days of Frederick Taylor, no longer applicable to the product of the intellect. Knowledge work is not repetitive, it is *iterative* and *reiterative*—that is, a process of the mind, a difficult place for metrics to have any meaning. Not many people would want a time-and-motion doctor who equated efficiency with quality medical care.

The task at hand is formidable, since the relationship between inputs and outputs is not as well defined in the knowledge era as it was in the Agricultural or Industrial Revolution. Thus, the goal is not to shun Frederick Taylor, but to learn from him. Specifically, he applied knowledge to knowledge, increasing the productivity of manual laborers around the world, in the same manner Adam Smith explained the specialization and division of labor. However, even some of Smith's insights are not effective in a knowledge environment, since, for example, Shakespeare could not specialize in writing the verbs while a colleague wrote the nouns of his many works.

The fact of the matter is that we do not know how to measure the productivity of a knowledge worker. And even if we someday figure it out, we have not won even half the battle. We would still need to know how to increase it. It does no good to admonish your team members to work *smarter*, not *harder*. It's not bad advice, it's just not very helpful—like telling people to be healthy, wealthy, and wise. We need to apply the same ingenuity and creativity Taylor did to the subject of manual workers to inspire knowledge workers to contribute their full potential.

We need new thinking and new models to *judge* the effectiveness of knowledge workers. Fortunately, Peter Drucker blazed the trail in this area, a modern-day Taylor for the knowledge worker. Wise executives will build on his wisdom to usher in the new era of the knowledge worker.

A FRAMEWORK FOR KNOWLEDGE WORKER EFFECTIVENESS

Knowledge workers may be a minority of the workforce, but they are the largest single group and the major creator of wealth. What made the traditional workforce productive was the system—whether it was Frederick Winslow Taylor's "one best way," Henry Ford's assembly line, or Ed Deming's Total Quality Management. The system embodies the knowledge. The system is productive because it enables individual workers to perform without much knowledge or skill. ... In a knowledge-based organization, however, it is the individual worker's productivity that makes the system productive. In a traditional workforce the worker serves the system; in a knowledge workforce the system must serve the worker.

> —*Peter Drucker, Managing in the Next Society, 2002*

Knowledge work is not defined so much by *quantity* as it is by *quality*. It is also not defined by its *costs* but by its *results*. Frederick Taylor started with the assumption that there was "one best way" to achieve productivity and it was not necessarily determined by the physical—or even mental—characteristics of the job. But in knowledge work, the traditional tools of measurement need to be replaced by *judgment*, and there is a difference between a measurement and a judgment: a measurement requires only a stick; a judgment requires knowledge and discernment.

Frederick Taylor did not attempt to measure the productivity of knowledge workers because there were not very many in his day.

He did not focus attention on how to prepare the workers to do the job better next time, because he developed systems and procedures that removed the need for them to use their imaginations. He substituted rules for thinking.

It took approximately a half century before companies began to learn that this made their organizations complacent and stupid—not the traits you want in an auto factory, let alone among knowledge workers. Knowledge work can only be designed *by* the knowledge worker, not *for* the worker. In a factory, the worker *serves* the system. The same is true in a *service* environment; but in a knowledge environment, the system should *serve* the worker.

Productivity measurements on knowledge work may be in their infancy, but Peter Drucker has left us a good starting place, especially in his book *Management Challenges for the 21st Century*:

> Work on the productivity of the knowledge worker has barely begun. In terms of actual work on knowledge worker productivity we are, in the year 2000, roughly where we were in the year 1900, a century ago, in terms of the productivity of the manual worker. But we already know infinitely more about the productivity of the knowledge worker than we did then about that of the manual worker. We even know a good many of the answers. But we also know the challenges to which we do not yet know the answers, and on which we need to go to work. *Six* major factors determine knowledge-worker productivity.
>
> 1. Knowledge worker productivity demands that we ask the question: *"What is the task?"*
>
> 2. It demands that we impose the responsibility for their productivity on the individual knowledge workers themselves. Knowledge workers *have* to manage themselves. They have to have *autonomy*.
>
> 3. Continuing innovation has to be part of the work, the task and the responsibility of knowledge workers.
>
> 4. Knowledge work requires continuous learning on the part of the knowledge worker, but equally continuous teaching on the part of the knowledge worker.

5. Productivity of the knowledge worker is not—at least not primarily—a matter of the *quantity* of output. *Quality* is at least as important [I would argue more important].

6. Finally, knowledge-worker productivity requires that the knowledge worker is both seen and treated as an "asset" [I would say volunteer] rather than a "cost." It requires that knowledge workers *want* to work for the organization in preference to all other opportunities (Drucker 1999: 142).

These factors are almost the exact opposite of what is needed to increase the productivity of manual labor, with the possible exception of number six. The word *manufacturing* is derived from *manufactory*, meaning "made by hand." Yet more and more of today's economic output is made by mind. Taylor's systems did not engage the mind; they actually were designed to disengage it, similar to flying an airplane on autopilot.

Drucker believed the main focus of the knowledge worker needs to be on the task to be done—with all other distractions eliminated as much as possible—and this is defined by the worker him- or herself. Asking knowledge workers the following questions (adapted from Peter Drucker and other sources) about their jobs is a rich source of learning a great deal about any organization:

- What is your task?
- What should it be?
- What should you be expected to contribute?
- How fair are those expectations?
- What hampers you in doing your task and should be eliminated?
- How could *you* make the greatest *contribution* with your strengths, your way of performing, your values, to what needs to be done?
- What *results* have to be achieved to make a difference?
- What hinders you in doing your task and should be eliminated?
- What progress are you making in your career?

- How is the company helping you to achieve your professional goals and aspirations?
- What does the company do right and what should it continue doing?
- What are the firm's weaknesses and what should it stop doing?
- What critical things should the firm start doing?

These are excellent questions for executives to ask the team members periodically, as it will focus the company's resources and attention on external opportunities, rather than on internal bureaucratic procedures, rules, and systems that probably do not add much value to the customer experience.

Recall that a business does not exist to be efficient; it exists to create wealth for its customers. The traditional focus on efficiency in an IC-based economy is misplaced. This is not to say that productivity is not important, rather that it should not be the talisman for guiding the company to its core purpose: the creation of wealth.

Efficiency can be taken to ludicrous extremes. For instance, I doubt any efficiency expert would have suggested to the Nordstrom brothers to place pianos and hire piano players in their department stores. What could this possibly add to efficiency? Yet, how *effective* is it in providing a competitive differentiation that Nordstrom can leverage to create a more enriching experience for its team members and customers?

Knowledge companies understand this dynamic. Disney and Apple know there is a vast difference between being efficient and being *persuasive*. Even the egalitarian-minded Ben & Jerry's understood that a business simply could not operate at—or price for—100 percent efficiency. The new companies that have created so much wealth in the past decades, from eBay and Intel to Microsoft and Google, did not get where they are by focusing on efficiency. They focused on creating wealth for their customers.

Why, then, do so many companies worship on the altar of efficiency, confusing being busy with being profitable?

It should be obvious at this juncture that executives who are responsible for knowledge workers are going to have to become much more comfortable with intuition, judgment, and discernment over measurements. You simply cannot manage people by numbers. Professor Henry Mintzberg—who defends the word *manager* over *leader*—tells the story of one student who asked him: "How can you select for intuition when you can't even measure it?" (Mintzberg 1989: 83). This is a sad commentary on the state of current MBA education. We seem to be turning out greyhounds in counting but ignoramuses in dealing with human beings.

Emotions are essential to good decisions, since "most people reason dramatically, not quantitatively," as Oliver Wendell Holmes once wrote. This is why people are inspired more by stories than spreadsheets and pie charts full of statistics. Martin Luther King didn't proclaim, "I have quarterly objectives," but spoke of having a dream.

So many leaders are worried that if they get rid of objective measures they will introduce subjective bias into the decision-making process. So what? That's exactly what needs to happen. We simply cannot measure the most important things in life. To get rid of bias we would have to give up judgment, which is too high a price to pay. Neurologist Antonio Damasio has studied brain-damaged patients, demonstrating that without emotion it is impossible to make decisions. Why would we want to disregard our human emotions? For as accurate or scientific as you can make any measurement, judgment and intuition are more important.

It is time to replace efficiency with *effectiveness*, and begin to measure what counts, rather than counting for the sake of counting. Frederick Taylor's time-and-motion studies have no place in the knowledge organizations of the future because it is not an accurate measurement of the *results* and *wealth* knowledge workers create for their customers. We need to create an environment of responsible autonomy, where workers will decide for themselves what and how to perform their jobs, while taking full responsibility and accountability for the outcome. For this to happen, leaders of the future are going to have to fend off the ghost of Frederick Taylor, since it is they who are ultimately responsible for creating conducive organizations that maximize the contribution of their knowledge workers. A good beginning is recognizing the implications of this attitude. After all, if the executives of a company do not treat their people like knowledge workers, are they, in fact, knowledge workers at all?

FAR FEWER KNOWLEDGE WORKERS THAN WE THINK?

I can tell a factory worker to show up at seven AM and be productive. But can I tell an engineer or researcher to have a good idea at seven?

—*Akio Morita, late cofounder of Sony*

The famed consultancy firm, McKinsey, divides American jobs into three categories:

1. *Transformational* (extracting raw materials or converting them into finished goods)
2. *Transactional* (interactions that can easily be scripted or automated)
3. *Tacit* (complex interactions requiring a high level of judgment) (*The Economist*, October 7, 2006: 4).

McKinsey further reports "that over the past six years the number of American jobs that emphasize 'tacit interactions' has grown two and a half times as fast as the number of transactional jobs and three times as fast as employment in general. These jobs now make up some 40% of the American labor market and account for 70 percent of the jobs created since 1998" (*The Economist*, October 7, 2006: 4). There is also no doubt that the tacit workers are creating the majority of value in most organizations.

How many executives are fully prepared to deal with the implications of these distinctions? Far too many are still treating their people like waiters and waitresses, including the metrics they are utilizing to determine their "productivity." But knowledge workers are chefs, not waiters, and it is time for leaders to recognize the difference.

My colleagues and I at VeraSage Institute spend the majority of our time working with, by any common definition, knowledge workers, at accounting, law, and technology firms; advertising agencies; consultancies; engineering, architecture, and software programming firms; and so forth. We educate them on the difference between manual (and service) workers and knowledge workers. In a way, it is a compliment to be told you are part of a new vanguard of wealth creation in the economy by being labeled a *knowledge worker*. People take pride and immediate ownership in the term; you can even see a demonstrable increase in their self-respect. It just feels good to be called a knowledge worker.

But I can always count on at least one of my colleagues to cause some cognitive dissonance, and Dan Morris has not let me down. He thinks I'm wrong about most professional firms being filled with knowledge workers; he believes the majority of them are more akin to factory workers in the days of Taylor and Ford. Now I know this is a heretical view, but Dan has assembled a very powerful argument to support his assertion. He does not deny that professionals have the *potential* to be knowledge workers. His argument is that they are not largely because of the incentives and structures of the firms in which they operate, which function more like sweatshops of yore.

This is a powerful argument, and it made me pause to reexamine my core assumptions about automatically asserting that just because people are credentialed professionals, or work with their heads more than their hands, they are automatically knowledge workers. There is no doubt they can contribute a certain amount of creativity and innovation to the jobs they perform and the customers they serve. But being a knowledge worker also requires that the leaders of your organization recognize and treat you like one. This is where Dan's more constricted definition of a knowledge worker is compelling.

Stephen Covey writes about exactly this in his book *The 8th Habit: From Effectiveness to Greatness*:

> ... It's the leadership beliefs and style of the manager, not the nature of the job or economic era, that defines whether a person is a knowledge worker or not. If he is not perceived as a knowledge worker, that is, if a janitor is not seen as the local expert on janitorial work, then he is a manual worker and not a knowledge worker (Covey 2004: 265–266).

I do not agree with this definition in its entirety. The major determinant of knowledge workers is that they *own the means of production*, and they apply knowledge to knowledge to create value. Covey's requirement of the leadership beliefs and style of management may be *necessary* conditions, but they are not *sufficient*, in and of themselves, to define knowledge work.

The same might be said regarding the knowledge worker's environment. The process of ethnography involves using multiple cameras to observe how workers interact in their environments to optimize spatial conditions. This has a certain ring of feng shui to it—that is, not at all scientific—but if it helps knowledge workers to be more comfortable in their environments, then it could be worthwhile.

Some companies have a "clean desk" requirement, thinking it helps to improve productivity if things are neat and orderly. This may be true for clerical workers, whose mission is to help the company run smoothly. But knowledge workers use information to change themselves. The paper piles and Post-It Notes strung all over your office are physical representations of what is going on inside of your head. If anyone interferes with your desk, they interfere with your thinking—not a wise intrusion just to obtain 1 percent greater efficiency.

I remain skeptical of ethnography and other environmental factors because, once again, true knowledge work transcends time and space. J. K. Rowling wrote part of the first *Harry Potter* novel in an Edinburgh coffee shop. In the old days, workers took their coffee to the office. With Starbucks and knowledge workers, we now take our office to the coffee.

Having said all that regarding leadership beliefs and environmental factors, when you consider the metrics used by most firms to measure their team members, they all come from the Industrial Revolution's command-and-control hierarchies. We have to replace these hierarchical structures for more *autonomy*—from the Greek word for "self-governance."

Dan further supports his argument by stating that leaders of knowledge workers:

- Understand that knowledge workers are paid for ideas, not hours, like union employees.
- Allow at least 15 percent of team member time for innovation and creating better ways to add value to customers. (This certainly destroys productivity under the old metrics.)
- Understand that *judgments* and *discernment* are far more important than *measurements* in assessing performance.
- Are focused on outputs, results, and value, not inputs, efforts, activities, and costs.
- Don't require time sheets that account for every 10 minutes of their day.
- Trust their workers to do the right thing for the firm and its customers.
- Recognize that individuals, not jobs, have value.
- Allow their workers to monetize the value of their output, through stock options or other incentives that share the wealth created by minds, not machines.
- Select workers who are passionate and self-motivated, and don't need constant supervision.

If these criteria describe your firm, congratulations, you are a true knowledge organization. Perhaps nothing illustrates the value knowledge workers can add to a business better than the announced purchase of Pixar by Disney on January 24, 2006, for $7.4 billion in Disney stock (Steve Jobs purchased Pixar in 1986 for $10 million). Disney will have to respect Pixar's culture and continue to let it make quality movies at its own pace, in its own way. Otherwise, if Pixar's creative talent leaves, "Disney just purchased the most expensive computers ever sold," according to Lawrence Haverty, a fund manager at Gabelli Asset Management. It remains to be seen if Disney can learn from Steve Jobs's philosophy: "You cannot mandate productivity, you must provide the tools to let people become their best."

Knowledge workers need to be able to monetize at least part of the wealth they create, which is based on contribution, not seniority or stultifying union-type job classifications. Throughout history, trailblazing innovations, from the jet engine to the iPod, are more likely to come from those team members under the age of 45. If stock options or other incentives plans are not offered to value and attract talent, firms will not be able to tap into the enormous wealth-creating potential of their knowledge workers.

There is an old military saying that instructs the soldier is entitled to competent command. Unfortunately, most professional firms that we at VeraSage have come into contact with around the world do not fit Dan's criteria, which is why he makes such a strong case that they function more like manual laborers—or service workers—than actual knowledge workers. After all, if one set out to find knowledge workers, you would naturally select professional service firms as the most likely place to find them.

I cannot count the number of times we have been asked by intelligent firm owners, "How would I know what my team members were doing if they didn't complete a time sheet?" This is not a question demonstrating fear over lack of control; this is the *illusion* of control. Someone can look great on a time sheet but do substandard work, have a poor customer service attitude, disrupt colleagues, or possess a myriad of other poor characteristics that cannot be captured on a time sheet. But because the leaders in these firms do not trust the judgment of the very people they hire, they feel they need to micromanage them. This is counterproductive. Knowledge workers cannot be told *how* to do their job, since many understand the job at hand better than their bosses. They cannot be held accountable for results if their methods are micromanaged. Fortunately, there are some enlightened companies that recognize the realities of employing knowledge workers.

SAMPLE KNOWLEDGE ORGANIZATIONS

Is a gardener or office janitor a knowledge worker? They are to ServiceMaster, a company that arguably provides more autonomy to its people than many professional firms. Steel workers at Chaparral Steel are expected to experiment, innovate new designs, and propose new product offerings, a prime example of a traditional smokestack company adapting to the actualities of a knowledge economy. Legendary customer service leader Nordstrom has on its Web site: "*Use good judgment*. We trust one another's integrity and ability. Our only rule: Use good judgment in all situations." This autonomy is one reason 76 of Nordstrom associates sold over $1 million in 2005 (www.recruitingsite.com/csbsites /nordstrom/index.asp, visited March 17, 2007). Richard Branson, founder of the eponymous Virgin brand, also understands leading knowledge workers: "People who work at Virgin are special. They aren't sheep. They think for themselves. They have good ideas and I listen to them. What is the point of hiring bright people if you don't use their talent?" (Branson 2006: 29).

Best Buy treats all of its associates as knowledge workers. A field executive for the company, who oversees dozens of stores and thousands of associates, remarked: "We unleash the power of our people and let them know they can make a difference by teaching them how to think, not just do what they're told" (Gandossy et al. 2006: 228). The advantage of this philosophy is it engages people's minds to find better ways to do their job, recognizing that good ideas are not just the responsibility of management but also those who are closest to the work itself, as this story illustrates:

> ... [A]n employee in the company's Corona, California, outlet observed that his store was incurring monthly losses of $4,000 to $6,000 in damaged televisions. In all Best Buy stores, employees were told to use shrink-wrap to protect televisions that were shipped back to distribution centers for repair or return to the manufacturer. A front-line employee concluded flimsy shrink-wrap was not able to safeguard the television from bumping around and breaking while in transit. After researching options, he found a $50 tool that would take the same shrink-wrap and twist it into a sturdy rope that could hold the televisions securely on their palettes during shipment. Working with his manager, they tested the idea and after four months had completely eliminated damaged television charges. On a $50 investment, the self-initiation of this employee led to nearly 100,000 percent return for the single store in just the first year (Gandossy et al. 2006: 227).

Walt Disney understood that ideas were not the sole domain of management: "I use the whole plant for ideas. If the janitor has a good idea, I'd use it." To this day, Disney

> ... believes that ideas for successful animated films are everywhere in the organization; they need only be drawn out and developed. Three times a year senior managers, including the chairman, vice chairman, and president of feature animation, attend a Gong Show, at which any employee, from secretary to senior executive, is permitted to pitch concepts and story lines. Pitches are limited to five minutes, and managers respond immediately—and bluntly—to all proposals. If the pitch is accepted, the presenter gets the normal fee for a first treatment, usually $20,000. The results? An extraordinary esprit de corps, not to mention the central concepts for *Hercules* and other animated features (Garvin 2000: 38).

Toyota, one of the world's 10 most profitable companies, is another company that understands ROI—that is, return on ideas. Senior adviser to the University of Toyota, Matthew E. May, explains in his book *The Elegant Solution: Toyota's Formula for Mastering Innovation* how Toyota implements one million ideas a year, from all levels in the organization. Working on an auto factory line may not be the most creative job, but Toyota's quest is for its employees to *be* creative on a daily basis. In conditions as close as the business world can get to a scientific laboratory experiment, Toyota transformed a General Motors factory in Fremont, California, known as New United Motor Manufacturing Inc. (NUMMI).

In 1982, under GM management, this plant had the worst quality and productivity record, double-digit defects in every car, rampant drug and alcohol abuse, an absenteeism rate of 20 percent, and a backlog of 5,000 union grievances. In February 1982, in the depths of Ronald Reagan's first-term recession, GM closed the factory and laid off the entire workforce.

In 1983, GM formed a joint venture with Toyota and reopened the Fremont plant, now to produce the Toyota Corolla and Chevrolet Prizm. Toyota hired back 85 percent of the union employees and instituted a no-layoff policy. In essence, you had the same workforce and the same plant and equipment, as well as all the other tangible manifestations of the old factory in place. By 1985, NUMMI "had the highest quality and productivity of any GM plant. Quality defects dropped from 12 to 1 per vehicle. Cars were assembled in half the time. Absenteeism dropped to 3 percent. Worker satisfaction and engagement soared. Operational innovation was on the rise, with employee participation over 90 percent and nearly 10,000 ideas implemented" (May 2007: 65). What was the difference? Not what Toyota does, but how Toyota *thinks*. Paul Guitierrez (a pseudonym), a career autoworker who works at the GM/Toyota plant, explains how palpable this change in philosophy was:

> Never in a million years would I tell you this work is creative. Then Toyota took over twenty years ago. They teach us their system then say to us, 'we want you to tell us how to make it better.' We went from 'just do your job' with GM to 'no one knows the job better than you' with Toyota. They teach us how to solve problems. They turn us loose in here! They say, stop the line anytime

if something's wrong. I was floored. They think I can make their systems better? They're giving me the power to stop production? That right there changed my life. All of a sudden, I'm looking for ways to fix problems, make improvements, basically get rid of anything that was stupid. Get rid of waste, they said. Perfect the operation, they said. So now all of a sudden I'm using my head, I'm the expert, I'm creating new procedures. There you go, creating. I guess there's an art to it, yeah. It's not like I carved a Corolla or anything, but I started getting some real pride back. Before, we didn't care, we were ashamed to say where we worked. We'd laugh when we saw a car that came out of here. Now we feel like, hey, I built that! The place got cleaned up. We stopped fighting. We all wore the same uniforms, even managers. We started thinking, hey, people are driving these cars, let's make them safe. My mark's all over this plant, like everyone else's. One year we did like eight thousand ideas. The job itself wasn't creative, never will be, but our job was to be creative. And I guess if you can be creative in this line of work, you can be creative anywhere (May 2007: 24).

These companies, among others, all have something else in common. They position talent based on strengths, not weaknesses. Even the most talented people have weaknesses along with their tremendous strengths; and since the firm is hiring to produce for its customers, it has to capitalize on each person's strengths and, in effect, make irrelevant—or downplay—his or her weaknesses. This creates an environment of meritocracy, one that does not squander resources on trying to solve problems but that pursues opportunities. As Peter Drucker explains in *The Effective Executive in Action*:

One should waste as little effort as possible on improving areas of low competence. It takes far more energy and work to improve from incompetence to mediocrity than it takes to improve from first-rate performance to excellence. And yet most people—especially...teachers and...organizations—concentrate on making incompetent performers into mediocre ones. Energy, resources, and time should go instead to making a competent person into a star performer (Drucker and Maciariello 2006: 132).

Like a good sports coach, leaders need to work with people's strengths, develop and challenge them further, and put them in positions that downplay their weaknesses. This is no easy task, which is why coaches of professional sports teams are such a rare breed of leaders. They do exactly that, day in and day out. And if one of their team members fails after several attempts, they usually take the blame, and rightfully so. That is what being an effective leader is all about. A leader's job is not to motivate his or her knowledge workers—they are already highly motivated to perform their best for the firm, the firm's customers, and themselves; rather, it is to not *demotivate* them.

Executives earn the cynicism of their associates. Who starts a new job with a negative attitude? Knowledge workers, in particular, tend to be fiercely loyal to their chosen profession and outside ethical canons, but rather less loyal to any one employer. Loyalty has to be earned, through providing them a fair return and helping them develop their intellectual capital in an environment that is conducive to continuous learning and that grants them the dignity and respect that knowledge workers deserve.

So many leaders actually seem frightened at the thought of removing command-and-control hierarchies, as if they would be relinquishing total control over their team. Worse, they believe the suggestion is the equivalent of giving the team members total freedom, and will create anarchy in the organization. But I am not suggesting freedom for people "to do their own thing"; that is not freedom, it is *license*. The flip side of freedom is responsibility. That means holding people accountable for the *results* they achieve, hardly a prescription for anarchy and chaos. When leaders feel they need to tightly control a knowledge worker, they have made a hiring mistake.

There is no better way to demoralize knowledge workers than to have them perform duties that interfere with the tasks they are qualified to do. In all probability, the best way to increase the effectiveness of most knowledge workers is by *removing* various tasks that distract them from their core specializations. We do not want surgeons piercing ears or nurses spending half of their time completing paperwork (a common complaint). Most knowledge workers could stop doing approximately one-fourth of the tasks with no demonstrable loss of value, according to Peter Drucker. This is precisely why Jim Collins writes in *Good to Great*: "'*Stop doing*" lists are more important than 'to do' lists. This leads us to two other rituals companies engage in that may very well be past their sell dates with respect to dealing with knowledge workers.

PERSONALITY TESTING AND PERFORMANCE APPRAISALS

I am combining these two tools together since they have the same antecedents, are widely used by companies around the world, and each lack empirical evidence endorsing their effectiveness. Once again, Peter Drucker was among the first to point this out:

> Appraisals, as they are now being used in the great majority of organizations, were designed by the clinical and abnormal psychologists for their own purposes. The clinician is a therapist trained to heal the sick. He is legitimately concerned with what is wrong, rather than with what is right with the patient. He assumes as a matter of course that nobody comes to him unless he is in trouble. The clinical psychologist or the abnormal psychologist, therefore, very properly looks upon appraisals as a process of diagnosing the weaknesses of a man (Drucker 1993: 83–84).

Personality testing possesses the same history. Companies use these tests for a variety of purposes, such as employment screening, assessing leadership potential, fostering corroboration and teamwork, and so on. The most widely used is the Myers-Briggs Type Indicator (MBTI), created by Pennsylvania housewife Isabel Myers. This particular test is utilized by 89 percent of Fortune 100 companies, given to 2.5 million people each year to identify strengths and enhance teamwork. She thought the test could bring about world peace. The Minnesota Multiphase Personality Inventory (MMPI), was developed in 1946 to sort mental patients into diagnostic categories. It was then expanded in an attempt to describe normal people. A 2003 survey conducted by Management Recruiters International discovered that 30 percent of companies administer some sort of personality test, equating to between 5,000 and 6,000 companies and 5 million people annually. Of course, popularity does not imply scientific validity. What's worse, most companies keep these tests confidential so the data cannot be scientifically tested to determine effectiveness.

These tests are also popular among consultants, who are paid good money to administer them in a convivial atmosphere. But the fallacy is that the tests measure what we're like and who we are, not what we know, believe, or what we can do. They confuse *labeling* personality with *understanding* it. These tests are reassuring confirmations of what people already know about themselves, what psychologists call the permanency tendency. They also tend to validate the positive characteristics we all believe we possess, the so-called Pollyanna principle. Companies might as well bring their people together to play with Ouija boards, which are equally entertaining while having roughly the same empirical validity. Annie Murphy Paul, former senior editor at *Psychology Today*, has written a scathing indictment against these tests, labeling them modern-day phrenology, in her book *The Cult of Personality Testing: How Personality Tests Are Leading Us to Miseducate Our Children, Mismanage Our Companies, and Misunderstand Ourselves*. Here a few of her more condemning facts:

> ... [A]s many as three-quarters of test takers achieve a different personality type when tested again, and that the sixteen distinctive types described by the Myers-Briggs have no scientific basis whatsoever (Paul 2004: xiii).
>
> The sly brilliance of using personality test[s] to label employees is that, by dint of answering the test's questions, employees appear to be labeling themselves. ... Under this banner of respect for individuality, organizations are able to shift responsibility for employee satisfaction onto that obliging culprit, "fit" (Paul 2004: 129).

And research has found little connection between indicator types and real-life outcomes. There is scant evidence that MBTI results are useful in determining managerial effectiveness, helping to build teams, providing career counseling, enhancing insight into self or others, or any other of the myriad uses for which it is promoted (Paul 2004: 134).

In 1968, ... *Personality and Assessment* was published. ... Its author [Stanford University psychology professor Walter Mischel] simply pointed out that personality tests don't do a very good job of predicting how humans will act. Mischel's review of the literature showed that the correlation, or statistical relationship, between personality tests and people's actual behavior was only about .30. This meant that less than 10 percent of the variance in a person's behavior was explained by personality as measured by personality tests (Paul 2004: 184).

Professor Erkko Autio, department of management at HEC Lausanne in Lausanne, Switzerland, pointed out the same defects with respect to the current fad of "emotional intelligence" in a letter to *The Economist*:

It might interest you to know that not a single serious study has ever been able to demonstrate a link between "emotional intelligence" and leadership effectiveness. The most robust and consistent single predictor of leadership effectiveness is, simply, intelligence. Emotional intelligence sells well, but scientific evidence supporting it is almost as solid as that supporting the effectiveness of homeopathy (*The Economist*, August 26, 2006: 14).

Professor Autio is certainly correct in the assertion that intelligent quotient (IQ) is a better predictor of executive effectiveness, as *The Bell Curve* has scientifically demonstrated. If you were confined to learning one number about an individual to predict their standard of living, you would be hard pressed to find a better one than their IQ. That being said, companies are not confined to knowing just one thing about their potential or existing employees. As Rabbi Daniel Lapin, an expert in explaining how the world really works, teaches us: "You are best understood and appraised by others on the basis of the things you *believe* rather than on the basis of the things you *know*" (Lapin 2002: 183). Or, I might add, rather than on the basis of your personality. Trying to simplify the spirituality and soul of a human life by labeling it with a personality type or an IQ is to disregard the uniqueness of individuals, which requires judgment and discernment far more than measurement. We are better off understanding people's *beliefs* if we want to even begin to understand how and why the Germans of the Third Reich could carry out their murderous orders in acquiescent servility, or the pilots who flew airplanes into buildings killing innocent civilians on September 11, 2001. We will discuss this concept more in Chapter 14.

Companies seem to have the same irrational faith in performance appraisals as they do in personality tests, since more than 90 percent of the academic studies done on this tool contain no evidence of its effectiveness (Coens and Jenkins 2000: 236). Most companies and employees are dissatisfied with the performance appraisal process, so it remains a curiosity why this methodology continues to exist. Consultant and author Peter Block fires this salvo at the process, in the Foreword to the must-read heretical book, *Abolishing Performance Appraisals: Why They Backfire and What to Do Instead*:

> Performance appraisal has become more than a management tool. It has grown into a cultural, almost anthropological symbol of the parental, boss-subordinate relationship that is characteristic of patriarchal organizations. Appraisals are undertaken in good faith, but there is no escape from their basic nature. Their nature is that the boss takes responsibility for the development of the subordinate and exercises that responsibility through a discussion of strengths and weaknesses of the subordinate. This is the exercise of sovereignty, regardless of how lovingly it is done. It makes no sense to talk of team- and partnership-oriented cultures, which the marketplace is now demanding, and still hold on to this artifact called performance appraisal (Coens and Jenkins 2000: xiii).
>
> Appraisals ... often have money on the table as part of the discussion, and this brings a weapon into play that gets in the way. When we combine compensation with a developmental discussion,

we undermine the openness and vulnerability that development requires, and all our ears can hear is the money (Coens and Jenkins 2000: xv).

Hopefully we can reach the point where we can talk about what is good for the individual and what is good for the organization without a coercive dimension to the discussion. We can create cultures where peers can be accountable to each other and bosses can be as open in hearing feedback as they are in giving it. This requires us to choose faith over fear. Faith that most people want to do well, do care about the institution, and are committed to their own learning. If some people violate our faith, then deal strongly with them as an exception, but it is no reason to create low trust practices for all that are needed for just a few (Coens and Jenkins 2000: xv–xvi).

Tom Coens, one of the co-authors of the book, is a labor lawyer and does an excellent job in dispelling the myth that appraisals are necessary for legal protection. The authors also point out these salient facts regarding the process:

Appraisal is not the system that drives pay, careers, and status; it is an incidental effect of those dynamic systems. Appraisal is primarily the paper-shuffling that sanctifies decisions already made (Coens and Jenkins 2000: 28).

This book is about starting over. Abolishing appraisal is *not* the goal—it's only an obstacle that stands in the way of the goal. Dropping appraisal gives us new freedom—the freedom to think in radically different ways about how to unleash the human spirit in our workplaces. The real goal is building a culture that makes this possible (Coens and Jenkins 2000: 303).

The appraisal tends to focus on weaknesses and not strengths. But good leaders—like good coaches—design performance processes and tasks around a person's strengths, and ignore—or make irrelevant—their weaknesses. The Peter Principle—which says that people get promoted to their highest level of incompetence—may make for funny "Dilbert" cartoons, but in reality, there is nothing funny about it. We should promote people based on their strengths, not their weaknesses.

Someone who receives a stellar annual review one year is subject to the *Sports Illustrated* jinx; that is, when an athlete makes the cover of *SI* one week, he or she usually does poorly the next. The explanation for this is not a jinx; rather, the athlete has usually performed at a peak level, which puts him or her on the cover in the first place. Inevitably, then, the next week's performance, even if above average, will fall below the standard that earned the athlete the original accolade. No doubt we need to acknowledge superior performance, and even reward it monetarily and in other ways—but we need to take a balanced view of a knowledge worker's contribution and development over the course of his or her tenure with the firm.

Another problem with the process is the "annual" aspect of it; a year is far too long a time frame to evaluate and give feedback to any worker, but especially a knowledge worker. In Chapter 12, I propose that organizations should be utilizing After Action Reviews after every task, which is a process developed by the U.S. Army and is an excellent tool that facilitates learning, development, and improvement.

Any organization of humans—be it a school, a nonprofit agency, a governmental unit, or a business—is going to have a bell curve of high, average, and below-average performers. One study found wide differences in performance for complex jobs (e.g., attorneys, physicians, and cartographers), where the top 1 percent of producers generated 2.27 times the output of average producers (Davenport 1999: 66). It is estimated that the best computer programmers are at least 12 times as productive as the average. Alan Eustace, a vice president at Google, says that "one top-notch engineer is worth 300 times or more than the average" (*The Economist*, October 7, 2006: 22).

Given human nature, not much can be done about this distribution, but what we can do is not exacerbate the problem of below-average workers by designing systems around their weaknesses at the expense of placing a ceiling over the heads of the superior performers. Public schools do this all the time. They "dumb down" the standards for the slowest learners, while letting those with above-average abilities stagnate and get bored. A business organization should not do this to spare the feelings of the less effective team members; rather, it should design processes and compensation systems that take into account different levels of performance. As Thomas Jefferson said, "There is nothing less equal than treating nonequals equally." Not adequately rewarding your high achievers is a prescription for their defection, as it is precisely the high achievers who are the most desired workers of your competitors. Over 71 percent of the firms in the *Inc.* 500 list of young, entrepreneurial, and fast-growing companies were started by individuals who duplicated or modified innovations at their former employers (Lev 2001: 13).

If you want high performers, you have to be willing to pay for them commensurate with the value they create, and this requires that companies stop viewing jobs as caste systems—as if there were a union pay scale depending on the job classification—and start rewarding the value of your team members' human capital contributions. Firms should strive to create a meritocratic environment that rewards risk taking and innovation, rather than rigid, stultifying union-type jobs that reward seniority, mediocrity, and complacency. It is not uncommon, for example, for salespeople working the floor of Nordstrom to earn over $100,000 per year; as they say, "Your performance is your review." Why do organizations insist on putting artificial ceilings over the heads of their team members, therefore defining performance standards down? Remove those barriers and allow your team to reach for new opportunities and heights.

Promotions are another signaling device to your team members, who watch very closely the behaviors that are rewarded when someone advances. Be careful who you promote and what behaviors they display, since what gets rewarded gets done. If it is based on cleverness, flattery, or politics, then the firm is destined to sink to those traits, since they'll be perceived as the way to get ahead. Once again, most likely the best question executives could ask themselves before promoting someone is whether they would want their son or daughter to work for the person.

Public recognition of high performance is also a cultural trait in most successful companies, such as Disney, Toyota, and FedEx. The distribution of rewards must be done publicly, and they must be considered credible and meaningful. An old military saying has it that a man wouldn't sell his life for $1 million, but will gladly risk it for a ribbon or Medal of Honor. Super Bowl champions display their rings with pride, long after the money they earned has been forgotten.

Business is based on performance and results, not personality traits and rankings on stale performance appraisals. The knowledge organization of the future must rethink these antiquated systems and replace them with more effective methodologies. This brings us to another area critical for the development and inspiration of knowledge workers: continuing education.

THE IMPORTANCE OF CONTINUING EDUCATION

Learning is not something that requires time out from being engaged in productive activity; learning is the heart of productive activity. To put it simply, learning is the new form of labor.
> —*Shoshana Zuboff, professor for leadership, ethics, and corporate responsibility at Harvard University Graduate School of Business*

Nobel Prize–winning economist Gary S. Becker, a leader in developing human capital theory, writes, "I focus on the allocation of time to three activities:

1. The production of nonmarket commodities (nonmarket time);
2. The production of human capital (investment time);
3. The production of earnings (labor market time)" (Becker 1980: 5).

Knowledge organizations must have a healthy respect for these three categories, so as not to make their team members feel as if they are not spending enough time in the production of earnings when they are investing in their human capital. In spite of this, is there any doubt that most organizations underinvest in Becker's second category in ruthless pursuit of his third category? The American Society for Training and Development figures that the average number of hours spent in a classroom for the average American worker is 26.3 (Peters 2003: 259). The average company spends between 1.5 to 3 percent of *payroll expense* on education. Of course, organizations don't learn, people do. An organization's capacity for learning is limited by its people's capacity to learn, or what industrialists call the *absorptive capacity* of the firm.

I have the good fortune to speak to thousands of owners of professional knowledge firms who confirm that they don't spend more than the minimum on their people's continuing professional education. For certified public accounts (CPAs), this equates to 80 hours every two years. According to the American Institute of Certified Public Accountants, the average CPA firm spends just .8 percent of its revenue on continuing education, approximately equal to what is spent for broadband internet service. However, companies like Accenture, the Big Four accounting firms, and consulting houses such as McKinsey, Bain & Co. spend approximately 6 percent of their *gross revenue* on education. How else do companies expect to increase the human capital and effectiveness of their knowledge workers if they don't invest in continuous learning? Sure, they can invest in technology or a better widget machine, but those are merely tools. They are the equivalent of having restrooms in your building, not competitive advantages that enable you to do better than your competitors. What counts is what knowledge workers know this year that they didn't know last year that is more valuable to the company or its customers.

Today, there are over 2,000 corporate universities—from Merck, 3 M, and Toyota, to Disney, McDonald's, and GE—validating the importance of education driving corporate strategy. As Peter Drucker said,

> I think the growth industry of the future in this country and the world will soon be the continuing education of adults. Nothing else is growing as fast. ... I think the educated person of the future is somebody who realizes the need to continue to learn. That is the new definition and it is going to change the world we live and work in (Beatty 1998: 147).

One of the objections to investing more in people's education is "they will leave—and possibly become an even stronger competitor." This is no doubt true, although a company faces the risk of their leaving anyway. In fact, based on the evidence, there is an increasing probability of people's leaving if you do not invest adequately in their education. But let us deal with the objection directly, since we hear it so often. Let me pose a better question: What if you do not invest in their education and they *stay*? The problem with this cost is it is hidden, since it does not show up anywhere on the company's internal measurement systems. I posit to you that this loss far exceeds both the cost of education and the risks of people leaving. Professor and management thinker Henry Mintzberg is quite unforgiving on this issue: "Why invest in people who might leave? I reverse this: If that is the organization's attitude, then its people will be inclined to leave! ... Any organization that balks at investing less than half a year's salary to improve the practice of its managers through education deserves the turnover of managers it probably gets. My advice to good managers in such situations is to find an employer who respects their talent" (Mintzberg 2004: 244–245).

Education highlights yet another problem for those faithful to Taylorism. When we are learning something new, our productivity—based on outputs relative to inputs—deteriorates, sometimes quite significantly. I know this from personal experience. When I was employed by a then–Big Eight accounting firm in the mid-1980s, I had a habit of putting my feet up in my cubicle and reading books. When partners or managers would wander by, they incredulously asked me if I was okay, following the advice of Ralph Waldo Emerson: "If a man sits down to think, he is immediately asked if he has the headache." I simply responded I was taking a mental break by reading. There was never a pleasant conclusion to these conversations, and I usually ended being assigned more work since I obviously had too much free time. What might have been a better question in a knowledge organization? What was I reading? How was it relevant to the firm or its customers? I wasn't reading a Harlequin romance novel, but usually some business or economics book that was quite relevant to our work, yet you'd never know it by the attitude of my superiors. In fact, one of the books was the inspiration for the one you are holding (*The Economy in Mind*, by Warren T. Brookes). I am convinced I never could have written any of my books while employed at an accounting firm, since it would have decimated my billable hours and realization rates. What a sad commentary for a profession that supposedly is full of knowledge workers, lending even more credence to Dan's argument that they are really nothing more than modern-day factories that haven't given up the ghost of Taylor.

Since knowledge workers tend to be highly competent people with high self-respect and sense of accomplishment, learning something new requires the admission of incompetence and substandard performance—not a pleasant state of affairs. It is similar to learning a new software program; there is an inevitable reduction in performance until the learning curve has been climbed and performance begins to exceed the prior peak. Those companies without a myopic focus on short-term efficiency and earnings are the ones most likely to attract and inspire the knowledge worker, such as Singapore Airlines—that overtook Southwest Airlines in market capitalization in 2006—which requires 11 days of education annually. By comparison, the average CPA and lawyer in the United States does approximately five days of education annually. Singapore's elder statesman Lee Kuan Yew used to say, "Trained talent is the yeast that transforms a society and makes it rise." This is also no doubt true in companies with knowledge workers.

The Container Store, a chain of eclectic retail stores enabling customers to organize their lives, has been named one of *Fortune's* 100 Best Companies to Work For from 2000 to 2007. According to its Web site:

> Customer service is The Container Store's core competency, so hiring people who are self-motivated and team-oriented with a passion for customer service is key. We place so much importance on service that every first-year, full-time salesperson receives about 241 hours of training—in a retail industry where the average is about seven hours. And training continues throughout an employee's career (www.containerstore.com/careers/store Experience.jhtml, visited March 18, 2007).

Turnover at the Container Store is approximately one-third the industry average for salespeople and one-sixth the industry average for managers. According to president Kip Tindell: "A funny thing happens when you take the time to educate your employees, pay them well, and treat them as equals. You end up with extremely motivated and enthusiastic people" (Low and Kalafut 2002: 171).

We return to the topic of education in Chapter 12, where we explore corporate universities. Before we leave, though, one more important distinction needs to be made with respect to education, especially in the context of knowledge workers. There is an enormous difference between training and education. The former deals with specific skills, while the latter deals with understanding, wisdom, and self-understanding. Dogs can be trained, too, which is why education is not simply a matter of someone's pouring knowledge into another's head. *Educere*, the root of *educate*, means to "draw out," not to stuff in, and the ultimate responsibility rests with the willing student, not the educator. As my VeraSage colleague Paul O'Byrne is fond of saying: "When my daughters were 12 years old, I was very happy that they had sex *education*, but *training* would have been a different thing!"

WHAT ABOUT WORK-LIFE BALANCE?

Work-life balance is politically correct for "slacker."
                                    —*Daniel D. Morris, founder, VeraSage Institute*

An enormous amount of ink has been spilled on this topic, usually along with the different characteristics of the Baby Boomers and Generations X, Y, and Z. One reason for this increased attention is that there are simply more generations interacting in the workforce today than in the past. One reason is life expectancy. The average knowledge worker today will outlive his employer, with an average active work life of approximately 50 years compared to the average organizational life of 30. This translates into the average worker today having many more jobs—and even careers—than those of his ancestors a century ago. This is why management thinker Charles Handy uses the metaphor of a "portfolio life"—putting together a packet of different jobs, clients, and types of work. He dismisses the very concept of work-life balance as misleading "because it implies that work and life are two different things. Portfolio thinking holds that most of life is work, some of it boring, some lucrative, some worthwhile in its own right. It is the 'work balance' that matters" (Handy 2006: 99).

Having the opportunity of a portfolio life is not determined by the year one was born, but the economic conditions one inhabits. We all stand on the shoulders of our ancestors. John Adams, America's second president wrote: "I must study politics and war that my sons may have liberty to study mathematics and philosophy and they in turn must study those subjects so that their children can study painting, poetry, music, architecture, statuary, tapestry, and porcelain." In an intellectual capital economy there is a far greater range of talents that can be rewarded. America's best-paid chef, Wolfgang Puck, earned $16 million in 2005 while Takeru "Tsunami" Kobayashi earned more than $200,000 a year for holding the title of the world's hot-dog eating champion (in *The Economist*, October 7, 2006: 23–24).

It may be an interesting academic exercise to create lists of the differences between the Baby Boomers and Generations X, Y, and Z, but knowing the personality traits between the generations does not necessarily assist a company in attracting or inspiring its knowledge workers. The real difference between the generations is that today's knowledge workers own more of the means of production in their heads than ever before, which gives them enormous market power in the economy. They also understand this fundamental fact better than their predecessors.

Organizations can lament the fact that Generations X, Y, and Z are not as loyal as their parents, but the fact of the matter is loyalty is a two-way street; it must be earned. No business deserves any loyalty, either from its customers or its associates, until it does something to earn it. Loyalty is not dead in the business world, but a *reason* to be loyal may be. The real question is, does the organization *deserve* the loyalty of its workers?

Dr. John Sullivan, who runs the human resources (HR) management program at San Francisco State University, whose Web site (www.drjohnsullivan.com) lists him as an "Author, Speaker, Corporate Advisor, Educator," is a refreshing voice in the field of "human resources." As an outspoken critic of socialism and egalitarianism, his views fly in the face of the conventional wisdom that festers deep in the souls of HR departments, with articles titled "Is Your HR Department Unwittingly A 'Socialist' Institution." He explains his philosophy:

> I'm a capitalist, not a social worker. Too many companies spend too much time trying to 'fix' their mediocre performers. They should spend more time recruiting and retaining great performers. It's like in sports. If your basketball team has Shaquille O'Neal, you've got a good shot at the title every year. But two six-foot-tall guards will never equal one seven-foot Shaq. It's HR's job to go out and find lots of Shaqs—and then to create a system that allows them to shine. Of course you need a 'system.' But a system without stars is not going to win" (Taylor and LaBarre 2006: 200).

You can see from whence Sullivan gets his best line: "Stars don't work for idiots." This is corroborated by the Gallup Organization's long-term study that finds an employee's relationship with his or her immediate supervisor is more important than pay or perks in determining turnover (Low and Kalafut 2002: 161). As I learned from the course at Disney Institute: "People don't leave companies, they leave bosses within those companies."

In a spasm of inspiration, my VeraSage colleague Dan Morris penned this shot across the bow of the ship of work-life balance on the VeraSage Institute's community blog:

> The thought just hit me. Merging a CBS News report I watched this morning about how slackers cost American businesses over $500 billion in lost efficiencies per year (I won't quibble with the estimate—even if it is a hyperbole of statistical abuse, the amount is clearly significant) and the book I was reading (*Juicing the Orange* by Pat Fallon and Fred Senn 2006) where these advertising executives were writing about connecting, in a global climate, a common business theme—they were writing about United Airlines and their ad campaigns and as an aside, I can't stop playing that damned Gershwin song in my mind as I write this so I guess something must be working—and how Americans are business and productivity focused while Europeans are more work-life balanced.
>
> And it struck me. Maybe that is the problem with this incessant discussion about how people desire a work-life balance; in as much as column inch after column inch of professional literature has been dedicated to this topic along with hour upon pabulum (and mundane) hour of seminars—led by the modern day charlatan the "executive coach"—has pummeled this mantra of this generation or that generation requiring greater work-life balance or they will leave firms for better pastures. Work-life balance is for slackers.
>
> This concept of stressing work-life balance is pure poppycock. It is just a concept that says people want an excuse to be slackers. What people really need is not more balance but more extremes. The human capital issue isn't one of balancing but one of creating extreme opportunities. People simply require a passionate reason to bust their butt on or for something and then to go play just as hard. The X-Games have street luge and it is not for the faint of heart or thin of skin. In this context of leveraging our human

capital, the extremeness of the sport is an example of a generation's demand from themselves to achieve success. Street luge is not for slackers. Work-life balance is for slackers.

It is not balance one seeks. It is opportunity. The opportunity to strut, to stretch, to leap, to fail, and to succeed. All at supersonic speed and with the bounding energy of a leopard in pursuit of her dinner. This drive is transferred into their pleasures. Rave parties. Extreme sports. Exotic vacations. All-night gaming. These up and comers—they work hard and they play hard. Work-life balance is not in their vocabulary. Work-life balance is for slackers.

And if balance is not what they are seeking, working to bring more of it only leads to certain failure. Unless the definition of balance is merely the mathematical concept of average or the economic concept of equilibrium, balance is clearly the incorrect word and if words matter at all, the wrong word communicates the wrong concept. Words matter. Work-life balance is for slackers.

So what are we (leaders) to do? First, recognize that work-life balance simply means the socialization of work. I do not want to work with socialists. I want to work with stars . . . and superstars at that. I enjoy associating with people that push the envelope—theirs and mine. I do not learn from slackers and success requires a learning culture. So lets hang out the "No Slackers Here" sign. Work-life balance is for slackers.

Leaders should determine how to push their human capital to achieve greatness. That means leaders have to understand their human capital and learn where they want to go and to grow. Then develop work and projects that catapults them further along their careers than they have any right to anticipate. Stop worrying about balance—balance is for tires. Think about extremes. Stop pandering to slackers. Great minds and great workers don't want to hang with slackers. Slackers are dead-weight anchors and need to be released to the competition. Work-life balance is for slackers.

That means it is just fine to set impossible deadlines. It is critical that their acumen, creativity, stamina, and quest for excellence are tested. Tested to the brink of failure. Then after they deliver, their leader sends them packing into some X-Game style adventure or pleasure opportunity with the only charge to "recharge" and get ready for the next "shock wave of working adventure." Slackers need not apply.

Every summer the news and trade press discuss the vacation and work policies of Europe versus the United States. This comparison includes days off, holidays, breaks, benefits, and the like. And the media promulgates that something must be wrong with the American way. Yet each and every year, the leading indicators surrounding productivity, patents, innovation, income, and overall opportunity are not pointed towards the slacker socialists, but instead to those damned unbalanced capitalists. Slackers don't create; they waste resources, are inefficient, and interfere with success. Work-life balance is for slackers.

Here is to all of those overworked and under-balanced stratospheric human capital investors out there. Do not look for balance—that leads to mediocrity. Search instead for opportunities to excel in both business and in life. For truly then will you find blue skies over that personal rainbow. And leave the slackers behind (www. verasage.com/index.php/community/comments/work_life_balance_is_pc_for_slacker/, visited March 24, 2007).

Dan has a point here. The opposite of work is not leisure, it is idleness. In a knowledge organization we should not confuse being busy with being profitable. The commitment level of a knowledge worker exists in their hearts and minds, which cannot be measured. As Homer Simpson explains to his daughter Lisa: "If adults don't like their jobs, they don't go on strike. They just go in every day and do it really half-assed." This attitude is significantly more possible than it was during the Industrial Era where a worker's output was determined by the rhythm of an assembly line. Organizations are still struggling with this new reality, given that the ghost of Taylorism is embedded in the theories of many leaders, a form of negative human capital.

NEGATIVE HUMAN CAPITAL

The first book in the Intellectual Capitalism Series, *Pricing on Purpose*, discussed Baker's Law in terms of customer selection: Bad customers drive out good customers. Two corollaries to that law are: bad team members drive out good ones, and bad leaders drive out good team members. Bad team members have a

12

STRUCTURAL CAPITAL: IF ONLY WE KNEW WHAT WE KNOW

> The only irreplaceable capital an organization possesses is the knowledge and ability of its people. The productivity of that capital depends on how effectively people share their competence with those who can use it.
>
> *—Andrew Carnegie*

Between 1644 and 1737, in the small northern Italian town of Cremona, lived Antonio Stradivari, who made over 1,000 violins, violas, and cellos; a harp; and a couple of lutes that bear his famous name. These instruments are the most sought-after, and expensive, in the world, regularly selling in the millions of dollars.

Today, even with all the advances in modern technology—with our precision equipment, lasers, computer-aided design, and analytical machinery—and notwithstanding gallant attempts by researchers for over a century, we still cannot replicate the musical quality of an instrument handcrafted over 300 years ago. The knowledge—known as "the Stradivarius secret"—has been lost.

According to the National Aeronautics and Space Administration (NASA), it has lost the knowledge of how it got to the moon. As one NASA manager admitted, "If we want to go to the moon again, we'll be starting from scratch because all of that knowledge has disappeared. It would take at least as long and cost at least as much to go back" (DeLong 2004: 11–12).

This process of creating and losing knowledge is nothing new, with the lost Library of Alexandria by 300 AD perhaps being the greatest example of lost intellectual and cultural capital in history. With the so-called Graybe Boom, the average age of the workforce in the rich world is increasing at the same time many of the Boomers are anticipating retirement, making them the first wave of knowledge workers to do so. Here are some of the pertinent statistics:

> Within the European Union the number of workers between 50 and 64 years of age will increase by 25% over the next two decades, while those between 20–29 will decrease by 20%.
>
> Nearly 20% of Japan's population is already over age 65, the highest percentage in the world.
>
> In the United States, workers between 55–64 will have increased more than half this decade, while 35-44-year olds decline by 10% (*The Economist*, February 18, 2006: 65).
>
> Between 1998 and 2008 in the United States, the 25–44 cohort will decrease from 51% to 44%, a 3 million decline (DeLong 2004: 11).

Ben Wattenberg, senior fellow at the American Enterprise Institute, has written a book challenging the conventional wisdom of the so-called "population bomb." The real demographic story is the declining birth rate around the industrialized world. Ted Baxter, the pompous anchorman on *The Mary Tyler Moore Show*, said he wanted to have six children so one of them could grow up and solve the population problem. There is a certain logic to this reasoning, but not in the way Baxter thought. In his book *Fewer: How the New Demography of Depopulation Will Shape Our Future*, Wattenberg makes the following observations, keeping in mind the caveat of the demographers' axiom that *projections* are not *predictions*:

> World population is now 6 billion, which will grow to 8–9 billion, then decrease, perhaps by many billions (Wattenberg 2004: 8).

The United Nations projects a world population of 2.3 billion in the year 2300, in its "Low" scenario, where its "Medium" scenario projects 9.2 billion. Economist Julian Simon would ask if we might lose a Mozart or Einstein (Wattenberg 2004: 149, citing the UN's biennial *World Population Prospects*, www.unpopulation.org).

I figure global population will not go much over 8 billion and then contract, way below the 15–20 billion forecasts a few decades ago. Demographic momentum works on the downside just as it does on the upside (Wattenberg 2004: 112).

The big demographic shifts come from fewer babies, not older adults (Wattenberg 2004: 118).

In 2000 there were 17 million people in the modern nations aged 85–99. The projection for 2050 is 62 million (Wattenberg 2004: 121).

Economist Hu Angang of Quinghua University says that getting old before getting rich is China's big twenty-first century problem: "We will have the social burden of a rich country and the income of a poor country. No country has faced the same circumstances before" (Wattenberg 2004: 123).

The fact is we don't really know what happens to an economy in a sharply shrinking demographic situation. Since the advent of modern economics, going back at least to the beginnings of the Industrial Revolution, there is no model for it (Wattenberg 2004: 135–136).

Economist Gary Becker has written that the number of children is an *inferior good*—that is, the demand for it decreases as one's income rises, and economist Julian Simon used to say that capitalism is the best contraceptive. What do all of these projections mean for economic wealth creation? As Wattenberg says, we do not have a model for precipitous population decline since for at least 650 years, since the Black Plague, the world's population has been increasing. One implication may be less disruptive innovations, since throughout history most innovations in the sciences, math, medicine, and industry were carried out by individuals with a mean age of 40 years (this is documented extensively in Charles Murray's scholarly book, *Human Accomplishment*, reviewed in Suggested Reading). Demographers call this decrease and aging of the population *diminishment*—what French demographer Alfred Sauvy said in the 1930s means "old people, in old houses, with old ideas."

Companies lose knowledge from people leaving, forgetting, retiring, and so on. Knowledge also becomes obsolete and must be constantly replenished. Given the coming demographic trends, how can knowledge organizations capture some of that valuable knowledge before it is lost, like the lost Library of Alexandria? No one knows what the cost of this lost knowledge might be. Furthermore, how can companies leverage the knowledge they do have? According to Betty Zucker of the Gottlieb School of Management in Zurich, as little as 20 percent of the knowledge in a company is actually ever used (Brooking 1999: 5).

THE ECONOMICS OF STRUCTURAL CAPITAL

One of the most important distinctions between the three types of intellectual capital—human, structural, and social—is that structural capital is the only one that is wholly owned by the company. Thus, it becomes critically important to capture and leverage as much tacit knowledge as possible from the human and social sources of intellectual capital (IC). Think of structural capital as the infrastructure within the company responsible for converting human capital into wealth for the organization. Economist Sidney Winter describes businesses as "organizations that know how to do things," while Karl Weick called institutions "compressed expertise" (Davenport and Prusak 1998: xiii, 11). Structural capital is what remains with the company after the human capital goes home at night:

- Organization structure
- Recruitment and remuneration policies
- Management information systems
- Intellectual property (patents, copyrights, trademarks, etc.)
- Documented systems, processes, performance management systems

Mentoring, Coaching, and Shadowing

Like the master/apprentice relationships in the guilds of yesteryear, mentoring, coaching, and shadowing is probably the most effective way to transfer deep tacit knowledge. Many companies have some form of mentoring program, but they are usually not designed with the specific intent of transferring tacit knowledge, though that might very well be happening at some level. I have always been skeptical of the effectiveness of these mentor and coaching programs since the company usually assigns the mentor. But this is not how mentors are selected, being thrust upon someone. It is a volitional relationship, one that is difficult to structure and plan with precision. Perhaps it is time to change the name of these programs to make their strategy more pronounced and specific: that of transferring knowledge. Shadowing—the process whereby a junior worker "shadows" the more experienced worker throughout the day—conveys a more precise objective.

Communities of Practice

Effective knowledge transfer requires *communities of practice* (CoPs) to leverage a firm's IC. These communities can be created through intranet sites, blogs (web logs), internal notes, discussion boards, databases, or Web portals. Each enhances the ability of knowledge workers to access the knowledge they need, when they need it. The systems can even have a ranking of the usefulness of the various knowledge, much the same way amazon.com lets its customers review, rate, and tag the value of the books it sells.

The blogosphere is an interesting case in point of how knowledge management has evolved from the early days. As of the end of 2006, *The Economist* estimated there were 57 million blogs in existence, while according to Technorati a new blog is created every second of every day. According to Pew, an American research organization, only 7 percent of bloggers say their main motivation in launching a blog is to make money. There are, no doubt, many other intrinsic rewards to blogging: ego, peer recognition, acknowledgment as an expert, communicating with like-minded people worldwide—the list goes on. There is also no doubt that a lot of blogs are worth what you pay for them. That said, viewed through the prism of a method to manage an individual's own IC, blogging is quite effective, as it is a place to store important bits of information and knowledge, while making connections to the knowledge of others. Some firm executives I've spoken to worry about the effect on productivity from their workers' blogging; but this is the ghost of Frederick Taylor. For starters, knowledge workers are going to blog with or without the permission of their "superiors," so firms better get used to the unexpurgated world of the blogosphere where standards of truth and honesty are an expected characteristic, and the slick, spun pronouncements of the public relations department are spotted, and chastised, instantly. As mentioned earlier, Web sites such as www.vault.com have sprung up, allowing prospective employees to read personal accounts of what it is really like to work for the companies they are considering joining.

CoPs require conversations, collaboration, commitment, connectivity, and capabilities, all of which can be handled effectively by blogs. Sharing specified knowledge across disperse geographical locations is another function of CoPs, especially in a world where telecommuting has become more popular. One of the reasons the human capital market is not as effective as the capital market is that human capital is hard to document and record, like accounting transactions. Blogs and other types of CoPs allows for a record to be maintained of the accomplishments and expertise of individuals. A blog can profile such individual attributes as education, hobbies, project experience, core competencies, who the person mentors and is mentored by, papers and books published, and so on. No doubt, in the future there will be software programs allowing knowledge workers to peer into this type of information and collaborate with anyone, anywhere in the world, who has the exact knowledge they need just in time. Too many companies today reward people for *having* knowledge, not *sharing* it, but in a knowledge economy it is the latter that will take on increasing importance to reap the full potential of knowledge workers. It must become part of every firm's culture, an expected part of their jobs.

For some, this is threatening, since hoarding knowledge has so often been rewarded by career advancement—the old rule that knowledge is power. This may have been true in the Industrial Era, but it no longer comports to the covenants of a knowledge economy, where *sharing* knowledge is power. Rather than hoarding knowledge as a way to advance, knowledge workers will more and more give away their knowledge and watch it expand and grow, enriching their own knowledge in the process. Paul Arden, a former advertising agency executive creative director, has some wonderful counterintuitive advice with respect to this philosophy:

> ... [P]eople are secretive with ideas. 'Don't tell them that, they'll take the credit for it.' The problem with hoarding is you end up living off your reserves. Eventually you'll become stale. If you give away everything you have, you are left with nothing. This forces you to look, to be aware, to replenish (Arden 2003: 30).

Though I am not enamored with the term *knowledge management*, I will continue to use the term since it is in the mainstream of business lexicon and will make it easier for those of you who want to further your understanding—by doing more research—of this important field. Knowledge management (KM) is, of course, nothing new. Standard operating procedures documented in a manual accomplished the same thing, long before computers were available. Knowledge exchange exists in every firm, but the problem is these tend to be ad hoc, imperfect, mismanaged, and underutilized. Codifying knowledge is intrinsically a human function, since no computer can summarize what is inputted into it. Thomas Davenport and Laurence Prusak, in their book *Working Knowledge*, distinguish between the *velocity* of knowledge—the speed at which knowledge moves through an organization—and the *viscosity* of knowledge—the richness of the knowledge itself. They also point out that what improves the velocity may very well dilute the viscosity (Davenport and Prusak 1998: 102).

Firms need to define their key technical know-how in each department, decide on a place where it should reside, and determine how to articulate it. In their book *Unlocking Knowledge Assets: Knowledge Management Solutions from Microsoft*, Susan Conway and Char Sligar outline the following useful key elements of an effective KM system:

> *Storage*. The system should include a repository to put Knowledge Assets (KAs). It might also have document tracking and version control, security, search, and rating capabilities.
>
> *Publishing*. The system should allow several people to view and access information while restricting who can create and publish the information. It might include tracking and search features.
>
> *Subscription*. The system should allow users to set rules regarding the information that will be automatically "pushed" to them. It might also be able to differentiate formats for certain participants, have an updating feature, and so on.
>
> *Reuse*. The system should provide a many-to-many publishing environment. It might include rating, restricting, and tracking features.
>
> *Collaboration*. The system should allow several contributors to work together to create a single piece of content and manage revision tracking. It might identify experts and their online availability, discussions, and so on.
>
> *Communication*. The system should capture and manage all forms of information exchange, including e-mail, phone, instant messaging, and face-to-face dialogue, and allow for spontaneous communication (Conway and Sligar 2002: 17).

It is an axiom of knowledge management thinkers that the best venue for exchanging tacit knowledge is around the coffeepot or the watercooler. Informal conversations among employees are rich with knowledge sharing. The old Industrial Revolution admonition, "Stop talking and get to work," changes to "Start talking and get to work" in an organization of knowledge workers. KM systems do nothing more than take some of this tacit knowledge and make it explicit by putting it in a location where people can find it when they need it. In a true KM system, each team member is a knowledge *consumer* and a knowledge *producer*.

Make no mistake, KM is not simply a new technological tool that can simply be installed into an organization; it is a *cultural* change in the way IC is perceived, created, shared, and sold. Adding a sophisticated KM software program to any organization, in and of itself, is not going to create any long-term sustainable advantage unless the firm also conveys the importance and expectation of sharing and reusing knowledge. Yet many KM initiatives are controlled by the information technology (IT) function in many companies and are measured by inputs rather than outputs. This is probably due to the fact that IT spending can be measured easier than knowledge codification, and the ROI is therefore more apparent. Another barrier to an effective KM culture is the ghost of Frederick Taylor. Codifying knowledge takes time, and on a day-to-day basis businesspeople lead frenetic lives, making it easier to overlook the importance of documenting what we know, since each instance is merely a grain of sand on the scale, a seemingly insignificant contribution to future wealth creation. But knowledge is cumulative, and over time that scale will tip in favor of accumulating valuable intellectual capital that can be reused.

My VeraSage Institute colleague Paul O'Byrne is a partner in O'Byrne & Kennedy, a 12-person chartered accounting firm in Goffs Oak, Hertfordshire, just to the north of London. Along with his partner Paul Kennedy, he has taken to heart the message of leveraging IC, creating a "knowledge bank" within their firm, wherein everyone is expected to make deposits and withdrawals. Paul calls this "building our invisible balance sheet," making the firm more valuable. Here is what he has to say on the subject of converting tacit to explicit knowledge:

A knowledge worker carries the means of production around in his own neck-top computer. Many professional firms have a black hole in their income statement where the IT department spends money on knowledge management. Now whether knowledge can indeed be managed is a matter of debate. We are presently on our sixth iteration of a software solution to capturing, categorizing, and accessing knowledge, which we call KnowledgeBank. One thing we have definitely learned over the years of trying to develop our own system of knowledge management is that it is a cultural, not an IT, issue.

A variation we have found effective is to make recordings of ideas and store those in the KnowledgeBank. For example, we may be with a customer and discussing pricing. It's all very well for any of our accountants to assert to customers they should put their prices up, but what to say? What analogies to bring? What insights to share? We have over the past four years been video recording our seminars, stories, and interviews that encapsulate some point in a memorable (if only a voyeuristic) way.

The greatest challenge in knowledge management seems to us to be tacit knowledge. Everyone understands the need for procedures, checklists, and precedents and these should indeed be formalized and shared. But what competitive advantage is there in that? Indeed, many of us buy these from the same sources, so there can be no competitive advantage. As many of the public think: many accountants *are* all the same.

A firm of knowledge workers worthy of the name is inevitably differentiated in the application of knowledge and the delivery of personalized service. This is a challenge for firms: can you only be good by recruiting brilliant people? Or can you recruit able people and leverage their skills by recognizing the tacit knowledge of the most effective practitioners and transferring it to them? But we don't know how to do this, or at least we never have. It's generally not wise to do so, since the normal insecurity of professionals means you guard your knowledge in the hope you will be thought indispensable.

Even if you can overcome the self-interest aspect and get buy-in to the idea of sharing knowledge, you have to form new habits of recognizing when we are applying things we "just know," synthesizing different experiences, insights from our wider reading or conversations, and thinking skills that are all examples of tacit knowledge we need to share, but don't know how to.

"Red polo syndrome" is the name I gave to the phenomenon that struck me when my wife bought a Volkswagen Polo. Suddenly, from nothing, the number of cars of that type on the road—painted the exact same shade of red—exploded. My wife can be something of a trend setter, but I had to know that those red cars had been there all the time, but I never noticed. I wasn't attuned to seeing them. I wasn't sensitized to seeing red Polos until I had an interest in them.

So it is with knowledge. It's there, floating around all the time, but until we had an interest and were desirous of seeing it, we didn't notice it, and it passed us by. Now, varying by individual and how we feel that day, we see knowledge all the time. Sometimes it's too routine to mention, sometimes not exciting in itself, but perhaps valuable nevertheless.

Like Paul says, valuable knowledge can exist all around us that has the potential to create great wealth, propelled by an idea, as the next section demonstrates.

LEVERAGING IC AND CREATING THE WORLD'S SECOND LARGEST CURRENCY

"Humorist Art Buchwald gave this advice to Judith Martin ("Miss Manners") when she was starting her career at the *Washington Post*: 'Never sell anything only once,' he told her, explaining that the material he used in his newspaper columns he repackaged and resold in hardcover books, then in paperback, then told and sold again on talk shows and in paid speeches. That's what distilled knowledge is all about" (Stewart 2001: 145).

The airlines certainly learned this lesson. Twenty-six years ago, in May 1981, American Airlines launched the AAdvantage frequent-flyer program, which has become its own currency as of late and almost instantaneously duplicated by all airlines. At the end of January 2006, collectively, almost 10 trillion miles were unredeemed worldwide by 180 million members, 120 million of which are U.S. residents. Valued at the midpoint market value of between 2 and 10 cents apiece, the global currency is worth $700 billion, more than all the U.S. dollar notes and coins in circulation (according to www.webflyer.com, accessed March 29, 2007). These miles are fought over in divorce battles, and two-thirds of passengers polled said they see their miles as the next best thing to actual cash. More than one in three Americans now collect them, and a little more than one-half of all miles are earned on the ground (through affinity programs with credit cards, hotels, rental car companies, telephone calls, etc.), generating approximately $10 billion for the airlines in 2001. All this value created from leveraging a reservation system, plastic cards embossed with a customer's name, a frequent-flyer number, and empty plane seats. This spectacular wealth generation was not created by an industry that believes it sells commodity passenger seat miles. More proof that ideas create wealth.

The contrast with "physical" capital could not be more revealing when examining the real leverage embedded in knowledge organizations. If an airline assigns a Boeing 777 to the San Francisco–London route, it cannot be used at the same time for the San Francisco–Tokyo route. However, the airline's reservation system, which is based on its structural capital and its social capital (customer and supplier capital, to be discussed in Chapter 13), can conceivably handle an unlimited number of customers. This is precisely why IC is a nonrival asset, as opposed to physical or financial capital.

In some instances, structural capital is latent and is not being used to its full potential. This example from DuPont illustrates how mature structural capital can be converted to a valuable product:

> [T]he DuPont Company, originally a manufacturer of gunpowder, was also an early champion of safety programs and safety education. Several years ago DuPont's CEO asked whether it would be possible to develop a revenue-producing activity using the Company's storehouse of safety knowledge. The result is what is now

called DuPont Safety Resources, which provides safety consulting services and training courses and sells a range of safety products (Harrison and Sullivan 2006: 61).

Both Pepsi and Coca-Cola leveraged their manufacturing processes, distribution channels, water use, manufacturing, and marketing to create the bottled water brands Aquafina and Dasani, respectively. Basic economics teaches that it is very difficult to sell something someone else is giving away for free, making bottled water an interesting anomaly, especially since water covers nearly three-fourths of the earth's surface. This $35 billion worldwide industry continues to grow as water quality concerns and fitness and health awareness increases.

One of the best examples of leveraging IC to create wealth was given by a straight man for a very funny woman—Desi Arnaz, Lucille Ball's husband. *I Love Lucy* was certainly one of television's first great sitcoms. Arnaz was born in Cuba in 1917, but it was not until the 1950s that Arnaz took a risk that was to have an enormous payoff. In return for a salary cut of $1,000 per each of 39 episodes, CBS gave the pair sole ownership rights over the show, since in 1951 most television shows were shot live and preserved only on kinescopes. Hence, television executives back then thought that yesterday's shows had as much value as yesterday's newspapers. *I Love Lucy* was the first show that was filmed, not shot live, so there was something worth selling after the original broadcast was over. Today, half a century later, a single episode goes for $100,000. Jerry Seinfeld learned from success, and has banked $225 million from the sale of his show's syndication rights. More recently, A&E purchased the rights to *The Sopranos* for a reported $162.5 million for 65 episodes, or $2.5 million per episode.

Considering the wealth inherent to stories and songs, supposedly the most ephemeral of products, it's not surprising that Scarlett O'Hara and Rhett Butler are worth far more than cars made in the same year as the movie *Gone With the Wind*, 1939.

Let us now turn our attention to another method of capturing tacit knowledge from humans and making it part of a firm's structural capital, utilizing lessons from the U.S. Army.

KNOWLEDGE LESSONS FROM THE U.S. ARMY

Let your future be lit with the knowledge of the past.
—*Sakichi Toyoda, founder, Toyoda Automatic Loom Works, predecessor to Toyota Motor Company*

You always learn by doing, but you also learn by learning, if you know what I mean.
—*Yogi Berra, When You Come to a Fork in the Road, Take It!, 2001*

During the month of June 2002, I had two long conversations with U.S. Army personnel, one an active sergeant in the Army Reserve, and the second a retired 20-year major, who happened to be reading the same book I was—*Hope Is Not a Method*—on a flight we were on together. We talked mostly about the Army's policy of doing After Action Reviews (AARs), which take place after every training event or mission. Both officers assured me that the Army's goal is never to reinvent the wheel—"The Army never wants to build the same bridge twice" is how one expressed it. In fact, the retired major expressed his incessant frustration with his company's inability to adopt the AAR so as to spread its knowledge internally (the main objection seemed to be "Why would we want to waste time doing that?"). Since that discussion in 2002, I have talked with many other military personnel from all branches of the service. They are all familiar with AARs, acknowledging the lasting learning that comes from using this innovative tool.

The Army's use of AARs began in 1973, not as a knowledge management tool but as a method to restore the values, integrity, and accountability that had diminished during the Vietnam War. Thinking back on my own career in public accounting, I became convinced that the AAR is a practice that would have many salutary effects in a knowledge organization. I began to think about how well my firm learned from past mistakes, or how often we would reflect on what we did, rather than just moving on to the next project. Being generous, I can say there was plenty of room for improvement. We were not taught how the *evaluation* is ultimately more important than the *experience*. But doing AARs only decreases the Taylorite productivity statistics with which executives are so enamored. The average worker is so busy *doing* they do not have the time to *reflect* on what they have done, let alone discover major breakthroughs. But action without reflection is meaningless, as the T. S. Eliot poem expresses well: "We had the experience but missed the meaning." In Latin, *reflect* comes from the verb meaning "refold," implying the action of turning things inward to see them in a different way. Reflection without action is passivity, but action without reflection is thoughtlessness. Combine experience with reflection, and learning that lasts is the result.

Perhaps we ignore innovations in the military because its mission—to break things and kill people—is so divergent from that of a civilian organization. But this is far too parochial an attitude; and once again we discover a useful practice from another sector. In fact, because the AAR is such a useful method for turning tacit knowledge into explicit knowledge, not to mention to foster learning and sharing of knowledge throughout the organization, I will quote at length from Gordon R. Sullivan and Michael V. Harper's book *Hope Is Not a Method: What Business Leaders Can Learn From America's Army*:

> An AAR takes place after every training event. Its purposes are simple: learning, improving, doing better the next time. The participants sit down with a facilitator called an "observer-controller" who has been with them throughout the event, and they discuss what happened. To do this effectively requires several things. First, there must be a fairly good basis for understanding what actually happened. ... Soldiers call this "ground truth." Combined with ground truth, there must be a fairly unambiguous understanding of

what should have happened, and that comes from having standards derived from doctrine.

Given those elements, it is possible to talk about an event in a way that focuses on improving team performance without getting caught up in individual performance, rank, position, or personality. By asking questions such as "What did you think I wanted you to do?" (as opposed to questions such as "How did you screw that up?"), one can get to the roots of both success and failure. This is not an easy process, and it generally takes a lot of time, maybe two to three hours to "AAR" a major event. The cost in time alone is heavy, but the outcome is a much more in-depth understanding of what happened. The return on investment, measured by improved performance, is very high.

The most difficult challenge is developing a culture that values this kind of learning. A colleague in industry once described an attempt to initiate a similar program in his company. He told me of a dialogue with a loading dock foreman who, in great frustration, finally said to him, "Look, I can either ship product or talk about it. Which do you want me to do?" The answer can only be "Both," but it is hard to make that answer a reality. It took a decade for the AAR process to become respected in the Army, for us to learn that you can do both—ship product and talk—and that carefully structured talking leads to more effective shipping or whatever. It is an investment that no one can afford not to make.

Today AARs take place in garrisons, on staffs, and in headquarters—everywhere soldiers gather to perform some task. My personal staff would hold AARs for me after a major event in which I had participated. I did not especially enjoy discussing the gaps in my own performance—especially when I felt pretty good about what I had done—but these AARs helped me improve, and they helped my staff learn to support me better.

For America's Army, the AAR was the key to turning the corner and institutionalizing organizational learning. You probably never become a learning organization in any absolute sense; it can only be something you aspire to, always "becoming," never truly "being." But, in the Army, the AAR has ingrained a respect for organizational learning, fostering an expectation that decisions and consequent actions will be reviewed in a way that will benefit both the participants and the organization, no matter how painful it may be at the time. The only real failure is the failure to learn (Sullivan and Harper 1996: 191–193).

Imagine the benefits of having a library of AARs for almost any type of project, process, or method the company may encounter. Imagine further creating a culture that rewards knowledge workers for taking the time to contribute to this stock of knowledge, and perhaps even determines its utility by tracking how many times particular AARs are accessed by others. Imagine further a culture that understands AARs are real work, where time is spent on not just *doing* the work, but also *improving* the way work is done. Perfectionist cultures, however, resist this type of candid reflection, as they tend to be intolerant of errors, and mistakes are associated with career risk, not continuous learning. The medical world has an appropriate axiom for mistakes made: forgive and remember. Jim Collins calls this "autopsies without blame" (Collins 2001: 88). Fear is another reason for learning not taking place, as this study demonstrates:

> A recent study of errors in administering drugs in hospitals, in fact, found higher reported error rates in units with greater openness and more sympathetic management. When environments were less supportive and errors were associated with blame or discipline—a search for the guilty, rather than a search for solutions—errors were much more likely to be hidden or suppressed. Fear does little to encourage learning (Garvin 2000: 41).

AARs mitigate fear, if they are used not as a method to place blame but to learn from mistakes so they do not happen again, and identify best practices so they can be spread throughout the organization. AARs should not be used for promotions, salary increases, or performance appraisals. This is an enormous advantage of AARs compared to the annual performance appraisal. AARs provide instant feedback, where in their absence a supervisor may delay feedback—and hence learning—to a once a year ritual.

Once an organization is comfortable dissecting the performance *after* each engagement, it will be better equipped to make plans and preparations *before* the next one. As a result, innovation, creativity, and risk taking will flourish as the firm constantly strives for improvement in an iterative process that respects and rewards learning. Here are the questions you need to ask in each AAR:

- What was supposed to happen?
- What actually happened (the "ground truth")?
- What were the positive and negative factors here?
- What have we learned and how can we do better next time? (from the Centre for Army Lessons Learned: http://call.army. mil, accessed March 30, 2007).

Each team member who worked on the engagement would participate in this process. The AAR is not a tool to fix blame or point fingers; it is a learning tool, designed to increase the effectiveness of the firm. Its role is to be *analytical*, not *critical*. It also fosters a true team environment and makes everyone responsible for the success of the engagement; moreover, it is a development tool that helps leaders to become more engaged in the success of their teams. If there are shortcomings, the AAR fixes the *problem*, not assesses the *blame*. Even if only one individual completes an AAR because there was no team on the engagement, it is still an effective way to spread learning and knowledge to other members of the firm.

The Army suggests that you divide your time in answering the AAR's questions into 25–25-50: That is, 25 percent reviewing what happened, 25 percent reviewing why it happened, and the remaining 50 percent on what to do about it and how can you learn from it to improve. The objective is not just to correct *things*, but rather to correct *thinking*, as the Army has learned that flawed assumptions are the largest factor in flawed execution. An AAR is more of a verb than a noun. It does not have to be a formal written report, it can be a conversation held among the team. If the project is large and important enough, a facilitator is recommended to get the most from the process. The AAR could be videotaped, audio recorded, or summarized later in a formal report, any of which could be deposited into the organization's knowledge bank. The Army also recommends answering the following summary questions to wrap up the AAR:

> What should the organization learn from this experience of what worked and did not work?
> What should be done differently in the future?
> Who needs to know these lessons and conclusions?
> Who will enter these lessons in the knowledge management system, or write the case up for future use?
> Who will bring these lessons into the leadership process for decision-making and planning? (from the Centre for Army Lessons Learned, http://call.army.mil).

Microsoft uses a modified version of the AAR process to do postmortems on new software releases. Boeing also uses this method:

> Boeing used this approach immediately after experiencing difficulties with its 737 and 747 plane programs. Both planes were introduced with much fanfare—as well as serious problems. To ensure that the problems were not repeated, senior managers commissioned a high-level employee group, called Project Homework, to compare the development processes of the 737 and 747 with those of the 707 and 727, two of the company's most profitable planes. The group was asked to develop a set of "lessons learned" that could be used on future projects. After working for three years, they produced hundreds of recommendations and an inch-thick booklet. Several members of the team were then transferred to the 757 and 767 start-ups. Guided by experience, they produced the most successful, error-free launches in Boeing's history (Garvin 2000: 101).

One wonders if Airbus could have benefited from this approach in the development of its Airbus 380 super jumbo jet?

In their *Harvard Business Review* article, "Learning in the Thick of It," Marilyn Darling, Charles Parry, and Joseph Moore discussed the After Action Review process, and added this interesting tool to it: The Before Action Review (BAR), which they say "requires teams to answer four questions before embarking on an important action:

1. What are our intended results and measures?
2. What challenges can we anticipate?
3. What have we or others learned from similar situations?
4. What will make us successful this time?" (Darling et al. 2005: 92).

Toyota's famous Toyota Production System uses both AARs and BARs. The former is embodied by the Japanese word *hansei* (hahn-say), which means reflection. As Matthew May explains in his fascinating book on Toyota, *The Elegant Solution*, the process is quite solemn:

> Hansei is not about confirmation. It's not about celebration of success. It's a sobering reality check, regardless of a project's outcomes. Were you to attend a hansei meeting following a resounding success at Toyota, you would be shocked at the tone of the meeting. It's stern and serious. Fine, the team greatly exceeded expectations. Guess what, that means they didn't understand their process. Their objectives should have been met (May 2007: 81).

Once again, let us hear from Paul O'Byrne and how his accounting firm, O'Byrne & Kennedy, utilize AARs:

> We were introduced to the concept of After Action Reviews (AARs) by Ron when he wrote about them in his book, *The Firm of the Future*. The concept of reviewing what has taken place with a view to learning from it makes total sense. Funny that it is so little practiced. From the moment we read about it, we decided to embrace this and set about designing a process to capture our AARs. The idea is to note what happened, consider what clues there were to its happening (things rarely come out of a clear blue sky), what we could have done about it, what implications

there are for product or service design or learning, and—often most valuable—what other things might be like this where we can apply the lessons learned.

Admittedly, the early days after introducing this were like a contest for "foul-up of the week." This was probably inevitable, as we all tend to focus on things that go wrong, but we wanted to learn from success, too, and introduced a system whereby for each "failure" AAR a team member would have to bring in a "success" AAR as well.

The significance of the AAR process for a firm of knowledge workers is blindingly obvious. In many organizations it is not healthy to confess your sins in public, better to hope they are not spotted. Fortunate for us, the partners in our firm made—and willingly reported—more fouls ups than everyone else put together. This leadership showed it was okay to admit fault, with the overriding objective one of learning so we can perform better next time. The sharing of knowledge, whether by means of AARs or in some other way, is a cultural process. If you believe in your knowledge workers, why wouldn't you want them to share their knowledge? As economists say, knowledge is a nonrival asset: If I give you my pen, you have it but I don't; but if I give you knowledge, you have it and I still have it. Interestingly, we have discovered that when we exchange knowledge, not only do we still have it, we often gain a new perspective that enhances it and makes it more valuable.

One innovative idea that came out of our AAR process was the concept of "badges." You remember, from Brownies or Boy Scouts? Visible recognition of knowledge and skills learned and tested, lovingly sewn onto your uniform. Part of the context of knowledge is the ability of the user to use it. Our newest trainee has needs that are significantly different from our most senior tax planner. They have different prior knowledge, different technological abilities, different people skills, and they'll be doing different work. Our junior recruit cannot possibly do complex tax planning, and our senior tax planner should not be doing basic tax returns. But they do (the latter case, I mean). As the team thought about it, there were lots of instances where this applied, so we set about mapping work to the knowledge and skills required to perform it. The point being, until you've got your personal tax return badge, you couldn't do all of a tax return unsupervised. Perhaps more significantly, if you've got your advanced tax planner badge, you have to turn in your personal tax return badge—your human capital is too valuable to be doing work that could be done by someone else. We see this concept of badges linking back in to our methods for categorizing our knowledge and to our work and resource planning.

In our role as educators, conducting courses and seminars around the world, my colleagues and I have always utilized AARs, usually right after the event (or even during breaks and lunchtime, to make corrections and improve). By engaging in this process, we often discover a clearer way to express a thought, give a better example, or discover a better way of structuring our material. These conversations are constant, effectively transferring an enormous amount of tacit knowledge between us. Much of this knowledge finds its way into our books, our blog posts, published articles, videos, and other forms of our structural capital.

There is enormous value in immediacy here. By the time you read the attendee evaluations from a seminar, it is too late, you are reading history, a lagging indicator; and while it can shed some helpful light on how to improve, it is never as useful as an AAR would be right after the event. What we want are *leading indicators* that can help us stay away from obstacles and problems or deal with them effectively when they do arise. To this day, within VeraSage Institute, everyone who performs a seminar, speech, or course, completes an AAR with a team member, which has resulted in enormous improvements in the way we present ideas to knowledge workers around the world. Without question, it is sometimes very uncomfortable to face your performance errors and mishaps; but how else are knowledge workers supposed to learn? By getting an annual review? Practical learning demands hands-on, experiential knowledge that only those closest to the engagement can capture and share. It's helpful to remember that McDonald's Big Mac, fried apple pie, large fries, McDLT, and

Egg McMuffin were all invented by local franchisees, not as part of a corporate headquarters strategy.

No doubt AARs and BARs take time, and will impair traditional Taylorite efficiency, at least in the short run. Once again, we can hear the objections from some executives on this note, who are myopically focused on efficiency rather than effectiveness and learning. Your firm's IC is the most important source of its long-term wealth-creating capacity. It must be constantly replenished and created to build the firm's invisible balance sheet. Constantly focusing on *doing* rather than learning, creativity, innovation, and knowledge sharing is the equivalent of eating the company's seed corn. As Socrates said: "The unexamined life is not worth living."

Capturing the tacit knowledge that exists in the heads of your human capital and making it part of your organization's structural capital will insure that your firm knows what it knows, and can deploy it quicker and at a lower marginal cost than the competition. It is IC that is the ultimate lever in the firm of the future, and firms have to begin to understand this fundamental economic truth of wealth creation. Sullivan and Harper summarize the importance and value of converting tacit to explicit knowledge succinctly:

> Earlier we argued that, as we face our external environment, "We don't know what we don't know." As we face our internal environment, it seems that the opposite is too often true: "We don't know what we *do* know." As an important organizational asset, knowledge is usable only if it can be identified and disseminated so as to contribute value. The challenge is to discover what is known in any part of the organization and, if it is valuable, make it known to all (Sullivan and Harper 1996: 206).

SUMMARY AND CONCLUSIONS

We have explored the necessity of capturing your firm's tacit human capital and creating structural capital as a result, which will stay with your firm even if your human capital should depart. We also discussed why it is so important to leverage your structural capital to create wealth both for the company's customers and itself. Pepsi and Coca-Cola's bottled water, along with the airline frequent-flyer programs, are both excellent examples of this process.

Is it not tragic that there are more knowledge workers today in the labor force than ever before, yet they are not really rewarded for thinking and reflecting because they are too busy doing and billing? It shouldn't be a crime to read a business at work or write on a blog—let alone conducting an AAR or BAR—but these tasks require us to shift our focus from efficiency to effectiveness, learning, and adding to our IC. The present unclear focus sends a mixed message to the firm's team members: executives say they understand the importance of IC, innovation, and creativity, but they aren't really willing to make the investments necessary to create more of it and to leverage it effectively. Part of the problem is that our traditional metrics focus on precisely the wrong things (since the old theory of the firm is itself flawed, as we saw in Chapter 4), and many companies haven't taken the necessary time to study the success of other IC organizations. In fact, I posit the following argument: most firms' legacy systems of measurements and reward systems—from productivity, efficiency, and other production-oriented metrics to our legacy accounting systems—have actually become negative structural capital in the context of becoming a firm of the future. As with negative human capital, these types of antiquated capital must be extricated from the organization to achieve its latent potential.

Now that we have covered the human and structural capital components of an organization's IC, let us now turn our attention to what is perhaps the least leveraged—and perhaps least understood and underutilized—form of a company's IC—its social capital.

13

SOCIAL CAPITAL: NO MAN IS AN ISLAND

> No man is an island, entire of itself; every man is a piece of the
> continent, a part of the main.... Any man's death diminishes me,
> because I am involved in mankind; and therefore never send to know
> for whom the bell tolls; it tolls for thee.
>
> —*John Donne, English poet*

Most people are familiar with Archimedes's saying, "Give me a
lever long enough, and I shall move the earth." What is often forgotten is that he also said he needed not just a lever but "a single
place to stand." Without a solid ground—a family, neighborhood,
a common corporate culture, rules of just conduct, private property statutes, social norms, and customs—we move nothing, we
do nothing, we become nothing. Yet, until recently, social capital
was an area that was largely ignored by businesspeople. We are
just beginning to understand the importance of societal influences
on human behavior and its impact on creating wealth.

Maybe one of the reasons social capital has been unobserved by
businesspeople is the persistent myth that capitalism depends on
rugged individualists, entrepreneurs who constantly challenge the
status quo with new ideas, services, and products that bring forth a
"perennial gale of creative destruction," driven by an impersonal
"invisible hand."

But just as no man is an island, neither is any corporation. Buying and selling are activities as ancient as the human race, and do
not have much to do with capitalism. What does make capitalism

unique is the fact that it is an organizing ethos, a corporate enterprise, a collective effort. It is far more dependent on social order, and is more social in nature, than its enemies—or its friends, for that matter—have yet to understand. The essence of capitalism is an organizing structure to house the division of labor, division of purposes, and a division of talents. That organizing structure is a *voluntary association*, registered in law as a *corporation*. The corporation transcends the life of any single individual, and it binds people cooperatively across time and space, voluntarily.

Even in biblical times "private property" existed; otherwise, "Thou shalt not steal" would have been meaningless. Corporate law was based on the law of the monasteries. The Benedictines were the first multinational corporations, selling wine, cheese, and honey all over Europe and the world. As Michael Novak explains:

> They also did it, interestingly enough, by being the first to be so efficient at it that they could live above subsistence. They lived on their own profits. They were such good farmers that they could give seven hours to prayer a day. They could work seven hours and pray seven hours because they were efficient businessman and they sold across many nations. Corporate law developed out of monastic law because it was the only model for something that lived longer than any individual and it was given to something more than subsistence living (Younkins 2001: 62).

No one raises their children to be *rugged individualists*. Rather, we raise them to work, play, and get along well with others of all different backgrounds. The sociologist James Coleman defines *social capital* as

> "[T]he ability of people to work together for common purposes in groups and organizations; the ability to associate with each other, that is critical not only to economic life but to virtually every other aspect of social existence as well" (Fukuyama 1995: 10).

A free market economy depends on the voluntary cooperation of many competing interests, not on the fable of the lone cowboy. Even Adam Smith understood the importance of social capital in creating the wealth of nations. In his first book, *The Theory of Moral Sentiments* (first published in 1759), Smith's opening paragraph begins:

> How selfish whatsoever man may be supposed, there are evidently some principles in his nature, which interest him in the fortune of others, and render their happiness necessary to him, though he derives nothing from it except the pleasure of seeing it (Smith 2000: 3).

Smith explicitly understood that impersonal market forces don't force people to become impersonal. Economic life cannot be divorced from the customs, morals, traditions, and habits of the culture in which it exists. Smith poses a thought experiment in his book that is quite intriguing: Suppose you could save 100 million people at the expense of losing your little finger. Would you do it? Most people answer yes, and Smith suggests this proves that people don't always act in their selfish and sordid interests, arguing that it is your conscience that made you do the right thing. It is not love of the strangers, per se, that made you give up your finger, but the love for the dignity and superiority of your character. We desire the external praise of others, and we desire to attain the internal respect and praise of *ourselves*. We ultimately want to be *worthy* of our praise—in other words, we desire to be *praiseworthy*.

In Oliver Stone's 1987 movie *Wall Street*, the Nietzschean anti-hero Gordon Gekko proclaims, "greed, for lack of a better word, is good," as if greed is the pinnacle of virtue for businesspeople. This view is commonly attributed to Smith. He never said, or wrote, any such thing. In fact, the term is properly credited to Bernard Mandeville (1670–1733), a Dutch psychiatrist and pamphleteer. In his work, *The Fable of the Bees* (1714), Mandeville claims "private vices are public benefits." Smith disagreed with this, calling it "wholly pernicious" and the thesis "erroneous."

Even more absurd are those who claim that Smith's theories are based on impersonal—or psychological—and ethical egoism.

Psychological egoism is the idea that everyone is always motivated to act in their own perceived self-interest, while *ethical
egoism* is a normative theory about what people ought to do; and
what they ought to do is always act in their self-interest, not concern themselves with the welfare of others. Yet, who subscribes
to these views? Taken to the extreme, this view would prevent
anyone from starting a family—indeed, it would be a dagger in
the heart of family life, marriage, friendship, and brotherhood.
Helplessness may be the only truly universal human experience,
since all of us pass through infancy. The human race would not
have survived one generation if every person acted as if he were
unconnected to any other person. Most parents would die for
their children, and this is not even considered heroic behavior
but, rather, quite ordinary. Couples are subject to what actuaries
call the *broken-heart factor*: the correlation of the death of one
spouse with that of the other in a relatively short period of time.
These characteristics are hardly those of a greedy, self-interested
population.

The development of human capital (HC) is obviously not an
individual process but a *social* process. Human skills grow and
develop only if one generation teaches the next, as Alvin Toffler's
potty training question illustrated. In a knowledge economy, at
some point, your fellow worker's HC becomes as important to
your earning potential as your own. If he or she is uneducated, a
ceiling will be placed on your potential. Nowhere is the concept
of how social capital affects—negatively in this instance—the
wealth of nations better epitomized than in the cost of the communist experiment. As measured in the loss of HC creation, including
the work ethic, entrepreneurship, habits, customs, risk taking, creativity, and trust, the communist dream is dead. Consider the HC
that has fled Cuba's negative social capital structure, as told by
British historian Paul Johnson:

> In fact, the Cuban community in the United States grew and flour-
> ished. By the second half of the 1990s, it had founded 750,000
> new businesses, become the richest and most influential political

lobby after the Jewish Lobby, and its 2 million members generated a Gross Domestic Product eleven times larger than that of Cuba itself, with 11 million inhabitants. Moreover, Miami, center of the new Cuban settlement, forming links with the entire Latin American society of the hemisphere, became in many ways its financial, economic, communications, and cultural center, hugely boosting American exports in goods and, still more, in services throughout the western half of the globe. In the long run, then, the grand beneficiary of the Cuban missile crisis was indeed the United States (Johnson 1997: 867).

This is precisely why it is often wryly noted that Fidel Castro did more to develop the southern United States than did air conditioning. It also helps explain why the Spanish philosopher Pedro Saenz Rodriguez said from exile in Lisbon a dozen years ago, "But if I wanted the American Constitution to prevail in Spain, I would import not the Constitution, but Americans" (Buckley 2000: 241). It is also why, when asked what one book he would put into the hands of a Russian Communist, then-president Franklin Delano Roosevelt replied: "The Sears, Roebuck catalog."

Culture matters. Cultures are not merely customs to be displayed in museums, but rather they are a particular way of accomplishing the things that make life possible. Social influences play a significant role in shaping human behavior. Economist Milton Friedman was fond of pointing out "there is no such thing as a free lunch." Yet he was the first to concede that capitalism was the ultimate free lunch, since all of us derive enormous benefits from the relatively few innovators, entrepreneurs, scientists, and other giants whose shoulders we all stand upon for our present standard of living. The value of the many innovations throughout history accrues far more to their users than their creators. We are just beginning to comprehend and study the importance of social capital, and how it affects the development of people's individual HC, and indeed their behavior, tastes, and preferences, as we will explore next.

IS THERE ANY ACCOUNTING FOR TASTES?

Man is a social animal.

—Seneca, De beneficiis

You like bowling; I enjoy golf. You prefer white wine; I savor red. You always purchase Fords; I purchase General Motors. The standard explanation for all of these human differences can be found in the English translation of the Latin proverb: "There's no accounting for tastes." But is that true? How do we acquire our various tastes? Is it custom, tradition, habit, or something else that explains individual preferences and why people behave the way they do? Economist Gary S. Becker has an explanation for individual preferences that explains a great deal of human behavior. In his book *Accounting for Tastes*, he argues that, in modern industrialized countries—where basic biological needs for food, drink, and shelter have been adequately provided for—the necessities of life have little to do with the consumption habits of the average person. "Rather," according to Becker, "these choices depend on childhood and other experiences, social interactions, and cultural influences" (Becker 1996: 3).

In addition to the pioneering work Becker has done in the area of HC, where he has argued that spending on such items as education, training, medical care, and so forth should be classified as investments, not merely consumption—as governments and corporations are wont to do—in this book, Becker expanded on his definition of *human capital* to embody two additional components:

> My approach incorporates experiences and social forces into preferences or tastes through two basic capital stocks. *Personal capital*, *P*, includes the relevant past consumption and other personal experiences that affect current and future utilities. *Social capital*, *S*, incorporates the influences of past actions by peers and others in an individual's social network and control system. A person's personal and social capital form part of his total stock of human capital (Becker 1996: 4).

In other words, the fact that you have, for example, smoked in the past will, more or less, determine your future smoking consumption—that is now part of your personal capital. But what made you smoke in the first place? Perhaps it was peer pressure, which is also part of your social capital, as Becker defines it. We all understand that word-of-mouth—and, with today's ubiquitous World Wide Web, word-of-mouse—advertising is the most effective. National surveys reveal that, three times out of four, most consumers rely on the advice of friends and family before making a purchase. Becker's theory of social capital explains why it is so powerful:

> Men and women want respect, recognition, prestige, acceptance, and power from their family, peers, and others. Consumption and other activities have a major social component partly because they take place in public. As a result, people often choose restaurants, neighborhoods, schools, books to read, political opinions, food, or leisure activities with an eye to pleasing peers and others in their social network (Becker 1996: 12).

Psychologists refer to *the principle of social proof*, which states that one means we use to determine what is correct is to find out what other people think is correct. Social proof is a major motivator of individual behavior, and this explains why organizations such as weight-reduction clinics rely on public commitment and peer pressure to change behavior. People who reveal their New Year's resolutions to their social peers are more likely to keep them. It also explains why television executives insist on using laugh tracks for sitcoms, even though most people say they don't like them. Experiments have found laugh tracks cause an audience to laugh longer and more often than they would in their absence. Bartenders will often "salt" their tip jars with a few dollars at the start of each evening to give the impression that tipping is proper behavior. Advertisers will often tout their product as the "fastest growing" or "largest selling," not to convince us the product or service is good, but only to imply many others think so, which seems proof enough.

It has been estimated that Tupperware Home Parties Corporation generates sales in excess of $2.5 million a day from an independent worldwide sales force of approximately 1.9 million. This success is easier to understand when you consider that Tupperware parties are usually thrown by friends rather than unknown salespersons. With this method, the hostess is relying on the attraction, affinity, warmth, security, and the obligation of friendship to make the sale. Mary Kay Ash used essentially the same strategy when she founded her cosmetics company, Mary Kay Cosmetics, in 1963 with her life savings of $5,000. She passed away on Thanksgiving Day in November 2001, at the age of 83, leaving a legacy with her corporation, which generated sales of more than $2.25 billion in 2006, and has generated double-digit growth every year since its founding. Her company has made more women millionaires than any other organization in history; after the fall of communism, it even made headway in Russia. In 1995, Mary Kay's top Russian sales director earned more money than then-President Boris Yeltsin. Today, more than 1.7 million independent beauty consultants in more than 30 markets leverage the principle of social proof to create wealth for their customers, and in turn, for themselves (http://www.marykay.com/company/company_companyinfor mation.aspx?tab=home, accessed April 1, 2007).

Another important qualification of social proof, as pointed out by Robert B. Cialdini in his fascinating book, *Influence: The New Psychology of Modern Persuasion*, is that, "We will use the actions of others to decide on the proper behavior for ourselves, especially when we view those others as similar to ourselves" (Cialdini 1993: 142). Witness teenagers whom adults tend to think of as rebellious and independent-minded. However, when you see them in a group, you realize how much they behave, talk, dress, and act the same as their friends and associates. They conform massively to their own peer pressures.

This background on the effects of social influence will help us explore how today's knowledge organization can leverage its social capital to create wealth outside of itself.

LEVERAGING SOCIAL CAPITAL

Noscitur a sociis ("He is known by his company")

—*Latin proverb*

Similar to HC—and the opposite of structural capital—a company does not own its social capital; at most, it can influence and monetize it. A company's social capital is comprised of the following elements:

- Customers
- Reputation and brands
- Referral sources and networks
- Suppliers and vendors
- Shareholders and other external stakeholders
- Joint venture partners and alliances
- Industry associations and formal affiliations
- Alumni
- Unions
- Corporate universities
- Open source—mass collaboration
- Cultural, moral, and ethical capital

One of the advantages of looking at a company's social capital in this manner is that it expands the boundaries of what a firm can leverage. The factors just listed give the company "a place to stand," to use Archimedes's phrase. In a knowledge-based economy, the old lines of distinction between a customer, supplier, vendor, and so on become blurred. It does not really matter whether a person or an organization is both a customer and supplier or member of a joint venture, as long as he adds value in the economic chain. For instance, as a writer, I am a customer, reviewer, and supplier to Amazon.com, and—hopefully—creating value in each role. Enabling me to participate in these multiple roles, Amazon is able to leverage its wealth-creating potential utilizing its social capital. Let us briefly tour each component of a company's social capital.

CUSTOMERS

There is only one boss: the customer. And he can fire everybody in the company, from the chairman on down, simply by spending his money somewhere else.

—Sam Walton

We discussed the *marketing concept* in Chapter 5, which Peter Drucker used to indefatigably point out that "there is only one valid definition of business purpose: to create a customer" (Flaherty 1999: 131). A business exists to create wealth for its customers, since the only things that exist inside of a business are costs, activities, efforts, problems, mediocrity, friction, politics, and crises. Drucker used to say, "There is no such thing as a profit center in a business, only effort and cost centers. The only profit center is a customer's check that doesn't bounce."

In a knowledge economy, a customer brings far more than just revenue to the relationship. They also contribute intellectual capital (IC), such as ideas for innovation, competitive intelligence, feedback, referrals, challenges, inspiration, and a host of other intangibles. Because these contributions can be positive as well as negative, customer selection is becoming increasingly important in IC-based companies. The goal should be to maximize total IC from customers, not just dollar volume or profitability. For example, Karl Sveiby, a pioneer in IC development, writes that the Danish management consulting firm PLS-Consult divides its customers as follows, rated on a scale as very much/average/not much:

- Those who contribute to image, references and/or new assignments;
- Those with challenging and widely educational projects that contribute to the firm's internal structure;
- Those who improve individual competence (Sveiby 1997: 178).

In this context, Sveiby also states: "The issue is not about effi-ciency but about effectiveness. Knowledge strategies focus on the potential of professionals to increase revenue rather than on the ability of managers to reduce costs, and they define revenue broadly—to include all the good things that come from their cus-tomers, including methodology, experience, and image, as well as money" (Sveiby 1997: 138).

I have coined a law, affectionately known as Baker's Law (which was explained in greater detail in the two previous books in the Intellectual Capitalism series, *Pricing on Purpose* and *Measure What Matters to Customers*): Bad customers drive out good customers. Since customers are the most important component of social capital, diligent customer selection is vital. The market share myth, discussed in Chapter 4, is still far too endemic in most executives' thinking. Bad customers are a form of negative social capital, and waste a company's precious capacity while subtracting from its value-creating capacity.

Jeff Bezos, founder of Amazon.com, understands how to lever-age the value of each customer. In 1999, Amazon launched its "Marketplace" program, which at the end of 2004 had more than 100,000 Marketplace sellers, generating nearly 40 percent of the company's sales volume (Anderson 2006: 93). Rather than attempting to leverage the social capital of big retailers, such as Toys "R" Us or Target, Bezos moved down to smaller retailers. Amazon is not just a bookseller or a marketplace, but a platform for each customer, and Bezos here explains what is required to become the most customer-centric online retailer:

> Three things: listen, invent, and personalize. Listen to what cus-tomers want, and figure out how to give it to them. The second thing we do is invent for customers, because it's not the customer's job to invent for themselves. The third thing is to personalize. This is the newest part of customer at the center. And we're talking about putting each customer at the center of his/her universe. If we have 17 million customers, we should have 17 million stores (Sanford and Taylor 2006: 138).

It goes without saying that no company "owns" its customers, yet they have the ability to greatly influence how those customers perceive its value. That said, all value is still subjective—like beauty, in the eyes of the beholder—and companies must continually create value for its customers or the market will ruthlessly put it out of business for wasting society's resources. And just as no company owns it customers, it also does not, ultimately, own its brand and reputation.

REPUTATION AND BRANDS

What people say behind your back is your standing in the community.
—*Edgar Watson Howe, 1853–1937*

An interesting marketing question is who really "owns" a brand? Can you really control what external parties think of you and your company? Should a business be allowed to sue a disgruntled customer who creates a *companynamesucks.com* Web site? No matter how much businesses would like to control the World Wide Web, the fact of the matter is the Internet was not created by businesses and it cannot be controlled by business, any more than it is controlled by the Department of Defense that originally created it. The Internet is a true conversation, connecting people with similar interests across all geographic boundaries. Companies no longer have a monopoly on what customers see and hear; customers now can get the true story—good, bad, and ugly—about any product or service from any other customer around the world, unfiltered by the corporate marketing and public relations departments.

According to Interbrand, a U.K. consultancy (www.interbrand.com), brand value may account for up to 25 percent of the world's financial wealth. One of the best illustrations of who really owns a brand is Coca-Cola's decision to remove Old Coke and begin offering New Coke. There was literally a customer revolt, proving beyond a shadow of a doubt that it is customers who ultimately decide the value of a brand. When Robert Goizueta, then CEO of

Coca-Cola, was asked what the lesson was from the New Coke debacle, he replied that he learned that Coca-Cola did not own its brand—the consumer did (Tedlow 2001: 105).

It is easy to confuse legal ownership with subjective value. No doubt, Coca-Cola legally owns full rights in its brand, which it can monetize to its benefit, yet it has no control—only influence—over the subjective value millions of customers place upon it. In 1999, there were allegations of "tainted Coke" in Belgium, which cost the company $34 billion in market value (Low and Kalafut 2002: 8). The Sears, Roebuck catalog was at one point in history a well-recognized brand; it is now extinct. Once an organization's brand and reputation begin to be perceived as adding no value, it is destined to become history. Your firm's reputation, and your individual reputation, exists solely in the hearts and minds of the customers you are privileged to serve. Their impressions become your reputation, as Rabbi Daniel Lapin points out with this thought-provoking example of how all value is subjective:

> Another reminder that money is really quite intangible, a mere symbol for something else, is the $9 billion that then-head of Ford Motor Company, Jacques Nasser, paid for two utter intangibles, the names "Jaguar" and "Volvo." Two brand names are worth $9 billion? That is correct. No factories were moved from England or Sweden to Detroit. No accumulated inventory of cars was shipped across the Atlantic. The owners of those two brands, Jaguar and Volvo, simply said the magic words, "The brand is now yours; send the check to my office." If three-quarters of the world's population were afflicted with amnesia on the day before the transaction closed, would the transaction have gone through? No, because the value of the brand name lies in the reputation built up over the years. If most customers have forgotten that Jaguar means "performance" and Volvo means "safety," then the names have lost their value (Lapin 2002: 271).

As these examples exemplify, real wealth does not lie in tangible things, but in the minds of people—the purest manifestation of mind over matter.

REFERRAL SOURCES AND NETWORKS

As with Tupperware and Mary Kay Cosmetics discussed earlier, most businesses are built on word-of-mouth referrals. These referral sources have to be constantly cultivated and rewarded for sending you business. As author Harvey Mackay pointed out: "If everyone in your network is the same as you, it isn't a network, it's an anthill." Developing a referral network takes time and resources, which usually comes at the expense of traditional measurements of efficiency. Investing in and cultivating a vibrant social network entails more risk and uncertainty since traditional return on investment calculations are difficult to conduct.

According to Frog Design, a strategic-creative consultancy:

> We are leaving the Information Age and entering the Recommendation Age. Today information is ridiculously easy to get; you practically trip over it on the street. Information gathering is no longer the issue—making smart decisions based on the information is now the trick. ... Recommendations serve as shortcuts through the thicket of information, just as my wine shop owner shortcuts me to obscure French wines to enjoy with pastas (Anderson 2006: 107).

From recommended reading lists on Amazon and Barnes & Noble, playlists for iPods, blogrolls to movie reviews, customer recommendations are the "post-filters" of the digital age. In the past, editors, music and studio executives, department store buyers, and advertisers largely determined what people read, listened to, watched, bought, and learned about. According to Chris Anderson's theory of the Long Tail, with the infinite shelf space of the digital world, people can have their first choice without the interference of these gatekeepers. Rather than gatekeepers *predicting* our tastes, post-filters, such as product tags on Amazon or Google will be able to *measure* it (Anderson 2006: 123). The book you are now reading would not be encoded by a librarian using the Dewey Decimal System but, rather, tagged for various points of interests by the readers themselves. This is a far more useful system, since different readers will find different parts of the book useful, or useless. Rather than the traditional top-down "taxonomies" of history's gatekeepers, the digital world has ushered in the era of the new collaborative process of "folksonomies," representing the users themselves filtering what is relevant or not. As Anderson says: "In a world of infinite choice, context—not content—is king" (Anderson 2006: 109).

An example of a company that has taken full advantage of leveraging its social capital network, by creating a virtual marketplace where you can become both a buyer and seller, is eBay, the Web's premier auction site. Founded by Pierre Omidyar, whose fiancée was a committed collector of Pez candy dispensers, he thought of a creative way to help her trade with similar collectors. Today, eBay claims a confirmed registered user base of 222 million, conducting more than 610 million auctions per quarter, as of the fourth quarter of 2006, giving new meaning to "garage sale" (www.ebay.com, accessed April 2, 2007). eBay estimates that 700,000 people earn a primary or secondary income selling items. None of these sellers owns eBay, yet consider how valuable it is to them—the essence of social capital.

Craigslist is another case in point of the power of networks, with over 450 sites in all 50 states and over 50 countries, and 15 million visitors each month. eBay now owns a 25 percent interest in the company. It is estimated that Craigslist, with 23 employees, located in a Victorian house in San Francisco's Sunset district, could fetch more than $100 million if it were put up for sale—a valuation of approximately $5 million per employee. When asked, "Why doesn't Craigslist focus more on generating revenue?" the answer given is: "We rely on local communities to suggest ways to make money without compromising Craigslist." This is a company with a clear understanding that growth for the sake of growth is the ideology of the cancer cell, which leads to the market share myth discussed in Chapter 4.

Al Lerner worked as a kid in his parents' candy store in Queens, New York. In 1982, he founded MBNA, the success of which is a testament to the power of social networks. Signing up affinity organizations—such as professional affiliations, associations, and other institutions people have more than merely a passing interest in supporting—and paying a small percentage of each credit card transaction to it, it has become one of the most successful credit card companies in history.

Similar to FedEx selling its innovative tracking system to other companies, General Motors' OnStar was made available to other automobile manufacturers, leveraging its structural and social capital across a wider platform. Seattle-based Jones Soda leverages its customer's social capital by putting their pictures on its soda bottles, along with their favorite sayings, quotes, and messages underneath the twist-off caps.

The possibilities for leveraging your referral sources and network are as limitless as the Internet itself. Bringing customers of like mind together, providing them with a community to express themselves and add value to one another is one of the awesome manifestations of the age of the Internet. And this thinking applies to not only your customers and referral sources, but also your suppliers and vendors.

SUPPLIERS AND VENDORS

We often do not view those to whom we cut checks as being able to add value beyond what we purchase from them; yet, the organizations with which a company does business sometimes have enormous wealth-creating potential when they are viewed as part of the firm's social capital. Suppliers such as consultants, attorneys, accountants, financial planners, real estate agents, funeral directors, scientists, doctors, stockbrokers, insurance agents, veterinarians, charities, and so forth, all offer opportunities for a firm to create innovative and dynamic marketing programs. Perhaps a joint seminar could be run with any of the preceding specialists, or a joint article written in their respective trade publications.

For instance, most firms distribute newsletters, an untapped resource for your suppliers and vendors. Some professional firms charge for their newsletters, under the theory that things people get for free are not valued. If a firm charges for its newsletters, maybe it would contain something of actual value, rather than canned recitations of recently passed legislation that no one wants to read in the first place. If a firm's newsletter is truly valuable, then suppliers and vendors would gladly pay for advertising space to offer their products and services. Most view this as unprofessional. However, the true test is what customers are willing and able to pay for, and in the firms that offer this type of newsletter, the customers appreciate it. Further, your business customers will appreciate the opportunity to advertise their products and services to your excellent customer base, just as you appreciate the referrals they send you.

Rather than pay airports for landing slots, European low-cost airline Ryanair actually receives payments from them by guaranteeing a minimum number of passenger traffic for airport shops and services, converting a vendor into a revenue source. Hewlett Packard relies on UPS to repair its printers. Minnesota-based Fender guitars are tuned in Holland by UPS, saving up to eight days of shipping delay while cutting costs.

SHAREHOLDERS AND OTHER EXTERNAL STAKEHOLDERS

Obviously, a company owes a fiduciary responsibility to its owners and other stakeholders who have an interest in its longevity, such as bankers, landlords, and other parties to whom it has made commitments. The communities in which the company is located also have a stake in its success. I am not arguing that these external stakeholders should have a say in the leadership of the business, only that they have an ancillary interest in a thriving business community. Because a company directly impacts the success of multiple businesses in the community, its sphere of influence is quite large.

That said, this is not an argument for so-called corporate social responsibility (CSR). Businesses are too often praised for what they do worst—social work, fighting inflation, reducing welfare roles, or making charitable contributions—and denounced for what they do best—creating jobs and wealth, and producing goods and services people desire. Milton Friedman's famous 1970 article, "The Social Responsibility of Business Is to Increase Its Profits," essentially argues that businesses should pursue profits justly and within the bounds of the law and norms of society. Friedman makes this argument because management personnel are acting as agents for the principals—that is, the shareholders of the company. For the agents to spend money and resources for "social" purposes denies the profits to the shareholders, who would then be free to donate and spend the proceeds as they see fit. Another argument, often ignored by Friedman's critics, is that a business does not have particular expertise—or a comparative advantage—in performing social work, but does have expertise and knowledge about producing, say, automobiles or copiers.

JOINT VENTURE PARTNERS AND ALLIANCES

No one company can do it all. Thus, joint ventures and alliances with other companies—some even competitors—are more and more common. Observe the airlines' use of alliances, such as United Airline's Star Alliance program, whereby it shares flights, gates, pricing, frequent-flyer miles, and other infrastructure with specific partners. From a historical perspective, accounting firms were the leaders of the alliance movement, since professional regulations in most countries required partnerships to be national (i.e., owned by a citizen of that country). As a result, the major accounting firms, in response to the needs of their global customers who required quality and consistency in the level of service, globalized through forming alliances.

Cyrus Freidheim, a consultant with Booz-Allen and author of *The Trillion-Dollar Enterprise: How the Alliance Revolution Will Transform Global Business*, succinctly states why alliances have the potential to leverage intellectual capital successfully:

> Alliances can be a profitable way to expand a business. In an acquisition or merger, the partners take all—the good and the bad, the pretty and the ugly, businesses that fit and the baggage, the profitable and the unprofitable, the core capability, and the unwanted branch in Somalia. Any problems, liabilities, warts, and unfinished business of the acquired company are yours, for better or for worse, from this day forward.
>
> In an alliance, you can carve out the piece you like. You can take the prime cuts of meat and leave the liver and the hooves behind. Alliances are about combining capabilities of two or more partners. We take advantage of your strength in the market and my technology, or your cost position and my distribution. We do as Pepsi and Lipton did with iced tea—Pepsi's distribution and Lipton's product (Freidheim 1998: 42).

Wal-Mart uses this strategy by renting out space in its stores to McDonald's. Not only does this reduce its internal cost of running snack counters, it obtains a continuous cash flow; and the higher McDonald's sales rise, the higher revenue per square foot is achieved in each store. It also increases store traffic and no doubt brought in some customers who would not have otherwise entered. Not only is this an effective leverage of Wal-Mart's tangible capital (its physical buildings), it also promoted an alliance that enhanced its social capital.

Charles Schwab also leveraged its social capital by creating an alliance with more than 5,000 independent financial advisers in a network it calls Schwab Institutional. Schwab was originally built around a do-it-yourself investment strategy until it learned in the 1980s, through market research, that a large percentage of investors wanted advice in managing their financial affairs. Leveraging its structural capital enabled it to increase its social capital by providing a full-service, turnkey system to independent advisers.

INDUSTRY ASSOCIATIONS AND FORMAL AFFILIATIONS

Capitalism might be based on ferocious competition, but that does not mean there are not many ways in which competitors can cooperate with one another. Obviously, there are thousands of industry associations, alliances, and affiliations all promoting and lobbying for their industry's special interests. This is the "art of association" that French observer of America Alexis de Tocqueville observed during his journey through America during the 1830s. By finding common points of interest, competitors can work together to advance their industry's wealth-creating ability. No better example of this exists than from my own backyard, the wine country in Napa County, also annulling the absurd analogy that business is about war. Jeffrey Pfeffer and Robert Sutton, both professors at Stanford University, explain:

> Following the business as war analogy can be similarly mislead-ing. The analogy implies that you would always aim to hobble and destroy competitors and avoid cooperating with other firms in your industry. If such logic had been followed, however, the Napa Valley might never have become such a prestigious winegrow-ing region. When Robert Mondavi started his winery in 1966, he worked to enhance the reputation and quality of *every* Napa win-ery, not just his own. Such cooperation set the stage for the famous "Judgment in Paris" in 1976, where prestigious French wine critics consistently mistook the California wines for French and ranked the California wines higher. Although no Mondavi wines were tasted, California winemakers from Chateau Montelena (the top white) and Stag's Leap (the top red) were quick to thank Mondavi for helping them succeed. Indeed, both winners—Mike Grgich and Warren Winiarski—had worked for Mondavi before leaving with his blessing to start their own wineries. Mondavi's generos-ity paid off: he and his company profited when the prices of *all* Napa wines skyrocketed after the 1976 "judgment." Yet if you

read a Harvard case by strategy researcher Michael Porter about Robert Mondavi Winery, it only considers how Mondavi competes with other California winemakers like Kendall-Jackson and Gallo. Apparently, Porter's narrow focus on the useful but incomplete "competitive strategy" analogy led him to avoid noticing (or mentioning) the cooperation that benefited Mondavi's company as he enjoyed the reputational spillover from the Napa Valley's growing prestige (Pfeffer and Sutton 2006: 35–36).

ALUMNI

In a knowledge economy, where the human capital investors own the means of a firm's production, it is simply not possible to retain them for life. But even when a knowledge worker no longer works *for* you, she can certainly still work *with* you. Professional knowledge firms have actually long understood that an ex–team member is a valuable future customer. "The goal is not to retain employees," says Cindy Lewiton Jackson, director of global career development and alumni relations for Bain & Company, a pioneer of the concept of Alumni networks, "the goal is to build lifelong affiliation." Katie Weiser, global director of alumni relations at Deloitte Consulting, adds, "Our people will be movers and shakers wherever they land next. We're planting seeds for the future" (Canabou 2002: 28).

Former team members can offer benefits to companies in many ways, as pointed out by Cem Sertoglu and Anne Berkowitch in *Harvard Business Review*:

> *Rehires and Referral Sources.* Companies used to go out of their way to avoid recruiting ex-employees. But that was always short-sighted. The facts are, it costs half as much to rehire an ex-employee as it does to hire a brand new person; rehires are 40 percent more productive in their first quarter at work; and they tend to stay in the job longer. . . . Perhaps even more important, alumni are known quantities; the risk of a costly mishire is almost completely eliminated. Alumni are also a growing source of referrals. Some companies even offer alumni compensation for referrals who are hired.

Suppliers of Intellectual Capital. Former employees can be great sources of ideas and intelligence, helping their old companies to stay abreast of new trends, technologies, and even investment opportunities. ... One major financial services company hires alumni as temporary workers during periods of high demand, and another company taps into the expertise of former employees as market research sources.

Ambassadors, Marketers, and Lobbyists. Former employees are just as likely to influence outside opinions about an organization as current employees—especially if they haven't been gone from the organization for very long. So building and maintaining goodwill with alumni can fortify the company's reputation, brand, and influence. ... [Some] companies are starting to use their alumni networks as low-cost test beds for new products and marketing campaigns (Sertoglu and Berkowitch 2002: 20–21).

Establishing and maintaining an alumni network is more than just sending out an occasional directory and setting up a Web site with potential job postings. It should contain its own value proposition and give alumni a reason to stay in it, such as sharing of intellectual capital, educational programs, invitations to firm events, and special gatherings.

UNIONS

As the economy began to shift to a knowledge economy, labor unions began a long systemic decline in relevance and membership. Today, only 12.5 percent of the total workforce belongs to a union, while a meager 7.8 percent of the private sector, down from one-third in the 1960s. Even as of 1900, only 3 percent of workers were members of unions. The only area where union membership is growing is in government employment, since the employer is technically not spending its own money—but rather the taxpayers'—providing little incentive to resist the demands of the public sector unions.

Despite their positive perception, labor unions have always suffered from inherent flaws, which the knowledge economy has brought to the forefront. One of the flaws is that they treat jobs as *ends*, meant to provide a "living wage" rather than as *means* to add value to the lives of others. An economy, or a company, does not exist to provide jobs, or lifetime employment, but to create wealth outside of itself. The old Soviet Union used to boast that it did not have unemployment, which was true in one sense. It had a lot of make-work jobs, underutilizing the talents and creativity of its human capital—except, perhaps, in the defense sector. But as we have seen, this is not the path to wealth creation.

Another inherent contradiction is the notion that the union is somehow in conflict with the employer, which is economically absurd. Unions are *sellers* of labor, while employers are *buyers*. Sellers and buyers do not compete with one another. Sellers compete with other sellers. Hence, the real tension in the labor market is not between the union and the employer—their economic interests are aligned—but between union workers and other workers, their real competition. In contrast to the popular perception, labor unions do not raise the wages of workers. Only increasing wealth can achieve that objective, a topic unions rarely speak to, let alone concern themselves with. Instead, unions raise the wages of *unionized* workers, at the expense of nonunionized workers.

The biggest weakness, though, of labor unions is their uninspiring purpose. As the developing nations have become wealthier, unions seem to be drifting into the future, clinging to an Industrial Revolution model that is dying while ignoring the realities of an IC economy. An uninspiring purpose can dissipate any organization, from a profit-seeking company to a not-for-profit organization. A company that exists solely to turn a profit is not the type of organization that inspires a high level of dedication and creativity, especially from knowledge workers. Likewise, a union whose only mission is to increase its wages will suffer the same apathy over time. C. Northcote Parkinson—author of the famous *Parkinson's Law*—diagnosed this feckless condition of labor unions 40 years ago, when he wrote *Left Luggage: A Caustic History of British Socialism from Marx to Wilson*, observing:

The weakness in Trade Union policy lay from the outset in its lack of idealism. The union leaders did not point the way to any ideal form of society. They merely wanted to see wage levels raised to the highest point which the employers could afford. This sort of demand was natural enough but it had no moral basis. It gave the worker no right to point the finger of scorn at the capitalist, whose motives were no more material and whose methods were broadly the same. To sell what you have to offer, whether goods or services, at the highest possible price is no crime against humanity—that being, within limits, what we all do. But our efforts to this end cannot be made to look particularly progressive or noble. There are sound reasons for selling anything at the maximum price, any other policy being foolish and often corrupt, but this practice can scarcely be raised to the ethical level of the Lord's Prayer. It is not even a principle for which many of us would be prepared to die in battle. Morally considered, it stands on a par with the buyer's urge to buy at the lowest possible price (Parkinson 1967: 20).

Labor unions spend far too much time attempting to solve problems rather than pursue opportunities, a mind-set that also afflicts many businesses, as we discuss in Chapter 14. It is not a prescription for success, as can be witnessed with the entitlement mentality of the European Union workforce, who believe wholeheartedly that the world owes them lifelong employment at a decent wage. Unions should focus more on keeping their members *employable*, rather than simply employed. One way to achieve this would be for them to invest in lifelong learning, another to reorganize themselves into a just-in-time labor force that constantly searches for ways to add value. In a knowledge economy, unions will become more and more insignificant and marginalized. They are an idea from the day before yesterday.

CORPORATE UNIVERSITIES

... [T]hat is what learning is. You suddenly understand something you've understood all your life, but in a new way.

—Doris Lessing, English writer

In 1955, after the opening of Disneyland, Walt Disney established Disney University, the purpose of which was to train Disneyland's then-600 cast members (Disney parlance for employees) "to be aware that they're there mainly to help the guest" (Disney parlance for customer). This education continues to this day, with all new Disney cast members required to attend a one-and-a-half day Traditions course. The wording is very precise They are not "orienting" their cast members, but rather passing down traditions.

Many companies have recognized they possess an enormous amount of intellectual capital used internally to educate their team members, so why not leverage this IC to the outside world and create a university? From universities at Motorola and Nordstrom to the Ritz Carlton Leadership Center and General Electric's Leadership Development Training, all these companies have found that offering educational opportunities to firm customers, referral sources, alliance partners, and so forth, is an excellent way to further broaden its sphere of influence. Other firms have established research institutes to provide leading edge thinking in a variety of areas. Further, as Peter Drucker pointed out, continuing education will be one of the largest growth industries in this century, as it is increasingly difficult for any knowledge worker to stay abreast of current developments in his field of specialty.

The growth of corporate universities, in fact, has been quite dramatic. In the mid-1980s, approximately 400 corporate universities were in existence, growing to 800 in 1995, 1,200 in 1997, 1,600 in 1999 to over 2,000 as of 2001, an increase of roughly 400 every two years (Allen 2002: 251).

Many of these universities exist to provide more than merely technical skills and training. Recognizing the importance of education in the traditional sense, they are challenging conventional wisdom, theories, and assumptions to search for more innovative ways to add wealth to the world. Mark Allen, PhD, and author of *The Corporate University Handbook*, provides this definition of the corporate university:

> A corporate university is an educational entity that is a strategic tool designed to assist its parent organization in achieving its mission by conducting activities that cultivate individual and organizational learning, knowledge, and wisdom (Allen 2002: 9).

There is an enormous difference between training and education, as discussed in Chapters 6 and 11. Especially in a knowledge organization, the goal should be to link learning to the firm's strategy. The goal is not necessarily just to transfer know-how, but how to think, and ultimately, to change the culture of the parent organization. Matthew May was involved with the founding of the University of Toyota, the purpose of which was "to continuously improve associate and dealer performance through lifelong learning" (Allen 2002: 15). He explains the assignment, along with the concept of learnership, in his book on Toyota, *The Elegant Solution*:

> It started with a ridiculous assignment: We need to translate the Toyota Production System for the knowledge worker. We really want to figure out how to bring the levels of employee productivity, engagement, continuous improvement and constant creativity found in our Toyota factories and warehouses to the corporate environment (May 2007: xii).
>
> Toyota is the ultimate learning organization....Sure, they have the explicit mechanisms like a corporate university, technical training centers, and knowledge management systems. Most big firms do.
>
> But that's not it. There's something much more subtle, much more tacit. Mastery—*perpetual learning*—is so ingrained in the organization that it's been declared by many to be part of the Toyota DNA. And what makes learning at Toyota so different is that the concept revolves around pursuing the right questions rather than securing the right answers. What drives learning at Toyota isn't a need to know. It's a need to inquire. To *understand*. That's a fundamental departure from how most define learning. Toyota doesn't confuse training with learning. And the most fascinating thing is that humility is at the base of it all. Toyota most respects wisdom and insight. They're in awe of it.

> What they teach isn't a hard skill. It's the softest skill known: *thinking*. ... because learnership truly represents the keys to the kingdom (May 2007: 72).

Universities that follow this philosophy usually report to the CEO, not the human resources (HR) department, since the ultimate goal is to shape the culture and strategy of the company. Corporate universities will play an increasing role in the knowledge economy, where the line of demarcation between learning, thinking, and doing is continuously intertwined. Inspired by the founding of Disney University, Pixar (now owned by Disney) established Pixar University, headed by dean Randy Nelson. Here's how he explains the university's purpose:

> We've made the leap from an idea-centered business to a people-centered business. Instead of developing ideas, we develop people. Instead of investing in ideas, we invest in people. We're trying to create a culture of learning, filled with lifelong learners. It's no trick for talented people to be interesting, but it's a gift to be interested. We want an organization filled with interested people (Taylor and LaBarre 2006: 230).

Pixar encourages *every* team member to devote up to four hours per week to their education. Nelson says, "Why teach drawing to accountants? Because drawing class doesn't just teach people to draw. It teaches them to be more observant. There's no company on earth that wouldn't benefit from having people become more observant" (Taylor and LaBarre 2006: 233). Nelson also understands the difference between knowledge workers and manual workers, where the Taylorite notions of "productivity" are irrelevant. As reported in *Mavericks at Work*, Nelson expresses a sentiment found throughout this book, which could be said about many professional knowledge firms that continue to confuse being busy with adding value:

> Randy Nelson is a fierce critic of Pixar's neighbors in the video game business, who, he says, "are eating their young by working nonstop. They finish one project and immediately start on another.

It's no surprise their products all look the same." Pixar's technical employees, in contrast, get paid for a 50-hour week with the expectation that they will work between 40 and 50 hours. What's more, workers planning to spend more than 50 hours a week on the job must get permission from their manager. Needless to say, at plenty of points along the four-year life of a movie, plenty of people ask for and receive permission to work beyond the weekly limit (Taylor and LaBarre 2006: 234).

Paul O'Byrne, whom we met in Chapter 12 where he discussed his KnowledgeBank and use of AARs to leverage his firm's structural capital, has also launched a university to expand this intellectual capital to a wider audience. Paul explains how this has helped enhance the value his firm is able to generate within a wider business community:

> For many years in our firm we had a concept that our customers wanted to learn more about business in general, not just their business in particular. The name of the town we are in is Goffs Oak (Hertfordshire, just to the north of London). We came up with the name of Goffs Oak Business School because we liked the acronym GOBS. As is so often the case with our innovations, it starts a little tongue-in-cheek. Partly this makes it seem non-threatening, an amusing diversion; looking sideways at things and the humor in things also inspires a lot of creativity, which also makes us pursue it more often.
>
> We recognized that many of our customers were running highly successful businesses but they did not have any formal business qualifications—indeed, some of our most successful customers had no formal credentials at all. Over the years, some customers had asked us to investigate courses they could take to enhance their skills. We examined these programs, many of which were distance or evening learning programs specifically designed for executives. However, as we looked at the typical MBA syllabus, we realized there was a vast amount of content that would just not be relevant to many of our customers. Increasingly, it dawned on us that because of the type of work we had done with our customers over the years, we knew significant amounts of knowledge we could happily teach them. As we listed these topics, and then thought of

others that perhaps a well-rounded owner-manager should know, we developed the syllabus for the GOBS MBA.

As with any other product, this needed to be packaged, marketed, and sold, and we set about talking to some of our more ambitious customers and worked with them as to what they would need to know before they committed to come to such a program, and what they would like to see in it. In November 2002 we got seven brave souls to sign up to a series of 10 monthly sessions, two hours each. Admittedly, we did not have all the sessions mapped out or even half of them, but we knew we had to teach them about finance (not just accounting), marketing, law, intellectual capital, and probably some other things.

And off we went, preparing furiously how to explain what we understand with our knowledge of accounting and finance, what we thought business owner-managers should know about law and marketing, strategy, communication and thinking skills. To break things up, we went on "field trips" where we all traveled to see another company and how it functioned in a given area. We ran it through the calendar year so the last session was in December and we had a graduation ceremony at lunch and a very happy and memorable ending, encapsulated by many photos.

The advantages flowing from meeting with your better customers monthly and having them meet each other were not all serendipitous. We expected they would enjoy meeting like-minded entrepreneurs in a non-work environment, and we expected they would like learning. However, the reinforcement of us as experts and the inevitable "... while I'm here could I have a quick word with you?" led to a deepening of the relationship, and more work of the type we sought. And of course there was pride and morale throughout the team of creating and having a tangible emblem of being both a teaching and learning organization.

Before we ended the first one, we started marketing for the class of 2004, asking one of the more lively attendees from the class of 2003 to address some prospects and persuade them of the value of the program. Now, the class of 2007 is well underway, only this time *none* of them are customers of the firm; they were simply attracted to the content. Of course we are meeting with these very open-minded, willing-to-invest, owner-managers every month and giving them knowledge that their existing accountants and business advisors have never even considered. Who knows where that may lead?

Maybe the best example of this philosophy is encapsulated by Infosys Technologies, "founded in July 1981 by seven people who shared the dream of building India's first company *of the professional, by the professional, and for the professional.*" Infosys was the first "Indian company to establish a formalized leadership institute,..." based on the belief that "the company is the campus, the business is the curriculum, and the leaders shall teach" (Gandossy et al. 2006: 164, 168).

An example of a research institute is the McKinsey Global Institute (MGI), which exists to cogitate over questions that reach far beyond whether any company will buy into a McKinsey proposal for consulting services. McKinsey associates—usually its best thinkers—serve one-year fellowships at the Institute, and are measuring world economics from the broadest perspective they can create. Here is how James O'Shea and Charles Madigan describe MGI, in their book *Dangerous Company: Management Consultants and the Businesses They Save and Ruin:*

> If one thinks of McKinsey as its own kind of nation, then this is its intelligence agency, a well-funded think tank that studies world economics in depth, then issues reports available to anyone who wants them. They are free of charge, but worth their weight in whatever currency you want to spend. They buy goodwill and page after page of publicity for McKinsey and help create the consulting relationships that will carry The Firm well into the twenty-first century.
>
> All the big consulting companies have think tanks that grind out reports. [Led by the collapse of the Soviet Union, and the move towards free markets and privatization] what we realized as a firm is that we were either going to have to invest to get better informed and to understand better what was happening in the world's economy and the global economy and really help our CEOs, or we were going to have to get out.

The Firm had two options: It had to buy into the study of economics in a big way, or it had to leave the field to the collection of academics and macroeconomists who were already talking to the business leaders of Europe. Ultimately what that meant is that it would have to abandon the potentially profitable path of consulting on economics and just stick to business.

Some of the partners were confused. *Why should McKinsey spend to create something new when it was already doing very well?* The answer rests partly in The Firm's inherent sense of curiosity about how the world operates, since it now operates on the same level. The unspoken answer, speculation invites, is that The Firm did not at all like the feel of being bested by a collection of economists and academics.

Why do anything different? That is always a challenge for successful organizations. Of course, what we tell our clients is that that is just the time when you invest and do something different to maintain that success. In a narrow sense, we were taking some of our own medicine.

And so the MGI was born and now runs on one tenth of 1 percent of McKinsey's revenues. It is deeper than the CIA in the sense that it can call on McKinsey partners everywhere in the world for their special expertise. It is aimed at making certain McKinsey never again faces questions about the global economy from savvy CEOs for which it has no answers. On the surface, it might seem like an academic exercise. But if it follows the course of [The Firm], undoubtedly it will become a magnet, not only for clients eager to take advantage of McKinsey's special expertise, but also for the consultants of the twenty-first century who will want to make their start, and perhaps their careers, at a company that presents truly global opportunities (O'Shea and Madigan 1997: 288–289).

Recognizing no matter how exceptional all of the previous elements of social capital discussed above are, even the best organization does not have a monopoly on IC within its walls. By connecting with others, companies can expand enormously the amount of IC they have access to that can be leveraged to create wealth. The open source movement embodies this concept like no other.

OPEN SOURCE—MASS COLLABORATION

None of us are as smart as all of us.

—Japanese proverb

Recall from Chapter 10 Sun Microsystems' chief scientist Bill Joy's law: "Most of the smartest people are never in your own company." Nowhere is that more true than in the music industry. During 1999, an 18-year-old Northeastern University student was bored with his classes and listening to his roommate complaining about how difficult it was to download music from the Internet. Seeking an opportunity, Shawn Fanning founded Napster. In the first three months of 2001, 2.5 billion files a month were being downloaded, validating the economist's theory of demand, which states that the lower the price, the larger the quantity demanded, especially a zero price. Naturally, the music industry litigated Napster out of business, claiming everyone who downloaded music from it was no different than a common criminal. Of course, viewed from another angle, when you have millions of potential customers breaking the law, you do not have a crime wave, you have a *marketing* problem.

The point is not to argue the highly contentious legal issues of copyright and private property law, particularly as it relates to digitally downloaded music files. The more precise point is the lack of understanding of value by the music company executives. By keeping their focus on the inside of their companies, they completely ignored the external value potential of easily obtaining music files. It took Steve Jobs of Apple to capitalize on this opportunity with iTunes—which at the time of this writing has a 70 percent market share on the legal downloadable music market—in an eerily analogous manner in which he capitalized on the personal computer opportunity invented at Xerox's Palo Alto Research Center, validating Mark Twain's line, "History doesn't repeat itself—but it does rhyme." Had the music company executives been focused on the outside of their companies—studying, analyzing, and innovating what their customers found valuable—they could have invested many millions into productive research and development rather than throwing away that sum down the judicial sinkhole. Yet the Napster saga is just one in a long history of revolutions taking place outside the confines of an existing industry, in what the Austrian economist Joseph Schumpeter labeled "creative destruction." The reason entire industries can be brought down is because competitors offer more value to the customer than the status quo.

Linus Torvalds, the Finnish graduate student who invented the Linux operating system, did not utilize a formal corporate structure, or third-party financial capital, to coordinate the most collaborative project in history. Much has been written about how the open source movement is a dagger in the heart of intellectual property rights, will squelch innovation, lead to anarchy, among much other hyperbolic pronouncements. Richard Stallman, the leader of the Free Software Foundation, innovated the idea of a general public license (GPL), which places a program into the public domain. He calls it "copyleft" because it does the opposite of copyright. Anyone can use the program, but if they make any modifications or improvements, they must share them with the rest of the users. Saying open source does not imply that it is "free." Many companies have created vast amounts of wealth selling and customizing the Linux operating system, so it should not be confused with being "free." Torvalds believes whether or not an innovation should be subject to a "copyleft" or the traditional copyright is the "abortion issue of technology. It should be up to the individual innovator to decide for herself or himself whether to GPL the project or to use a more conventional approach to copyright" (Torvalds and Diamond 2001: 195). As a firm believer in the "spontaneous order" of the free market, I agree with this position. Google, Amazon, and salesforce.com are all built upon the foundation of Linux, but each is proprietary, since the GPL applies only to software distribution, not Web-based applications. The marketplace is certainly big enough for different types of operating systems, and unfettered competition is the best way to produce the most innovations, despite Bill Gates's and Microsoft's pronouncements to the contrary.

Torvalds logically understood that with a million eyeballs on his project, all software bugs would disappear. He posted his project on a listserve because he wanted feedback and praise, not to mention the chance to work with the best programmers in the world. Following Bill Joy's Law cited above, Torvalds instinctively knows that the best programmers do not work in any one company. The *Not Invented Here* syndrome is alive and well, Torvalds writes, because "open source ... is unforgiving. It shows who can get the job done, who is better. You can't hide behind managers. Open source is the best way of leveraging outside talent" (Torvalds and Diamond 2001: 232). So why would people contribute to a project such as Linux or Firefox, the latter another open source Web browser developed by some 800 volunteers from Google and Sun Microsystems, which has gained approximately 10 percent of the browser market? There are many other motivations beyond money: recognition, respect, reciprocity, ego, esteem of others, and jobs (since employers do spot talent by searching the programming code).

The success of Linux not only demonstrates that no man is an island, it also shows that no man works alone. Peter Drucker summarized concisely how this type of mass collaboration will change the shape of organizations in the future: "The corporation will survive—but not as we know it. Organizations are critically important as organizers, not as employers" (Edersheim 2007: 155). Procter & Gamble (P&G) has taken this very principle into what it calls "Connect + Develop" to describe how it will innovate new products in the future, as contrasted with the historical research and development. This is not merely an experiment, it is embedded in the company's strategy. P&G's CEO, A. G. Lafley, explained it this way:

Historically, over 90 percent of our innovations have come from inside our own organization. I want to see 50 percent or more coming from external partnerships. I honestly believe we can increase our innovative capacity fivefold by collaborating more effectively with external partners. I want to create an environment in which there is an open market for ideas, for capital, and for talent. More specifically, an environment in which big ideas can attract the capital and talent they need on the strength of the idea itself no matter where it comes from (Harrison and Sullivan, 2006: 123).

New products such as Mr. Clean Magic Eraser, the Crest Spin-Brush, and Swiffer Dusters have been built on ideas outside of P&G labs. Lafley is well on his way to achieving his 50 percent goal, now that P&G gets approximately 35 percent of new innovations from this strategy. Jeff Weedman, vice president of external business development for P&G, says: "At P&G we have moved from *Not Invented Here* to *Proudly Found Elsewhere*" (Harrison and Sullivan, 2006: 48). Consider some other examples of how mass collaboration is changing the nature of work, innovation, and wealth creation:

Innocentive (www.innocentive.com). Created by Eli Lilly, Innocentive is an online scientific forum of some 90,000 registered scientists located in 175 countries. If a scientist solves a particular problem, he or she is paid up to $100,000. Eli Lilly posts up to 100 problems a week and has attained a 4 percent solution rate, which is relatively high for R&D problem solving. P&G, Dow Chemical, DuPont, NestlePurina, and Boeing, among others, have all used Innocentive as a way to expand the brains of their internal R&D departments and leverage the social capital that exists outside of their walls.

NineSigma (www.ninesigma.net). According to its Web site, "NineSigma was founded in 2000 by Dr. Mehran Mehregany, Goodrich Professor of Engineering Innovation, Case Western Reserve University. The company's core mission is to work on behalf of our clients to source innovative ideas, technologies, products and services from outside their organization quickly and effectively by connecting them with the best innovators from around the world" (http://www.ninesigma.net/about-us, accessed April 4, 2007). Where Innocentive acts as a spot market for ideas and solutions, since the scientists never know the identity of the company that has posed the challenge, NineSigma, acts as a broker between the scientist and the company, taking a percentage of the contract that is entered into between the two parties.

Myelin Repair Foundation (www.myelinrepair.org). Scott Johnson was diagnosed with multiple sclerosis (MS) in 1976, and after 30 years scientists are no closer to finding a possible cure. Johnson believes it is because the academic model is serving the wrong customer, progress being measured by papers published and grants received rather than bettering the quality of life for the patient—a classic example of measuring inputs and ignoring results. Here is how the company describes its Accelerated Research Collaboration model:

The Myelin Repair Foundation (MRF) is a non-profit medical research foundation dedicated to accelerating basic medical research into myelin repair treatments that will dramatically improve the lives of people suffering from multiple sclerosis (MS).

To achieve this goal, MRF has developed a unique business/science hybrid model for medical research that is speeding the time to drug discovery by as much as 200%. This new research model, called the Accelerated Research Collaboration (ARC) model, is based on three key elements:

Collaboration: Bringing the best researchers together MRF has brought together five of the world's leading neuroscientists approaching the study of myelin from five different perspectives— immunology, genetics, developmental biology, molecular biology and proteomics—in an outcome-driven research plan.

Acceleration: Speeding up the research process. Since beginning its research program in 2004, the MRF scientific team has identified more than a dozen new myelin repair drug targets and 10 new research tools/assays that may be applied to all neurological disease research. MRF has filed for eight patents on these discoveries. When compared to the world's greatest research universities, the MRF scientific team has had five times as many invention disclosures and more than three times as many patent applications per million dollars in research expenditures.

Results: Driving discoveries into the drug pipeline. MRF has an aggressive intellectual property (IP) protection program that enables the organization to more effectively engage with pharmaceutical companies and to license discoveries for further drug development and clinical trials. Licensing revenues will be invested in ongoing research programs.

Revolutionizing All Medical Research

MRF's ARC model has the potential to speed all medical research, bringing treatments to those who suffer from other chronic or debilitating diseases for which there are no effective treatments or cures (http://www.myelinrepair.org/about/, accessed April 4, 2007).

Wikipedia (www.wikipedia.org). Founded in 2001, the online encyclopedia now has over 1.7 million articles in English, roughly 12 times the size of the print version of the Encyclopedia Britannica. There are over 75,000 active contributors in more than 100 languages. The word *wiki* is Hawaiian for "quick," but Wikipedia contributors view it as meaning "what I know is..." Sure, there are bound to be errors in some of the entries, but with so many eyes checking them, the chances of them not being corrected is slim.

The Goldcorp Challenge. Inspired by Linux and the open source software movement, former chairman and CEO of Goldcorp, Inc., Rob McEwen, decided to try something radical. He made available on the Internet full data on one of his mines in the Red Lake district of northwest Ontario, Canada. He invited geologists and engineers from all over the world to analyze the data and submit innovative drilling plans to extract the precious metal, offering a prize of \$500,000, divided by 25 semifinalists and 3 finalists selected by a panel of judges. The rest of the industry thought he had lost his mind, but McEwen understood that smart people did not have to work *for* his company to work *with* it. Here is a leader who understands how to leverage social capital, in his own words:

> Gold mining is an old industry, a tired industry. The pace of change is glacial. Traditionally, mining companies have worried about how strong your back is, not how big your brain is. We wanted to do something that no one in the industry had done, to tap into the intellectual capital of the whole world (Taylor and LaBarre 2006: 63).

Over 1,400 participated in the challenge, whereas 140 submitted detailed drilling plans, with over half the targets being new discoveries for Goldcorp.

Scientists are far more effective when they collaborate with other scientists rather than working in isolation, even as they pursue their own individual projects. Since real science progresses by dissent, not consensus, this collaboration is essential to advancing knowledge. Michael Polanyi, the scientific philosopher who delineated tacit from explicit knowledge, who we met in Chapter 9, described this coordination and collaboration by mutual adjustment of independent initiatives as a "Republic of Science." He offers this metaphor of solving a puzzle:

> Imagine that we are given the pieces of a very large jigsaw puzzle, and suppose that for some reason it is important that our giant puzzle be put together in the shortest possible time. We would naturally try to speed this up by engaging a number of helpers; the question is in what manner these could be best employed. The only way the assistants can effectively co-operate, and surpass by far what any single one of them could do, is to let them work on putting the puzzle together in sight of the others so that every time a piece of it is fitted in by one helper, all the others will immediately watch out for the next step that becomes possible in consequence. Under this system, each helper will act on his own initiative, by responding to the latest achievements of the others, and the completion of their joint task will be greatly accelerated.

> We have here in a nutshell the way in which a series of independent initiatives are organized to a joint achievement by mutually adjusting themselves at every successive stage to the situation created by all the others who are acting likewise (Polanyi 1974: 50–51).

As all of the examples in this section reveal, we are just beginning to tap into the power of leveraging social capital. While politicians and pundits can ponder the effects of outsourcing, leaders should focus on the limitless opportunities represented by *insourcing* ideas from outside their company's walls. To forego these opportunities because of the *Not Invented Here* syndrome is to abdicate the fundamental responsibility of an enterprise to create wealth for society while allocating intellectual capital and resources to their highest valued use. Of course, all of this social capital rests on the cultural, moral, and ethical capital of a society, which we explore next.

CULTURAL, MORAL, AND ETHICAL CAPITAL

I have spent my whole life under a Communist regime, and I will tell you that a society without any objective scale is a terrible one indeed. But a society with no other scale than the legal one is not quite worthy of man, either.

—*Alexander Solzhenitsyn, commencement address, Harvard University, 1978*

A people's manners and morals are more important than the law, and beyond doubt these are what constitute the culture of a society, or an organization. The University of Pennsylvania's motto is: *Leges sine moribus vanae*, "Laws apart from moral habits are empty." Certainly, no one would deliver a eulogy praising a person for avoiding criminal misconduct and honoring contracts. Greek statesman Plenides said "to live a moral life, you must do more than required, and less than allowed." Simply because a particular law is voted for does not make it moral, as Apartheid, the Fugitive Slave Act of 1850, and the election of Hitler prove.

It is common today to speak of "medical ethics," "bioethics," "accounting ethics," and so forth. Yet many philosophers deny there are different ethical consequences for these various disciplines. In his 1981 article in *The Public Interest*, "What Is Business Ethics?" Peter Drucker challenges the concept of a separate ethics for business:

> If "business ethics" continues to be "casuistry" its speedy demise in a cloud of illegitimacy can be confidently predicted. Clearly this is the approach "business ethics" today is taking. Its very origin is politics rather than in ethics. It expresses a belief that the responsibility which business and the business executive have, precisely because they have social impact, must determine ethics—and this is a political rather than an ethical imperative.
>
> What difference does it make if a certain act or behavior takes place in a "business," in a "non-profit organization," or outside any organization at all? The answer is clear: None at all.
>
> Clearly, one major element of the peculiar stew that goes by the name of "business ethics" is plain old-fashioned hostility to business and to economic activity altogether—one of the oldest of American traditions and perhaps the only still-potent ingredient in the Puritan heritage. There is no warrant in any ethics to consider one major sphere of activity as having its own ethical problems, let alone its own "ethics." "Business" or "economic activity" may have special political or legal dimensions as in "business and government". . ., or as in the antitrust laws. And "business ethics" may be good for politics and good electioneering. But that is all. For ethics deals with the right actions of individuals. And then it surely makes no difference whether the setting is a community hospital, with the actors a nursing supervisor and the "consumer" a patient, or whether the setting is National Universal General Corporation, the actors a quality control manager, and the consumer the buyer of a bicycle.
>
> Altogether, "business ethics" might well be called "ethical chic" rather than ethics—and indeed might be considered more a media event than philosophy or morals (Drucker 1981: 22–23, 31, 33–35).

The Josephson Institute of Ethics provides a useful definition of ethics:

Ethics is about how we meet the challenge of doing the right thing when that will cost more than we want to pay. There are two aspects to ethics: The first involves the ability to discern right from wrong, good from evil, and propriety from impropriety. The second involves the commitment to do what is right, good and proper. Ethics entails action; it is not just a topic to mull or debate (Maxwell 2003: 23–24).

Honesty and ethical standards do not always pay off, at least in the short run. The costs can be high to do the right thing, but these costs are worth paying. For a company, reputation is a priceless asset, and the loss of that reputation is the single biggest risk a company faces. Consider the Johnson and Johnson Credo, which the company turned to during the two Tylenol poisonings in 1982 and 1986, which had a cumulative effect of $140 million in write-offs (http://www.jnj.com/our_company/our_credo/index. htm;jsessionid=RQUXI1QGKCCKQCQPCCGSU0A). Founder R.W. Johnson wrote this Credo in 1943 and it has often been cited as a precedent for ethical decisions made since then. The Ten Commandments are not the *The Ten Suggestions*, and J&J's Credo is carved in stone at the company's New Brunswick, New Jersey, headquarters, reminding everyone that ethical principles are timeless.

Dr. Samuel Johnson wrote, "There are few ways in which man can be more innocently employed than in getting money," and John Maynard Keynes agreed, stating, "It is better that a man should tyrannize over his bank balance than over his fellow citizens." No doubt businesses act in a social context, as do all individuals, and should be held accountable for doing the right thing for the right reasons. None of this is inconsistent with the pursuit of profit and meeting human needs and wants. Parents do not raise their children to become rugged individualists, and no company was built by the efforts of a single human being. Ethical conduct, integrity, trust, and honesty are not just moral principles, they are also major economic factors, a vital component in any organization's social capital, and one all businesses should be judged against and held accountable for. We would have no need to study ethics if we were like Robinson Crusoe, living on a deserted island, since there would be no one to be just or unjust to. It is because we have to live among others that ethical conduct is necessary. This takes us back to where we started—no man is an island—and now we have come full circle in our exploration of social capital. Let us put it all together in one last innovative model, to see how one organization has implemented these ideas to create wealth for its customers.

PUTTING ALL YOUR SOCIAL CAPITAL TOGETHER: THE CONCIERGE SERVICE MODEL

My VeraSage Institute colleague, Dan Morris, has long believed social capital is the least leveraged of all of the intellectual capital in most businesses. He has borrowed a very old concept from the hotel industry to change this situation in his accounting firm—what he calls the Concierge Service Model. In effect, Dan wants his best customers to call him for *anything* they need, *anytime*, *anywhere*. The logic is not to offer a "one-stop shop," but rather a "first-stop shop" experience for your customers. We have already seen the suggestion the only true scarce resource in today's information-rich and knowledge-intense economy is people's *attention*. The Concierge Service Model was devised for your best customers to think of your firm first for any need or want they might have.

Dan's firm has helped people get Super Bowl tickets, five-star restaurant dinner reservations, theater tickets, a plumber, a new roof, an automobile, a doctor or dentist for newcomers to town, and so forth. The theory is that you already know someone in your network who can satisfy the customer's need or want. Is it not better to recommend them to someone in your network, effectively leveraging your firm's social capital? If you trust the people within your network, this will be a win-win situation all around—your firm will be offering higher value, your customers will appreciate the additional business you send their way, and the customers will be satisfied and, most likely, have their expectations exceeded. If no one in your network can satisfy the customers' need, chances are they know someone who can. And even if it turns out no one can satisfy the customer, isn't it nice to know your customer is thinking of your firm first for anything that he or she may desire? You are putting "velvet ropes" around the customers, helping to ensure that they do not let a potential competitor penetrate the sphere of your influence, while increasing their switching costs.

This service mentality has the salutary effect of raising your firm's collective consciousness with respect to its best customers, while offering a better experience to them. You move through the following levels in order to provide a full-service concierge:

- Awareness
- Familiarity
- Knowledge
- Understanding

Once you move to a level of understanding of your customers' wants, desires, hopes, aspirations, future goals, and so on, the Concierge Service Model becomes easier to facilitate. It does entail some risk; you have to refer businesses you know are excellent value providers, but your customers are an excellent source for this talent. You also have to reserve capacity for these first-class customers, so the firm is not able to handle as many customers as a firm of equivalent size. Yet Dan does not let the risks overshadow the opportunities of offering this dynamic service model. He knows that it increases customer loyalty, he can charge a premium price for offering this service, it deepens the relationships throughout the firm's social capital base, and instills the mindset among his team members that they are not just a technical professional firm, but a total-solutions firm, providing an enormous competitive differentiation in the marketplace.

CONCIERGE SERVICE MODEL

by Daniel D. Morris, CPA, Partner, Morris + D'Angelo; Founder, VeraSage Institute

The Concierge Service Model (CSM) reflects my analysis of the ultimate value proposition for leading customers. This model is not designed for a company's rank-and-file customers. Rather, it is specifically designed to provide a complete service solution for any unfulfilled need or want to those customers who desire a higher level of service from our firm.

The CSM has been established to leverage a company's depth of intellectual capital and related social capital to enable its team members to deliver solutions within and outside of their core areas of expertise.

Leading customers, those customers who provide either current or future significant profits, are both extremely valuable and extremely valued. I determined our firm's best customers were the envy of all of my competitors, and my competitors were certainly willing to impact my customers' purchasing decisions.

In order to provide additional control over the relationship between our firm and our customers, I started to leverage knowledge, relationships, and information that was outside of our normal and daily routines.

It started out by solving simple issues like suggestions for anniversary gifts, preferred restaurant ideas, and travel destinations. Although we are not retailers, restaurateurs, or travel agents, our combined 35 years of business experiences along with our 80 years of life experiences allowed my founding CPA firm partner and I enough knowledge to share with our better customers those special items, locations, and events we had found that made dramatic impact and improved our lives.

As word spread among and between our leading customers, referral sources, and professional colleagues, we were more and more frequently approached by our customers for our advice and opinions on areas outside of our core competencies (accounting, tax, and general business advisory services) and we were enjoying this increased respect and confirmation of our abilities to match a customer want with a desired outcome.

We started to experiment with our service offerings and our pricing by segmenting our customers into differing groups and requiring a price premium for these concierge services. Those customers that opted for our premium level of services recognized that, through our direct sources of several hundred current customers and nearly a thousand key contacts in our relationship database, we were their "hub" for nearly any information and opinion for which they were searching.

Our most challenging requests have included acquisition (without paying a scalper's premium) of Super Bowl tickets, sold out Broadway Shows, dinner reservations at fully booked restaurants across the country, and itineraries, including recommended accommodations, for travel on nearly every continent.

We have also provided access to emergency medical treatment for customers and their out-of-town guests. These services were for our hometown while we were traveling. As Harvey Makay explained, 2:00 A.M. is a terrible time to learn that you need a referral to a doctor. What we have learned is that our network of customers, team members, referral networks, and professional associations is an excellent source for effective and efficient solutions and advice for our customers.

The CSM has provided our firm with additional protections from encroachment by aggressive competitors, enhanced the personal and professional lives of our customers and their loved ones, and has provided both financial and emotional enrichment for all of our team members.

Nothing can compare to helping others achieve their dreams. Through our continuous process of developing our social and knowledge networks, we will continue to be our customers' leading source for happiness and problem solutions, and by so doing we will preserve our pricing advantage and insure our future.

SUMMARY AND CONCLUSIONS

Your organization's social capital—customers, reputation and brands, referral sources and networks, suppliers and vendors, shareholders and other external stakeholders, joint venture partners and alliances, industry associations and formal affiliations, alumni, unions, corporate universities, open source collaboration, and cultural, moral, and ethical capital—not only represent a lever to help you move the earth, but also provide a solid place on which to stand. As with other nonrival assets, an organization's social capital is not limited by physical time or space. In fact, it takes advantage of Metcalfe's Law of the computer industry and the Telecosm, which states the value of a network increases as the square of the number of users connected to it—that is, connections multiply value exponentially. Everyone in your organization's social network is a producer, consumer, and supplier of intellectual capital.

Gary Becker's theory—as well as that of others studying this area—of social capital recognizes the dominant role it plays in our lives and the lives of our customers and ourselves. No one exists in a vacuum. We are all heavily influenced by our family, friends, colleagues, neighbors, and so forth. The knowledge firm of the future will begin to leverage this inexhaustible source of IC to create value for everyone who comes into its sphere of influence, and it will become more effective in attracting the type of people it wants to work with and for, and improve the quality of its social, not to mention financial, life.

It is now time to turn our attention to the other side of the intellectual capital coin. Far more than we may care to acknowledge, we are guided by our beliefs more than what we know. Let us learn why.

14

KNOWLEDGE VERSUS BELIEFS

Our knowledge is a drop, our ignorance a sea.
—William James, American psychologist and philosopher

Al Qaeda is an example of an organization that effectively leveraged all of the elements of intellectual capital—human, structural, and social—to achieve its objectives on September 11, 2001. As wicked as it is to write about their evil mission in a business book, one has to admit that they leveraged an array of intangibles, specific knowledge, alliances, and networks, along with one of the oldest tools known to man—the knife. In terms of the destruction per person it was able to inflict—the immoral equivalent of profit per person perhaps—the results were a validation that the capacity for intellectual capital (IC) is just as great to destroy wealth as it is in creating it. Like technology itself, knowledge can be used for both good and evil. Consider these two statements:

> "In everyday life a person with a clear-cut life goal, which he strives to reach in all circumstances, will always be superior to others who are aimless."
>
> "We are participating in a New Economy, and the rules have changed dramatically. What you own is not as important as what you know."

I would venture to guess most readers are nodding their head in agreement with these two statements, especially the second in the context of what we have been exploring in this book. Does it change your opinion on the veracity of these statements to know from whence they came? The first was written by Adolf Hitler in his unpublished sequel to *Mein Kampf*. The second was from the "Letter to Shareholders" in the 1999 Enron Annual Report.

We have hinted at the topic of negative intellectual capital throughout this book. Obviously, not all knowledge is created equal. We have also discussed how knowledge can become obsolete. Throughout, we have discussed legacy systems from the Industrial Era that are holding organizations back from reaching their full potential in an IC economy. Some examples of negative IC are:

- Avoiding change
- Not experimenting
- Taylorite micromanaging, especially knowledge workers
- Resisting ideas from employees
- Bureaucratic rules and procedures that add no value, and may even destroy value
- Lack of risk taking
- Confusing efficiency with effectiveness
- Underinvesting in the future while overinvesting in the present
- An unclear, unarticulated, or uninspiring purpose

This is by no means an exhaustive list. Every reader, I am certain, would be able to add several negative traits of their organizations that hold them back. All of these examples raise an interesting dichotomy: Which guides us more, what we *know* or what we *believe*?

At the end of World War II, English writer and prominent socialist H. G. Wells wrote, "Human history becomes more and more a race between education and catastrophe." Wells was a socialist who believed knowledge alone would create a more peaceful world. But surely before they became the aggressors in World War II, the German people were among the best educated in the world—with their universities to become the model for America's—and the Japanese among the most literate. For as valuable as knowledge and education are—and they have been given a prominent role in this work—it is imperative to bear in mind that man is guided far more by his beliefs than his knowledge. How else does one begin to explain why people fly airplanes into buildings? Rabbi Daniel Lapin makes this point quite cogently in his book, *Thou Shall Prosper*, helping his readers understand how the world really works:

> You are best understood and appraised by others on the basis of the things you *believe* rather than on the basis of the things you *know*. For example, during the twentieth century, Jews again learned the importance of this principle. They learned that what the Germans of the Third Reich *believed* was far more important a guide to their actions than the things they *knew*. After all, Germany was a society whose universities had produced the world's most accomplished scientists, like Max Planck, and great philosophers, like George Hegel. Germany was a society that had produced writers like Heinrich Heine and musicians like Ludwig van Beethoven. Nonetheless, it was their beliefs about a superrace and the genetic inferiority of Jews—beliefs that had little to do with facts—that won the day and changed the course of history.
>
> Most of the really important adventures on which you embark depend on belief and faith. For instance, when you marry, you seldom do so on the basis of incontrovertible facts: You don't walk down the aisle knowing for certain that you are going to live happily ever after in a state of permanently wedded bliss. And you don't enter the state of matrimony knowing everything there is to know about your spouse. You marry on the basis of belief and faith.
>
> ... For an entrepreneur, starting a business far more closely resembles marriage. ... Faith is key (Lapin 2002: 183).

Indeed, all enterprise is an act of faith, a faith in the future, faith in the ability to humble yourself before others and solve their problems, create real value, investing in an unknown future where predetermined returns are uncertain—supplying before you can demand. Hence, all organizations are built and operated on a worldview—what Peter Drucker called "The Theory of the Business." We are ruled by our theories and worldviews far more than we are willing to admit. Accumulated knowledge certainly guides this theory, but ultimately any business is subject to the same process as a scientific theory—that of falsification.

PROFITS COME FROM RISK AND UNCERTAINTY

The only way to look into the future is use theories since conclusive data is only available about the past.
> —*Clayton Christensen, et al., Seeing What's Next: Using the Theories of Innovation to Predict Industry Change*, 2004

In Chapter 5, we discussed how profits are derived from risk. At this point, we will add uncertainty as well, the difference being that risk can be measured by assigning a probability (such as the chance of a coin's coming up heads is 50%), whereas uncertainty cannot be calculated at all. From an entrepreneur launching a new business to an existing organization introducing a new product, both are acting on a theory that ultimately will be subject to falsification in the marketplace. Peter Drucker explained this process in one of his many *Harvard Business Review* articles entitled "The Theory of the Business" (September-October 1994, reprinted in Drucker, 2003). Since the macroeconomic environment of nearly any developed country is comprised of millions of businesses, the aggregate marketplace is a laboratory where multiple hypotheses get tested, where customers spending their own money ultimately falsify the theory of any one particular firm. All ideas and theories are, ultimately, subjected to this authentication process.

For all of our advances in management thinking and the thousands of business books published each year claiming the path to success with some new fad, there is simply no economic theory that can predict which particular company will succeed and which will fail. If there were, competition itself would serve no purpose. And competition is incredibly risky and full of uncertainty. Throughout history, man has developed various institutions to deal with risk management, including:

- *Domestication of wildlife* —allowed the change from hunting to agricultural society.

- *The family* —allows greater productivity without increasing risk.

- *Private property* —barbed wire, the barking dog, laws and institutions to protect it.

- *Contracts* —allow parties to bind themselves to take certain actions if a risk did materialize.

- *Trade* —continuous expansion of voluntary exchange.

- *Arbitrage* —middlemen who take risk on future prices.

- *Insurance* —Originating in the maritime industry, insurance was the first business based solely on risk management; were it not available, a vast array of risky activities would not take place.

- *The corporation* —According to Nobel laureate Ronald Coase, a firm is created to perform tasks collectively at less cost than could be done individually through the market.

- *Accounting* —to record historical transactions and, more recently, the heroic attempt to assign static value to a dynamic concern.

- *External monitoring* —banks, credit rating agencies, credit scoring, and so on.

- *Derivatives* —transactions that derive their value from some underlying asset, reference rate, or index. During the Great Depression, "speculative excesses" were blamed, and financial contracts called *privileges* were outlawed. Not until deregulation in 1981 were they legalized, and upon reappearance were known as *options* (Culp and Niskanen 2003: 277–284).

The above institutions, with the exception of the corporation, are all conserving institutions, all with the mission of preventing change or slowing it down. Only the business enterprise is a desta-bilizing institution, organized for creative destruction. This is why economic dynamism and growth depends on innovation and the entrepreneur, because as organizations age they tend to regress to stability and homeostasis, not change. This is the reason most innovations take existing industries by surprise, as Harvard pro-fessor Clayton Christensen has documented so well in his work (see the Bibliography and Suggested Reading).

The buggy whip manufacturers did not invent the automobile, and slide rule companies were taken out by the calculator, and so on, as the history of all innovations show. Henry Ford famously said, "If I had listened to my customers, I would have given them a faster horse." Without the risk takers in society, growth would slow immeasurably. Discovery and innovation always take us by surprise; otherwise, we could run the economy with bureaucrats and our immense computational power—an idea falsified by the former Soviet Union. George Gilder articulates this point well:

> Knowledge emerges not from chaos, or fixity, but from conditions of uncertainty. Under capitalism power flows to precisely the peo-ple who are willing to stake their money not on gambles or sure things but on testable hypotheses, thus generating knowledge and wealth for society.
>
> Entrepreneurs are trustworthy because they accept a moral code of testability and falsifiability rather than one based on sentiment, sanctimony, good intentions, good press, good luck, good looks or guarantees (Gilder 2002).

Thomas Sowell also explains the importance of risk, along with its associated costs:

> Although risks may be calculated mathematically, as in the actuar-ial tables of life insurance companies, the cost of a given risk is no more objective than any other cost. Some people can sleep soundly with their rent unpaid, and creditors threatening to repossess their car or attach their salary. Other people worry about their money in a government-insured bank account. In between are numerous gradations of individual concern for a given risk, and therefore a

different psychic cost paid in carrying that risk, or different financial costs paid to reduce the risk. For example, bondholders may accept a lower rate of return than stockholders as the price they pay to reduce the risk of losing their investment.

If risky activities like drilling for oil wells (most wells have no oil) were financed by nervous people, the cost would be much higher than if such activities were financed by devil-may-care types who are happy to be able to dream of striking it rich some day. For an optimal distribution of risks, knowledge must somehow be communicated through the system as to who is more willing and who is more reluctant to bear the various levels of risk which are inherent in undertaking different economic (or other) activities. This kind of knowledge is far too specific and changing to be reduced to a science or to be mastered by "experts" (Sowell 1996: 61).

It is simply impossible to know how to do something until you attempt it. In a free market system, it is the leap, not the look, that generates the indispensable understanding and the necessary knowledge to generate wealth. A world where companies are "built to last" exists only in book titles, not in the "perennial gale of creative destruction" necessary to propel the economy forward. For my part, I would not want to live in a world where companies last forever. This is the ideology of communism and socialism, not a vibrant and dynamic free market economy. If a business is no longer creating wealth for its customers, I want the market—meaning sovereign customers—to ruthlessly drive it out of business for wasting society's resources. I do not want to inhabit a world built from the economist's perfect competition model, where businesses do nothing but crank out commodities on a "level playing field," with no ability to affect prices, output, or customer preferences. How dreadfully boring. No innovation, no dynamism, no growth.

I look forward to the *destruction* capitalism produces as much as I do the *dynamism*. Silicon Valley may be a font of creativity, but only because it rests atop a mass cemetery of bankrupted hypotheses—many more ventures fail than succeed—falsified by the sovereignty of the customer. Henry Ford wrote, "The man who is too set to change is dead already. The funeral is a mere detail" (Ford 1922: 239). The same applies to companies, which is why capitalism creates prosperity—it has a built-in falsification process whereby companies, like scientific experiments, can be proven wrong and removed from wasting society's oxygen. It is not survival of the fittest; it is survival of only those firms that continue to add more value to society than they consume.

This is one of the problems with benchmarking, business books, and consultants. They study only the survivors, those companies with a track record of success, measured usually by financial accounting statements. But as Phil Rosenzweig points out in his insightful book, *The Halo Effect*, "So many of the things that we—managers, journalists, professors, and consultants—commonly think *contribute* to company performance are often attributions *based on* performance" (Rosenzweig 2007: 64). If consultants applied the same logic to war, they would conclude that no one ever dies since they only observe and study the living.

Since no one can know with any certainty which enterprise is going to succeed, beliefs are far more powerful than simply what we know. And it is also those very same beliefs that are so difficult to alter in the face of changing conditions. Without an authentication process, we simply could not progress. As we learned in Chapter 6, science is one way to validate knowledge, utilizing the scientific method of observation, categorization, prediction, and confirmation. Even within science, old theories can take centuries before being replaced by better theories, as the example of germ theory proves.

The physicist Max Planck wrote, "A new scientific truth does not triumph by convincing its opponents and making them see the light, but rather because its opponents eventually die, and a new generation grows up that is familiar with it." This statement has often been interpreted as "science progresses funeral by funeral." This seems a rather pessimistic view of mankind's progress, as if we had to line up our elders and shoot them to advance. Yet, sometimes it seems so. How else do we account for all of the negative and obsolete IC discussed throughout the Intellectual Capitalism Series—cost-plus pricing, a ruthless focus on efficiency, Taylorite thinking, and measuring for the sake of measuring, confusing cause and effect?

I do not have a conclusive answer to this question; but I do believe it is largely because we are guided far more by our beliefs than our knowledge; and since our beliefs are part of our theories of how the world works, we relinquish them only after some traumatic experience, or the difference between our beliefs and reality is simply too great to ignore—in other words, people change not when they see the light but rather when they feel the heat. This is precisely why entrepreneurs are so essential to growth and wealth creation. Existing organizations that have done something well millions and millions of times are usually not the best vehicles to perform something new for the first time. Jack Welch put it this way: "Change has no constituency." Niccolo Machiavelli said it even better in *The Prince*: "Innovation makes enemies of all those who prospered under the old regime, and only lukewarm support is forthcoming from those who would prosper under the new." John Perazzo, in his book *The Myths That Divide Us*, sums it up nicely:

> It requires courage to cast the accumulated myths of a lifetime to the wind. Our natural desire for simplicity, certitude, and the approval of others occasionally causes us to defend even our most flawed worldviews as if our very lives depended on them. Dead belief systems are difficult to bury, for in doing so we enter a world we do not recognize; we watch the carefully crafted towers of our understanding crash down in ruins; and we lose an integral piece of the only reality we have known, reinforced and imprinted on our minds by a thousand voices, internal and external (Perazzo 1999: 17).

This discussion on risk and uncertainty sets the stage for another aspect of what is becoming increasingly a marginalized body of knowledge, yet it is clung to with ferocity and has far too much dominion in the running of enterprise. Prepare to challenge the most sacred of cows in the business world, what the nineteenth-century German writer and scientist Johann Wolfgang von Goethe described as "among the loveliest inventions of the human mind." As a recovering CPA, I think it is necessary to challenge my colleagues' worldview by questioning whether accounting is really as relevant as they believe.

DEBITS DON'T EQUAL CREDITS

But Ric, in the real world debits don't equal credits.
> —*Dan Morris, in an inspired moment at dinner with Ric Payne,*
> *founder of Principa, and Ron Baker*

Goodwill is the word we use to label our ignorance.
> —*Paul O'Byrne, chartered accountant, partner, O'Byrne and*
> *Kennedy; senior fellow, VeraSage Institute*

On December 21, 2006, George Gilder wrote on his blog about the last time he saw Peter Drucker speak (http://blog.gildertech. com). It is such a profound piece that goes to the heart of how accounting is becoming increasingly irrelevant to the spirit of enterprise, it is worth quoting in full:

> The last time I saw Peter Drucker, he was keynoting a *Forbes* conference in Seattle for CEOs. In the auditorium at the International Trade Center next to the bay, they had wheeled out the great man to the middle of the stage in a great fluffy easy chair. Close to 90 years old—at the end of the previous century gazing toward the next—he was the numinous name and Delphic presence at the conference. Everyone leaned forward to hear what he had to say.
>
> Then a gasp shook the rows of CEOs. The conference management stood there stricken, unable to move: "For the Love of Malcolm's motorcycle ...What is this?" The CEOs sat popeyed.
>
> The hoary sage's balding pate flopped back in the chair as if he had fallen asleep ... or worse.

Perhaps *Forbes* had erred in staking a major conference on an aging guru seemingly well over the hill and in parlous health.

Then his entire body fell forward. I was ready to run up to catch him if he should tumble toward the crowd. But he somehow caught himself. His eyes opened, and he looked out intently at the throng of CEOs. Everyone sighed with relief. He was awake. He had their attention.

Drucker growled: "I have just one thing to tell you today. Just one thing ..."

Wow, I said to myself, it better be good.

"No one," he continued, "but *no one* in your company, knows *less* about your business than your *See Eff Oh*."

Huh?

This was the era of the heroic Chief Financial Officer (CFO). Scott Sullivan of Worldcom, Andy Fastow of Enron, clever, inventive folk like that. You remember them. Across the country, CFOs were in the saddle. CEOs would not move without consulting them.

What could Drucker have meant?

He was stating law number one of the Telecoms.

Knowledge is about the past. Entrepreneurship is about the future. CFOs deal with past numbers. By the time they get them all parsed and pinned down, the numbers are often wrong. In effect, CFOs are trying to steer companies by peering into the rearview mirror. Past numbers do not have anything much to do with future numbers. As Ken Fisher puts it in his new book *The Only Three Questions That Count*, "Stock prices [and by extension other business numbers] are not serially correlated."

Moreover, CFOs tend to focus on internal problems. But most internal problems cannot be solved internally. Determining business outcomes are decisions made by customers and investors and both are outside the company and not directly managed by the company. Their views can change in an instant, casting all the existing numbers into oblivion. To reach customers and investors takes outside vision and leadership, not internal problem solving.

Tech companies should not try to solve problems. Solving problems sounds good, but it is a loser. You end up feeding your failures, starving your strengths and achieving costly mediocrity. Don't solve problems—that's the CFO's forte and pitfall. Pursue opportunities (http://blog.gildertech.com/index.php?/archives/36-Law-Number-One-of-the-Telecosm.html, accessed December 28, 2006).

A lot of rules have been added since the Venetian monk Luca Pacioli published the first accounting textbook, *Summa de arithmetica, geometrica, proportioni et proportionalita*, in 1494, introducing double-entry bookkeeping. It was a creation for future accountants that was as big as the invention of zero for mathematicians. Unfortunately, one could also make the argument that it was the last revolutionary idea to come from the accounting profession. As quoted in *Intellectual Capital*, David Wilson, CPA and partner at Ernst & Young: "It has been 500 years since Pacioli published his seminal work on accounting and we have seen virtually no innovation in the practice of accounting—just more rules—none of which has changed the framework of measurement" (Stewart 1997: 58).

The balance sheet dates from 1868; the income statement from before World War II. Generally accepted accounting principles (GAAP) fits an *industrial* enterprise, not an *intellectual* one. Currently, GAAP measures the cost of everything, and knows the value of nothing. As Robert K. Elliott pointed out in an essay entitled "The Third Wave Breaks on the Shores of Accounting":

> [GAAP] focuses on tangible assets, that is, the assets of the industrial revolution. These include inventory and fixed assets: for example, coal, iron, and steam engines. And these assets are stated at cost. Accordingly, we focus on *costs*, which is the *production* side, rather than the *value created*, which is the *customer* side (Stewart 1997: 58).

The profession of public accounting as we presently know it came into existence in Great Britain in the 1850s with the introduction of the companies acts and the bankruptcy acts, legislation designed to protect shareholders and promote capital accumulation during the early stages of the Industrial Revolution. In the decades following the U.S. Civil War, British chartered accountants came to the United States to monitor the capital investments of the Old World in the New World.

But the traditional accounting model is over 500 years old, and it is in bad shape. Financial statements presented in accordance with GAAP are based on a liquidation value of a business, essentially historical cost assets less liabilities—a heroic attempt to assign static value to a dynamic and going concern. The income statement was set up to account for the most important cost in an industrial society: cost of goods sold. But in an IC economy, cost of revenue is less meaningful. In the Industrial Age, there was not much of a lag between the creation of inventory and the realization of its value from a transaction. In the knowledge economy, however, creation can precede transactions, sometimes by years or decades, as with software and pharmaceutical research and development (R&D). Even though IC is the main driver of wealth, you will look in vain to find it in the traditional GAAP statements—the balance sheet, income statement, and statement of cash flows. Increasingly, these statements are being referred to as the "three blind mice."

Coca-Cola's brand name alone was estimated to be worth $67 billion in 2006, according to Interbrand, a London consultancy that calculates the value of brand names by comparing the premium priced earnings of branded products with what could be earned by a generic equivalent (you can find more information at www.interbrand.com). Some critics, such as *Harvard Business Review* editor and managing director Thomas A. Stewart, have asserted:

> Most important, the case against conventional accounting has become—it seems to most observers—open and shut: It's incontrovertibly true that present financial and management accounting does not give investors, directors, the public, or management the information they need to make informed decisions. It is time, once and for all, to drive a stake through the heart of traditional accounting, which is draining the life from business (Stewart 2001: xiv).

Abraham Briloff, a professor of accounting at Baruch College and irritant to the auditing profession, contends that accounting statements are like bikinis: "What they show is interesting, but what they conceal is significant." According to Dr. Margaret Blair, in a study for the Brookings Institution, in 1978, 80 percent of a company's value could be attributed to its tangible assets; by 1988, only 45 percent; in 1998, only 30 percent (Harrison and Sullivan 2006: 4). In effect, 70 percent of the average company's value *cannot* be explained by traditional GAAP financial statements. The consulting firm Accenture has arrived at the same conclusion with respect to the value of companies listed on the Standard & Poor's (S&P) 500. Adding more arcane and picayune rules to GAAP, or converging existing GAAP with international accounting standards, will not solve this problem. The accounting model is suffering from what philosophers call a *deteriorating paradigm*—the theory gets more and more complex to account for its lack of explanatory power.

These shortcomings of GAAP explain why Larry Page and Sergey Brin, cofounders of Google, wrote, in effect, their worldview in their "Letter from the Founders: An Owner's Manual for Google's Shareholders." This letter was written at the time of Google's initial public offering in 2004, and it clearly illustrates that Page and Brin had a definite theory of their business, while understanding that the archaic accounting model should not be the talisman to guide their company:

> Many companies are under pressure to keep their earnings in line with analysts' forecasts. Therefore, they often accept smaller, predictable earnings rather than larger and less predictable returns. Sergey and I feel this is harmful, and we intend to steer in the opposite direction.
>
> Our long term focus does have risks. Markets may have trouble evaluating long term value, thus potentially reducing the value of our company. Our long term focus may simply be the wrong business strategy. Competitors may be rewarded for short term

tactics and grow stronger as a result. As potential investors, you should consider the risks around our long term focus.

We will make business decisions with the long term welfare of our company and shareholders in mind and not based on accounting considerations.

Although we may discuss long term trends in our business, we do not plan to give earnings guidance in the traditional sense. We are not able to predict our business within a narrow range for each quarter. We recognize that our duty is to advance our shareholder's interests, and we believe that artificially creating short term target numbers serves our shareholders poorly. We would prefer not to be asked to make such predictions, and if asked we will respectfully decline. A management team distracted by a series of short term targets is as pointless as a dieter stepping on a scale every half hour.

We encourage our employees, in addition to their regular projects, to spend 20% of their time working on what they think will most benefit Google. This empowers them to be more creative and innovative. Many of our significant advances have happened in this manner. For example, AdSense for content and Google News were both prototyped in "20% time." Most risky projects fizzle, often teaching us something. Others succeed and become attractive businesses (http://investor.google.com/founders_letter.html, accessed February 8, 2007, pp. 2; 3).

In all fairness to accounting, it never was meant to predict value prospectively, only to record transactions retroactively. In effect, accounting can only measure exchanges *after* they have taken place. This is why accounting can only record the "goodwill" of a business until after is has been sold. Accounting has no way to place a value on that goodwill until a transaction takes place. That is why my colleague Paul O'Byrne says *goodwill* is the name we give to our ignorance, since to value goodwill *before* a business is sold would require a theory, since theories are the only way to peer into the future. The best an accountant can do is to extrapolate the past into the future, and unless one believes that the future is going to be the same as the past, this technique is fraught with hazards. This was Drucker's point at the CEO conference in Seattle. CEOs have to create the future, not relive the past, and the only way to do that is with a theory of the business.

Financial statements are examples of *lagging* indicators, as they report on where a particular business has been. This may or may not be useful in determining where the business is heading. Real-time financial statements would rise to the level of what economists call *coincident* indicators, since they would track present performance. But what every business should develop is a set of *leading* indicators that would enable them to get a sense of where the business is heading. Yet the accounting profession proffers little help in achieving this objective, for a very fundamental reason: Accounting is not a theory.

Developing leading indicators requires evolving a set of falsifiable theories the business can test to determine the relationship between those indicators and future financial performance. When Fra Luca Pacioli introduced double-entry bookkeeping in 1494, it was no doubt a revolutionary concept, as it allowed businesses to expand beyond familial and geographical boundaries. Accounting to this day states, quite rightly, that debits must always equal credits. That is, it is an identity statement, expressed in the following fundamental accounting equation taught in every beginning bookkeeping course:

$$\text{Assets} - \text{Liabilities} = \text{Owner's Equity}$$

An identity statement is true by its very definition. It is an equation that can explain nothing but itself. It is not a theory. A demand curve is an example of an identity statement: the summation of how much product customers would purchase at various prices. The supply curve is the same: a summation of how much product businesses would be willing to provide at various prices. It was not until economists combined these two identities into the scissors of the well-known supply-and-demand graph—inserting some assumptions along the way—that they posited the *theory of supply and demand*. This allows them to predict future price movements in the economy. The principles of accounting also do not comprise a theory; rather, they are simply a set of guidelines, rules, and procedures for measuring financial items such as assets, liabilities, revenues, and expenses, grounded by standards such as relevance, reliability, and materiality.

One cannot use the accounting equation to predict the future performance of a business any more than one can use the federal government's budget deficit, or trade deficit, as a predictive tool. It is not the equation or the measurement that provides the usefulness; it is the context of the assumptions behind it that matter. Charles Handy sheds some light on the historical influence of the accounting curriculum in Britain's business schools:

> The best preparation, however, for a management role in business was generally thought to be an accountancy qualification. In preparing my report 'The Making of Managers,' I unearthed the intriguing fact that Britain had 168,000 qualified accountants compared with four thousand in West Germany, six thousand in Japan and twenty thousand in France. We didn't need or use that many accountants. The great majority were not working as accountants at all, but as nonfinancial managers in business organizations. There is nothing wrong with the accountancy training—for accountants. But accountants are taught to give priority to the visible financial costs and assets, not to the less quantifiable human assets, which they regard as costs. They focus on the past rather than the future, because that alone can be accurately measured and audited. Their training regards risk, uncertainty and the unknown as undesirable. People management, at that time, had no place in the curriculum, for money and its measurement was all that mattered. The accountancy profession had, accidentally, become the business schools of Britain. No wonder our economy was lagging behind that of our competitors (Handy 2006: 59–60).

I am not prepared to draw the conclusion that Britain's lagging economic performance is tied to accountancy education, but I have no doubt of the accounting profession's inability to take the lead in movements such as the Balanced Scorecard, which attempts to look at more indicators than merely historical financial performance metrics. They have begun some initiatives in this area, but they have been half-hearted at best, nor have they been very successful in changing the accounting model, as we shall see later. Is it any wonder so many companies provide pro-forma financial statements to their users? In any other discipline, this would be a leading indicator that the information you are providing is not as valuable as it could be, but the accounting profession is not innovative. After all, its last true innovation—financial statement compilations and reviews, two lesser services to the flagship audit—came in 1978, a nearly 30-year innovation curve, and counting.

    Robert K. Elliott, former partner at KPMG and past chairman of the American Institute of Certified Public Accountants, summarized the state of the accounting profession, explaining what it needed to do to stay relevant in an intellectual capital economy:

> ... I think we have to look at the scope question in terms of the historical sweep of the adequacy or inadequacy of the accounting model. I would like to address the issue from an historical perspective. Before the Industrial Revolution when we were in the agricultural era, the information professionals were the scribes. They were the people that could read and write. They wrote down the accountability records and kept the contractual memos. Preceding industrialization, a necessary condition was the development of accountancy, which was a much more elaborate way of keeping records and of analyzing and interpreting and figuring out what happened. When that happened the scribes went away. In one sense, there were no professional scribes anymore, but in another sense we all became our own scribes. We all learned how to read and write and document things. Now we come to the Industrial Revolution and we have these accountants, who keep records and sum up financial transactions. I would submit that as we move toward the Post–Industrial Era the accountant goes the way of the scribe. We don't have a class of accountants anymore. In effect we all become our own accountants. We all do the data entry and the analysis necessary to reach our own conclusions. And what has to happen is there has to be an emergence of a new professional class

that is focused not on just keeping records or summing up transactions but on the strategic use of knowledge to create value. And that becomes the new playing field. As accountants, we have an historical opportunity here to reposition ourselves into that space; you can put any other name on it if you like. Or we can go the way of the scribes—the way of the people whose function has been absorbed into the fabric of what everybody can do for him or herself. Much of the work we used to do in the accountancy profession is now done by those who would have been our clients by using *Intuit* or *Peachtree* or *TurboTax* or something like that. We have to move up the value chain to higher value activities, which are those involved not about the production and summarization of information but about the use of information in order to make wise wealth creating decisions. And that's the shift we have to make. Now, that's the good news because we have the opportunity to see the need and reposition ourselves. The bad news is that history doesn't provide many precedents for entire professions or businesses transforming themselves into a new wealth creation paradigm. Frequently they have expired. Their function has gone away and they with it. But the opportunity still exists for us to transform our profession (Jensen 2002: 20–21).

Will accountants go the way of the scribes? Is there a prospect for real financial reporting model reform, or are we condemned to a 500-year-old model that increasingly ignores IC?

FINANCIAL MODEL REFORM

Financial statement accounting today is where physics was a century ago. By that time, it was obvious that Newton's laws failed to explain gravity, the behavior of atoms, and so forth. Consistent with all scientific progress, once some of Isaac Newton's theories were falsified, Einstein replaced them with his theory of relativity. Unfortunately, accounting is not subject to the scientific method, mostly because it is not a theory.

This is not for lack of effort on the part of the accounting profession. Various alternative models have been proffered, but each is found lacking because it is glued upon the identity equation. For example, some commentators have suggested a formula similar to this:

Market Value = Book Value (GAAP) + Intellectual Capital

The problem with this is that they are different measurements. Book value only captures value *realization*, whereas IC is about value *creation* in the future. Bill Swirsky, vice president of the Canadian Institute of Chartered Accountants, explains how the Institute has dealt with IC and traditional financial statements:

> Our early efforts were focused on "shoehorning" IC into traditional financial statements. In 1997, however, we came to the conclusion that trying to put IC into financial statements was bound to be unsuccessful for a variety of reasons. Further, we realized that financial measurement for intangibles produced an inaccurate answer to the *wrong* question: What is the financial value of the firm's IC? We concluded instead that the right question was: How can we measure the value that organizations create? We came to realize that traditional accounting is based largely on recording transactions, and in so doing (quite well) what it actually measures is the *realization* of value that was previously created through R&D and other forms of innovation.
>
> Thus the Value Measurement and Reporting Collaborative (VMRC) came to be, comprising the accounting institutes of Canada, the United States, Australia, South Africa, and Germany … we now call the New Paradigm Initiative (NPI). The purpose of NPI is twofold: in the short term, to identify and categorize all of the current approaches for measuring value; and to provide measurement professionals with a comprehensive listing of methods, including an assessment of what each does well (Harrison and Sullivan 2006: 98–99).

In addition to the NPI, there is also the Enhanced Business Reporting Model, and each of the Big Four accounting firms have their own initiatives as well. Individual countries are also promulgating regulations that require companies to disclose supplemental information on IC. Denmark was the first country to require such disclosure with the passage of the Danish Financial

Statement Act, 2003. In addition to disclosing a description of the firm's IC, it also requires a description of the firm's environmental impact along with its objectives for reducing and/or preventing negative environmental effects. There is also a movement in Germany to create a "knowledge balance sheet" (*Wissenbilanz*), reporting on important IC companies own or control. You can find more information on these initiatives in the Resources section at the back of this book.

As encouraging as some of these programs are, in my opinion they are doomed to fail, for a very fundamental reason: Accounting is not a theory, but intellectual capital is. The philosopher Wittgenstein wrote "Whereof one cannot speak, thereof one must be silent." We are asking far too much of accounting if we expect it to be able to do anything other than record historical transactions. To peer into the future, whether it is with key predictive indicators, valuing brands such as Interbrand does, or estimating the future wealth-creation capability of IC projects, all require a theory. The accounting profession simply does not possess the IC to posit and test theories. All they seem to be able to accomplish is to pile more rules and procedures onto an already outdated reporting model. We are so busy polishing our glasses—the old model—we are not putting them on to see the new realities in front of us.

Enron and the other spate of accounting scandals from the early 2000s were not so much about fraud, malfeasance, misfeasance, or other crimes, but rather the increasing *irrelevance* of the traditional accounting reporting model. Enron's legerdemain is not what caused it to fail. Its financial deception allowed it to remain in business for longer than an otherwise similar firm engaged in accurate financial disclosures, but this is a question of *timing* alone and not *causality*. The financial statements were simply lagging indicators of bad business decisions. Had Enron been reporting leading indicators, perhaps the market could have responded sooner.

Compounding the mistake was the passage of the Sarbanes-Oxley Act of 2002 (SOX), which will not restore relevance to GAAP. All it does is pile burdensome and costly regulations onto a decrepit reporting model. This is the equivalent of Baron Munchausen's struggle to extract himself from a swamp by pulling on his own hair.

I see three possible roads for the accounting profession to travel into the future. On the first, it can do nothing, which is usually the road traveled most by stagnating industries. Thinking that the past will somehow equal the future, the leaders simply see no reason to change. No doubt the profession would survive in some shape, since a lot of its work is governmentally mandated, but it will relinquish its status as the premier financial profession if it chooses this path.

On the second road, outsiders could replace the profession—the "perennial gale of creative destruction" Schumpeter wrote about. Accountants would go the way of the scribes. In some instances, this is already taking place with respect to key predictive indicators, social and environmental audits, brand valuation, and other IC frameworks, being performed by consulting firms and even nongovernmental organizations (NGOs), as detailed in *The ValueReporting Revolution: Moving beyond the Earnings Game* (see Bibliography). This is unfortunate since the accounting profession should be out in the forefront in these areas, but it has simply rested on its past successes.

Finally, on the third road, the profession could innovate and become its own creative destroyers. Why not relinquish its monopoly on offering auditing services, opening up the field to competition from banks, insurance companies, and any other industry that wanted to attest to financial statements? Why should the audit be a state-granted monopoly? Open it up and let the free market innovate new solutions to attesting to the financial performance and risk position of companies. The goal is to protect the public, disclose relevant financial information, while dealing with the principal-agent dilemma; yet there are myriad ways of accomplishing these objectives, we don't have to suffer with a one-size-fits-all monopoly offering from an increasingly ossified profession. Insurance companies and banks could innovate new products, the stock markets could also enter the fray, perhaps by hiring auditors themselves and thereby remove the major conflict of interest—the fact that auditors are paid by the very companies they are supposedly auditing. SOX did nothing to deal with this conflict. There are so many permutations of what an unfettered free market could accomplish in this arena, it cannot even be speculated what types of new and dynamic ways investors could be assured of receiving timely and accurate financial information, and even insured against the risk of audit failure if they chose to be. Additional governmental regulations will only slow this innovation down further. Heavily regulated industries are rarely hotbeds of innovation; if the computer industry were as heavily regulated as accountants and auditors, we would have Vacuum Tube Valley, probably located in West Virginia.

Another innovative tool being used by some companies are so-called *information markets*. These markets are proving useful in three areas: forecasting, decision making, and risk management. In effect, people are putting up their own money to predict future outcomes. The most famous example is the Iowa Election Markets, which have outperformed election polls 451 out of 596 times across a wide variety of elections. Hewlett Packard, Goldman Sachs, Microsoft, and Eli Lilly have all created internal information markets to forecast sales, predict which drugs are likely to be successful, and other profit-making decisions. Prediction markets exist on the weather, horse racing, the Oscars, movie box-office receipts, legislative outcomes, economic indicators, initial public offerings, and a host of other uses. At one point, the government floated the idea of using them to forecast terrorism. Economists and other policy experts have made great strides in their understanding of these markets, how to structure them, eliminate distortions, and make them quite effective. There is still much to learn, but the early successes are encouraging.

Information markets are an effective way to avoid "group-think," since groups often amplify errors, whereas markets correct them. Imagine, for example, if interested investors could pay for access to an internal information market for Apple's forecast of sales for its new iPhone. Would this help investors make better decisions? Would it provide more meaningful and relevant information, allowing interested parties to peer into the future rather than just analyze the past, as with the traditional financial statements? Accounting information will never be able to provide such knowledge, no matter how much it is tweaked and manipulated, since it is not a theory. Perhaps the stock markets could require their listing companies to establish such markets, since they have an incentive to capitalize on the information generated. Those companies that participated might incur a lower cost of capital. Open competition would ultimately determine if this type of information is valuable. For more background on information markets, see the book review of *Information Markets*, edited by Robert Hahn and Paul Tetlock, in the Suggested Reading and Resources sections, for a listing of information market Web sites.

Information markets are simply a microcosm of the larger marketplace, where we know there is no better way for innovation and new knowledge to diffuse throughout society than to have entrepreneurial experiments take place to satisfy the needs and wants of consumers. Ask yourself which products and services have gotten dramatically better over the past decades—computers, financial services, telecommunications, the Internet, automobiles, trucking, airlines, electronics, and so on—and which have stagnated and left the consumer with little or no freedom to choose among competing offers—Social Security, the public school system, Medicare, the Postal Service, and the financial statement audit, to name just a few. The difference between these two sectors is the extent of regulation and barriers to entry, which stifle creativity, innovation, risk taking, and experimentation.

None of these three paths will be very pleasant for the accounting profession, since any of them will no doubt cause disruption of the status quo. But can there be any doubt that the current accounting reporting model is the Edsel of our time? Is it not incumbent on the profession to shape its own destiny, rather than being relegated to part-time governmental bureaucrats destined to comply with the ever-increasing tax code, GAAP, and SOX rules and regulations? The only way to get the accounting profession to reform itself is to open it up to competition, forcing it to innovate and respond to the very people it is designed to protect—the public.

In the meantime, company's should take Drucker's advice and leave history and problems to the chief financial officers, while the rest of the C-suite focuses on opportunities and creating the future we all, eventually, inhabit. This future is shaped by the beliefs and worldviews we all walk around with. For despite all of our advancements in knowledge, the act of enterprise is still an act of faith. It is unpredictable. It has to be, for if it were completely controllable, it would be unnecessary.

SUMMARY AND CONCLUSIONS

Milton Friedman told a wonderful story that may illustrate what we need:

> A young nun was out driving a car down a superhighway and ran out of gas. She remembered that a mile back there had been a gas station. She got out of her car, hiked up her habit, and walked back. When she got to the station she found that there was only one young man in attendance there. He said he'd love to help her but couldn't leave the gas station because he was the only one there. He said he would try to find a container in which he could give her some gas. He hunted around the gas station and couldn't find a decent container. The only thing he could find was a little baby's potty that had been left there. So he filled the baby potty with gasoline and gave it to the nun. She took the baby potty and walked the mile down the road to her car. She got to her car and opened the gas tank and started to pour it in. Just at that moment, a great big Cadillac came barreling down the road at 80 miles an

hour. The driver was looking out and couldn't believe what he was seeing. So he jammed on his brakes, stopped, backed up, opened the window, and looked out and said, "Sister, I only wish I had your faith!" (Poole and Postrel 1993: 10).

If we constantly reinvigorate, revitalize, and challenge our worldviews, there is no limit to what we can achieve, as long as we do not lose faith in ourselves. The manifestation of our beliefs is expressed in the overarching *purpose* of the organizations we work with, the topic we turn to next, thereby concluding our exploration of intellectual capital.

15

PURPOSE

Anybody who's running a business has to figure out the higher calling of that business, its purpose. Purpose is about the difference you're trying to make—in the marketplace, in the world.
—Roy Spence, cofounder and president, GSD&M

Purpose is bigger than tactics. Purpose is bigger than strategy. It is a choice to pursue your destiny—the ultimate destination for yourself and the organization you lead. Purpose is your moral DNA. It's what you believe without having to think.
—Nikos Mourkogiannis, Purpose: The Starting Point of Great Companies, 2006

Everyone has a purpose in life. Perhaps yours is watching television.
—David Letterman

Imagine you had to give a commencement address to a graduating class of students who were about to enter your chosen occupation. What would you say to them? What would be the main message you would want them to walk away with and remember for the rest of their lives? If you have ever had the privilege of being asked, you know this is a daunting challenge. How can you possibly sum up the main lessons you have learned in your years on this planet in a 30-minute speech? I feel exactly the same way about writing the conclusion to this book.

Some would say the purpose of life is *happiness*. Happiness is not a frivolous or selfish concern, but rather a serious subject, and a noble goal. It is also a uniquely human aim. Aristotle believed the ultimate end of being human was *eudaimonia*, which is sometimes translated as "happiness," but is perhaps closer to "fulfillment," "flourishing," or "success" (Mourkogiannis 2006: 32). Aristotle associated it with a *type* of happiness, based on virtuous conduct and philosophic reflection. John Stuart Mill wrote in Chapter 2 of *Utilitarianism*: "It is better to be a human being dissatisfied than a pig satisfied; better to be Socrates dissatisfied than a fool satisfied." But how does one define, or measure, eudaimonia, or happiness? Nobel Prize–winning economist Paul Samuelson tried to do just that in his ubiquitous and famous economics textbooks, where he presented the following equation:

$$\text{Happiness} = \text{Consumption} \div \text{Desire}$$

At first glance, this appears to be crassly materialistic, but it does not have to be viewed that way. It can also describe Buddha-like levels of serenity—reduce your desire to zero and happiness becomes infinite. There now exists an academic discipline committed to understanding happiness, known as "subjective well-being." This new science uses psychology, physiology, and neurological studies. A lot of it is meant to deepen our understanding of human behavior, taking it beyond the economists' assumption of rational man. New indices of well-being are being developed, such as Australia's *Measures of Australia's Progress*, created in 2002 (www.abs.gov.au) and the World Database of Happiness (www.eur.nl/fsw/research/happiness). Along with others, these measures try to supplement the traditional gross domestic product (GDP) measurement with other measurements, such as literacy, life expectancy, environmental damage, and so on. Richard Layard, a member of the British House of Lords, makes a case that happiness should be a goal of public policy, in his book *Happiness: Lessons From a New Science* (2005). So far, what has been learned is there is, indeed, a link between income and happiness, but only up to a point (around

$15,000 GDP per person). Beyond that, the correlation is more tenuous. I have severe misgivings regarding some of the methods and public policy prescriptions arising from this discipline. Indeed, this entire book is a testament to the salutary effects of creating wealth. After all, to argue that *reducing* income would increase happiness seems nonsensical. That said, I do believe the question of happiness is important in understanding the motivations of why people work.

It has often been observed that if you define your happiness by your level of success, you can never achieve enough success to make you happy. Studies of lottery winners show the happiness effect wears off after about two years (Coyle 2007: 112). When one works simply to make money, the work is rarely joyful or meaningful, which is why so many people volunteer at not-for-profit organizations where they feel they are making a significant contribution. The acid test to determine if you love what you do is to ask yourself: Would you continue to work if you won the lottery? The Chinese philosopher Lin Yutang made this keen observation in his book *The Importance of Living*:

> From my own observation of life, ... the great humbugs of life are three: Fame, Wealth and Power. There is a convenient American word which again combines these three humbugs into the One Great Humbug: Success. But many wise men know that the desire for success, fame and wealth are euphemistic names for the fears of failure, poverty and obscurity, and that these fears dominate our lives (Yutang 1998: 102).

The relationship between the humbugs Yutang mentions and happiness is indeed tenuous. Witness Hollywood actors who achieve all three and burn out at relatively young ages or seem to live in wealthy misery. We seem to have become richer and less happy. Michael Novak says, "The aftertaste of affluence is boredom." Maybe this is why Andrew Carnegie wrote, "The man who dies rich dies disgraced," arguing that the rich should give away their money before they die. Carnegie worked diligently to achieve his own advice, spending the last 17 years of his life giving away his vast fortune, some $332 million (Rockefeller, by comparison, gave away $175 million). Even with his Herculean efforts, Carnegie could not give away his money fast enough, for by the time he gave away approximately $180 million, his fortune had grown—through the magic of compound interest—to a sum nearly as large as where he started, which is why he transferred what remained to the largest philanthropic trust ever before known, the Carnegie Corporation. All told, he had given away 90 percent of his fortune, 80 percent going to support the human mind in universities, libraries, institutes, schools, grants and pensions for college teachers, and so forth. Not too bad for someone born quite poor in the town of Dumferline, Scotland, in 1835, whose family immigrated to Pittsburgh, Pennsylvania. Bill Gates and Warren Buffett are destined to follow in the footsteps of Carnegie, each pledging their fortunes to the Bill and Melinda Gates Foundation.

How would this affect your commencement address? Oscar Wilde wrote, "No man is rich enough to buy back his past." All in all, if I were restricted to four key topics in a commencement speech, they would be: *vocation, intellectual capital, adventure,* and *legacy*.

VOCATION: WHAT IS CALLING YOU?

Business is a demanding vocation, and one is not good at it just by being in it or even by making piles of money. The bottom line of a calling is measured by pain, learning, and grace. Having a good year in financial terms is hard enough; having a good year in fulfilling one's calling means passing tests that are a lot more rewarding. The difference is a little like being drafted into the army and, instead, volunteering for the Green Berets. Doing anything as a calling—especially doing something difficult—is a lot more fulfilling than merely drifting.

—*Michael Novak, Business as a Calling: Work and the Examined Life, 1996*

Most of us have had career goals. A vocation, however, is something quite different, and is usually not discovered until later in life, after many paths have been followed. Vocation originates from the Latin *vocare*, meaning "to call." It literally calls you to contribute your talent, energy, passion, enthusiasm, and desire to the work you love and believe in.

I recall a fortuitous phone conversation I had with a remarkable woman, Dr. Sheila Kessler, several years ago. She is a consultant for more than 100 of the Fortune 500 companies, a former California Baldrige Quality Award examiner for the California Council on Service and Quality (CCQS), and author of nine books; she has worked and consulted in 54 countries. Every time I have the good fortune to speak with her, my intellectual capital rises immeasurably.

During our conversation Sheila asked the question: "How many [large] companies do you truly admire?" This goes far beyond merely patronizing them, but more relates to whether I would want a son or daughter to work for them. It is an excellent question, and for all of her experience—with literally thousands of companies around the world—she said there are perhaps 20 that would make her list. *Only 20?*

As I thought about it, I could not name more than 20 myself. Although Sheila's and my list differ on the companies we truly respect, is it not a sad commentary we cannot name more? What is worse, when I recently spoke with her as I was working on this chapter, her list has not expanded, nor has mine. We also both believe the level of service from large organizations has deteriorated over the past decade or two, which is quite sad. This is a very philosophical question, because it caused me to think deeply about the business education most of us have received at universities, continuing education courses, seminars, conferences, and especially from the books we read. It seems as if, at various times and places, different companies are held up as models to emulate for different purposes—Disney, Nordstrom, and

Ritz-Carlton for customer service; Southwest Airlines for managing customers' expectations and competing on low price; 3M, Apple, and Hewlett Packard for innovation; and so on—and I am guilty of this as well in this book. But reflecting on my education, I would have to say I have learned more from business autobiographies and biographies than all of the business books I have read *combined* (with the exception of those by Peter Drucker).

The history of business is the history of dreamers and entrepreneurs, those rare individuals who cast aside the security of a paycheck, mortgage everything they have, and chase a dream that ends up creating our futures. The factories and technologies of tomorrow—that may be nothing more than a glimmer in the eyes of a garage tinkerer—will at some point rise up and supplant the old order, disrupting the status quo and making a mockery of static income distribution tables. It is the sophomore dropout who starts a software company and creates the world's standard operating system—Microsoft's Bill Gates. It is the perseverant student who charges against the odds despite receiving a "C" on his term paper and launches a company that, most likely, every reader of this book has used, or uses, on a regular basis—Fred Smith's FedEx.

The tempo of business is not one of stability and order, but rather of disequilibrium and instability. Stability exists only in the graveyards. Ralph Waldo Emerson once wrote: "An institution is the lengthened shadow of one man." Mike Vance, former Dean of Disney University, tells this story of Walt Disney's final hours in 1966 in his book, *Think Out of the Box*:

> At Disney studios in Burbank, California, Mike could gaze out of his office window, across Buena Vista Street, to St. Joseph's Hospital where Walt Disney died. The morning he died, Mike was talking on the telephone when he saw the flag being lowered over at the hospital around 8:20 A.M. His death was preceded by an amazing incident that reportedly took place the night before in Walt's hospital room.

A journalist, knowing Walt was seriously ill, persisted in getting an interview with Walt and was frustrated on numerous occasions by the hospital staff. When he finally managed to get into the room, Walt couldn't sit up in bed or talk above a whisper. Walt instructed the reporter to lie down on the bed, next to him, so he could whisper in the reporter's ear. For the next 30 minutes, Walt and the journalist lay side by side as Walt referred to an imaginary map of Walt Disney World on the ceiling above the bed.

Walt pointed out where he planned to place various attractions and buildings. He talked about transportation, hotels, restaurants and many other parts of his vision for a property that wouldn't open to the public for another six years.

We told this reporter's moving experience, relayed through a nurse, to each one of our organizational development (OD) groups . . . the story of how a man who lay dying in the hospital whispered in the reporter's ear for 30 minutes describing his vision for the future and the role he would play in it for generations to come.

This is the way to live—believing so much in your vision that even when you're dying, you whisper it into another person's ear (Vance and Deacon 1995: 30).

Soon after the completion of Walt Disney World, someone said, "Isn't it too bad Walt Disney didn't live to see this?" Vance replied, "He did see it—that's why it's here."

I do not mean to imply that it is only entrepreneurs, or men and women of incredible foresight and tenacity, who should be held up for emulation and education. I will admit a personal bias for entrepreneurs (and entrepreneuses), because I consider them to be more interesting to study than the CEO of an established company. But you can learn from both. This is also not to imply that an organization is the result of only one person—for it certainly is not. As we have explored throughout, the amount of social and human capital that is required to build a Microsoft, FedEx, and Disney—not to mention have them outlive their founders' lives—is staggering, a feat against all odds. Most of the day-to-day business in our worldwide economy is carried out in the more prosaic fashion of the local barber, and with the skilled precision of the oncologist.

It is also too simplistic to say that all any business of the future needs is an excellent vision statement, or the right type of culture, or adequate leadership. No doubt these are all important, but they are not enough to ensure inspired wealth creation. In the introduction to the paperback edition of their book, *Built to Last: Successful Habits of Visionary Companies*—an objective, again, I do not share—James Collins and Jerry Porras define purpose as, "The organization's fundamental reasons for existence beyond just making money—a perpetual guiding star on the horizon; not to be confused with specific goals or business strategies" (Collins and Porras 1997: xx). Business is all about purpose, those internal beliefs and worldviews that define who we are and what we want to accomplish. When a company has a strong purpose, its people do not have to be "aligned" with a strategy because they already believe in and are inspired—meaning, literally, *to breathe in*—by what they are accomplishing. This is even more important when it comes to attracting and inspiring knowledge workers, who are more loyal to their profession or occupation than any one employer. They simply can no longer be bribed to do their best work.

We have already mentioned Johnson & Johnson's credo in the last chapter. The company will tolerate mistakes but not "sins," defined as a breach of the credo. A true purpose cannot be compromised, only adhered to or surrendered. The difference between a purpose in a company like Johnson & Johnson and Enron is putting these values in action, even when it costs more than it wants to pay. It is a rare company that survives the ages by putting greed and profits ahead of creating wealth for the customers it is privileged to serve. Money simply is not enough of an inspiration to partake in work that serves a larger purpose, as a visit to any local charity or Salvation Army office should teach us. In fact, it would be interesting to ask people how many charities they would be willing to work with and compare it to the number of companies they highly regard. No one has pictures of money hanging on their office walls, but rather those things we care most deeply about—family, friends, colleagues, communities, trophies, and memories that acknowledge the achievements in our lives for what we contributed, not what we earned. Bill O'Brien, former CEO of Hanover Insurance, sums it up well: "The fundamental problem with business is that they're governed by mediocre ideas. Maximizing the return on invested capital is an example of a mediocre idea. Mediocre ideas don't uplift people. They don't give them something they can tell their children about. They don't create much meaning" (Senge et al. 2005: 169). Some of the more inspiring companies' core purposes are:

Fannie Mae.   To strengthen the social fabric by continually democratizing home ownership.

Hewlett-Packard.   To make technical contributions for the advancement and welfare of humanity

Mary Kay.   To give unlimited opportunity to women.

McKinsey.   To help leading corporations and governments be more successful.

Sony.   To experience the joy of advancing and applying technology for the benefit of the public.

Wal-Mart.   To give ordinary folk the chance to buy the same things as rich people.

Walt Disney.   To make people happy.

Charles Schwab.   We are the guardians of our customer's financial dreams.

Even former Pope John Paul II understood the importance of creating wealth and generating a profit for the owners of the business. In his 1991 encyclical *Centesimus Annus* ("The Hundredth Year"), Pope John Paul II approves of profit (quite a change from the prior viewpoint of the Catholic church) but also admonishes that profit is not to be considered the sole indicator of the success of the business—capitalism is not a system merely of *things*, but about the human spirit as well:

> The church acknowledges the legitimate role of profit as an indication that a business is functioning well. When a firm makes

a profit, this means that productive factors have been properly employed and corresponding human needs have been duly satisfied. It is possible for the financial accounts to be in order, and yet for the people—who are the firm's most valuable asset—to be humiliated and their dignity offended. This is morally inadmissible [and] will eventually have negative repercussions on the firm's economic efficiency. The purpose of a business firm is not simply to make a profit, but is to be found in its very existence as a community of persons who in various ways are endeavoring to satisfy their basic needs and who form a particular group at the service of the whole of society. Profit is a regulator of the life of a business, but it is not the only one; other human and moral factors must also be considered, which in the long term are at least equally important for the life of the business.

One trait that separates humans from animals is that humans know they have a past and a future, and they are willing to invest to improve the future, even though they know as mortals they will not be around to enjoy the fruits of those investments. Animals are not wealthy or poor; they are either well fed or hungry. History remembers the *builders* and *creators* of wealth, never *consumers*. In a sense, there is a free lunch, since each generation is living off the accumulated intellectual capital of its ancestors. Walt Disney was certainly a builder who created and shaped the future by building a purpose-driven company:

> You reach a point where you don't work for money. ... When I make a profit, I don't squander it or hide it away; I immediately plow it back into a fresh project. I have little respect for money as such; I regard it merely as a medium for financing new ideas. I neither wish nor intend to amass a personal fortune. Money—or, rather the lack of it to carry out my ideas—may worry me, but it does not excite me. Ideas excite me.
>
> I could never convince the financiers that Disneyland was feasible, because dreams offer too little collateral.

The U.S. Marines recently ran a television commercial expressing the difference between a job and a calling, with the voice-over announcing: "We don't accept applications. Only commitments."

Airline pilots understand this, recognizing the exits exist for the passengers. Each individual's calling is unique, and certainly passion is no substitute for talent. A higher purpose is measured by the renewed energy it gives us, even when it involves drudgery. There is no greater joy than watching someone engage in their true calling with their entire mind, body, spirit, and soul.

CONTINUOUSLY DEVELOP YOUR INTELLECTUAL CAPITAL

The illiterate of the 21st century will not be those who cannot read and write, but those who cannot learn, unlearn, and relearn.

—*Alvin Toffler*

One of the central themes of this book is that, as a knowledge worker, your intellectual capital (IC) is what enables you to create wealth for others, and in turn for yourself. Like any other form of capital, however, IC is subject to obsolescence and must be constantly renewed. The most skilled are constant students, willing to look at the world in absolute wonder and think about why things are the way they are. Continuing professional education will be one of the major growth industries in the coming decades, since IC is constantly being developed, making it nearly impossible to keep up with in your area of specialty.

Remember, though, that your IC is more than your human and structural capital. It also consists of your social capital, the relationships that will have a profound impact on the rest of your life. If you think the Pareto Principle is true in a business setting—that is, that relatively few control the majority—think about it in terms of your personal life. Meeting someone and falling in love takes relatively little time but will have a major impact on your future. Or meeting a colleague or mentor who will point you in a totally new direction. You are whom you associate with. I do not feel the need to tell you things you already know; suffice it to say, do not pollute your social capital with people who have a zero-sum mentality and believe you can only gain if someone else loses. Develop relationships with a mentor and with individuals you truly admire and respect, whether they are colleagues, authors, or just a friend in whom you can confide. To expand your sphere of IC, become a mentor to a younger person and guide him or her with your accumulated wisdom.

ADVENTURE

We are perishing for want of wonder, not for want of wonders.
—*G.K. Chesterton*

Profit comes from taking risks since we live in a world of *dynamic disequilibrium*, where the only equality is in the graveyard, to paraphrase a German proverb. Not content to let the past stand in the way of the future, we all engage in a never-ending cycle of creative destruction. Change is our middle name, and we will continue to embrace and accept it as the progress it represents. We tear down the old order every day, in business, science, literature, art, architecture, cinema, politics, and the law.

George Gilder, writer, economist, and eclectic thinker, wrote of the ultimate conflict in *Wealth and Poverty*:

> In every economy, as Jane Jacobs has said, there is one crucial and definitive conflict. This is not the split between capitalists and workers, technocrats and humanists, government and business, liberals and conservatives, or rich and poor. All these divisions are partial and distorted reflections of the deeper conflict: the struggle between past and future, between the existing configuration of industries and the industries that will someday replace them. It is a conflict between established factories, technologies, formations of capital, and the ventures that may soon make them worthless—ventures that today may not even exist; that today may flicker only as ideas, or tiny companies, or obscure research projects, or fierce but penniless ambitions; that today are unidentifiable and incalculable from above, but which, in time, in a progressing economy, must rise up if growth is to occur (Gilder 1981: 235).

Virginia Postrel adds to this observation in her book *The Future and Its Enemies*:

> How we feel about the future tells us who we are as individuals and as a civilization: Do we search for *stasis* — a regulated, engineered world? Or do we embrace *dynamism* — a world of constant creation, discovery, and competition? Do we value stability and control, or evolution and learning? ... Do we see technology as an expression of human creativity and the future as inviting? Do we think that progress requires a central blueprint, or do we see it as a decentralized, evolutionary process? Do we consider mistakes permanent disasters, or the correctable by-products of experimentation? Do we crave predictability, or relish surprise? These two poles, stasis and dynamism, increasingly define our political, intellectual, and cultural landscape. The central question of our time is what to do about the future (Postrel 1998: xiv).

Buying — and even reading — a book about change is easier than actually implementing change. If you think of the future as a threat, you will never innovate. In order to try something new, you must stop doing something old. Ultimately, the power of the ideas in this book rest in their implementation. Those who are most complacent and comfortable with the present — or worse, a nostalgic past — are likely to remain trapped inside it forever. It is the uncomfortable and dissatisfied ones who take the risks and ultimately create our future.

A new idea should terrify us, challenging our worldview, the very core of our beliefs. And while many new ideas might need to be rejected the way a healthy immune system kills off foreign intruders, of course, this is where we must strike a healthy balance between the status quo and doing something new, or we would never have gotten the first airplane off the ground. In a business setting, constant experimentation is its salvation. What would you think of a company that had the following characteristics and beliefs?

- No official structure, organization chart, no business plan, or company strategy; no mission statement, long-term budget, fixed CEO or human resources department (don't need a mother and father of everyone in the company); no career plans, job descriptions; no one approves reports or expense accounts, and supervision or monitoring of workers is rare indeed.

- Instead of dictating [our company's] identity, [we] let our employees shape it with their individual efforts, interests, and initiatives.
- On-the-job democracy isn't just a lofty concept, but a better way to do things. ... People are considered adults in their private lives, at the bank, at their children's schools, with family and among friends—so why are they suddenly treated like adolescents at work? Why can't workers be involved in choosing their own leaders? Why shouldn't they manage themselves? Why can't they speak up—challenge, question, share information openly?
- If we have a cardinal strategy that forms the bedrock for all these practices, it may be this: Ask why. Ask it all the time, and always ask it three times in a row.
- We have been known to place ads reading: "We have no opening but apply anyway. Come and talk about what you might do for us, and how we might create a position for you."
- [The company's] *Lost In Space* program, assumes young recruits don't know what they want to do with their lives. So do what you want, move where you want, go where your interests take you. At the end of a year, anyone you've worked for can offer you a job.
- Telling people that the company trusts them and then auditing them makes it impossible for them to feel secure. ... We don't require expense accounts because of what they say about character. We've learned that peer control is as effective as reporting and auditing. ... Even in cases of fraud, we shun audits or policing procedures because we feel that responsibility and peer interest are stronger than

any internal controls (and that was before the collapse of Arthur Andersen, the king of audits and controls!).

- Most people flourish under freedom, flexibility, and responsibility. Most who have left [the company] have been managers.

- No management works quite like self-management. And working at [the company] means self-managing as much as possible. It isn't nearly as frightening as it sounds. In the end, it's self-interest at work. It requires conceding that managers don't—and can't—know the best way to do everything. People who are motivated by self-interest will find solutions that no one else can envision. They see the world in their own unique way—one that others often overlook.

- The world desperately needs an "Age of Wisdom," and workplaces would be an inspiring place to start. At [the company] we have little to teach and even less to "sell" in a packaged form. We're just a living experiment in eliminating boredom, routine, and exasperating regulations—an exploration of motivation and passion to free workers from corporate oppression. Our goal is helping people tap their 'reservoir of talent' and find equilibrium among love, liberty and work. ... Once people learn to do that ... I know we'll be alright (Semler 2003: 3, 4, 5, 62, 78, 116–117, 150, 175, 275).

After a speech the owner of this company gave, he was asked, "... Can you please tell us what planet you're from?" These beliefs defiantly challenge the conventional wisdom of management practices. As someone whose mission it is to bury the billable hour—a form of cost-plus pricing—and eradicate time sheets from professional knowledge firms, I can attest to how difficult it is to challenge long-held beliefs. But the preceding go much further than these two relatively simple objectives. They force us to challenge nearly everything we think we know about how to properly run an organization. This 50-year-old company, by the way, employs 3,000 people in three countries (some of them union members); engages in manufacturing, professional services, and high-tech software; and had revenues of $160 million in 2001—up from $35 million in 1994. If you had invested $100,000 in this company 20 years ago, it would now be worth almost $6 million (Semler 2003: ix).

When I discuss this company in presentations, I am met with a *staring ovation* of disbelief. As a Persian proverb teaches: "When the heart is willing, it'll find a thousand ways, and when it's unwilling, it'll find a thousand excuses." This visionary leader knew what type of future he wanted for his company, and he was willing to pay the price to achieve it. Is this the type of company—and leadership—you would want one of your children to work for? In the spirit of adventure, I implore you to read the two books by Ricardo Semler, cited above, and discover for yourself the possibilities of creating a better future.

LEAVING A LEGACY

No person was ever honored for what he received. Honor has been the reward for what he gave.

—*Calvin Coolidge, 1872–1933*

Aristotle devised a "deathbed test," to imagine our last day of life on earth and to consider how we would evaluate ourselves. In *The Seven Habits of Highly Effective People*, Stephen Covey lays out the second habit: "Begin with the End in Mind." He has you imagine being at your own funeral. What would you want people to say about you?

If you study business biographies and autobiographies—which former British Prime Minister Benjamin Disraeli labeled "life without theory"—you quickly discover successful cultures have been the result of original thinking. And it is precisely those cultures where original thinking is stimulated and encouraged that leave behind the richest legacies. Think of Walt Disney and the impact he still has on the company he founded, embodied in the continuously asked question: "What would Walt do?" Ben Franklin's epitaph, which he wrote, reads:

> B. Franklin, Printer; like the Cover of an old Book, Its Contents torn out, And stript of its lettering and Gilding, Lies here, Food for Worms. But the Work shall not be wholly lost, For it will, as he believ'd, appear once more, In a new & more perfect Edition, Corrected and amended By the Author.

What do you want your legacy to be? Part of any writer's legacy will be his books, which in Voltaire's words will have provided him "the great consolation in life [of saying] what one thinks." You have read my beliefs, values, and convictions (from the Latin word *convictum*, "that which is proven or demonstrated"). I have attempted to demonstrate the superiority of the new Business Equation over the old one. It challenges the wisdom of the ages because truth is not defined simply by seniority.

I have offered you a testable hypothesis, one that is subject to the falsification principle described by Karl Popper, which is how all scientific knowledge progresses. As a writer, I would desire nothing more than having my theories and ideas accepted as part of the conventional wisdom—not to mention next practices—of the knowledge economy. I have stated what I believe to be the truth, and I am now ready to accept the consequences, hoping that what is false will be exposed and that what is true will be admitted.

The thesis of this book has been that wealth is created by intellectual capital, a process of the inexhaustible human mind and spirit. The Mexican author Gabriel Zaid wrote, "Wealth is above all an accumulation of possibilities." These possibilities lie hidden in the womb of the future, waiting to be discovered by human imagination, ingenuity, and creativity, manifested in free enterprises dedicated to the service of others. I would not want it any other way.

BIBLIOGRAPHY

Albrecht, Karl, and Ron Zemke. *Service America! Doing Business in the New Economy*. Homewood, IL: Dow Jones-Irwin, 1985.

Albrecht, Karl. *The Power of Minds at Work: Organizational Intelligence in Action*. New York: AMACOM, 2003.

Albrecht, Karl. *Social Intelligence: The New Science of Success*. San Francisco, CA: Jossey-Bass, 2006.

Allen, PhD, Mark, Editor. *The Corporate University Handbook: Designing, Managing, and Growing a Successful Program*. New York: AMACOM, 2002.

Anderson, Chris. *The Long Tail: How Endless Choice Is Creating Unlimited Demand*. London: Random House, 2006.

Arden, Paul. *It's Not How Good You Are, It's How Good You Want to Be*. London: Phaidon Press Limited, 2003.

Baker Ronald J., and Paul Dunn. *The Firm of the Future: A Guide for Accountants, Lawyers, and Other Professional Services*. Hoboken, NJ: John Wiley & Sons, Inc., 2003.

Baker, Ronald J. *Professional's Guide to Value Pricing*. 6th ed. Chicago: CCH Incorporated, 2005.

Baker, Ronald J. *Pricing on Purpose: Creating and Capturing Value*. Hoboken, NJ: John Wiley & Sons, Inc., 2006.

Baker, Ronald J. *Measure What Matters to Customers: Using Key Predictive Indicators*. Hoboken, NJ: John Wiley & Sons, Inc., 2006.

Bastiat, Frederic, *Economic Sophisms*. New York: The Foundation for Economic Education, Inc., 1996.

Beatty, Jack. *The World According to Peter Drucker*. New York: The Free Press, 1998.

Becker, Gary S. *Human Capital:A Theoretical and Empirical Analysis, with Special Reference to Education*, 2nd ed. Chicago: University of Chicago Press, 1980.

Becker, Gary S. *Accounting for Tastes*. Cambridge, MA: Harvard University Press, 1996.

Becker, Gary S., and Guity Nashat Becker. *The Economics of Life: From Baseball to Affirmative Action to Immigration, How Real-World Issues Affect Our Everyday Life*. New York: McGraw-Hill, 1997.

Beinhocker, Eric D. *The Origin of Wealth: Evolution, Complexity, and the Radical Remaking of Economics*. Boston, MA: Harvard Business School Press, 2006.

Bernstein, Peter L. *Against the Gods: The Remarkable Story of Risk*. Hoboken, NJ: John Wiley & Sons, Inc., 2001.

Berra, Yogi, with Dave Kaplan. *When You Come to a Fork in the Road, Take It!: Inspiration and Wisdom from One of Baseball's Greatest Heroes*. New York: Hyperion, 2001.

Bethell, Tom. *The Politically Incorrect Guide™ to Science*. Washington, DC: Regnery Publishing, Inc., 2005.

Birla, Madan. *FedEx Delivers: How the World's Leading Shipping Company Keeps Innovating and Outperforming the Competition*. Hoboken, NJ: John Wiley & Sons, Inc., 2005.

Block, Peter. *The Answer to How Is Yes: Acting on What Matters*. San Francisco: Berrett-Koehler Publishers, Inc., 2003.

Bornstein, David. *How to Change the World: Social Entrepreneurs and the Power of New Ideas*. New York: Oxford University Press, 2004.

Boulton, Richard E. S., Barry D. Libert, and Steve M. Samek. *Cracking the Value Code: How Successful Businesses Are Creating Wealth in the New Economy*. New York: HarperBusiness, 2000.

Bowie, Norman E. *Business Ethics: A Kantian Perspective*. Oxford, UK: Blackwell Publishers Ltd., 1999.

Boyle, David. *The Sum of Our Discontent: Why Numbers Make Us Irrational*. New York: Texere, 2001.

Branson, Richard. *Losing My Virginity: How I've Survived, Had Fun, and Made a Fortune Doing Business My Way*. New York: Three Rivers Press, 1998.

Branson, Richard. *Screw It, Let's Do It: Lessons in Life*. Milsons Point, NSW, Australia: Random House Australia, 2006.

Brookes, Warren T. *The Economy in Mind*. New York: Universe Books, 1982.

Brooking, Annie. *Corporate Memory: Strategies for Knowledge Management*. London: International Thomson Business Press, 1999.

Buchholz, Todd G. *New Ideas from Dead Economists: An Introduction to Modern Economic Thought*. New York: Plume, 1990.

Buckley, William F. Jr. *Let Us Talk of Many Things: The Collected Speeches*. Roseville, CA: Forum, 2000.

Callahan, Gene. *Economics for Real People: An Introduction to the Austrian School*. Auburn, AL: The Ludwig von Mises Institute, 2002.

Canabou, Christine. "Gone, But Not Forgotten." *Fast Company*. May 2002: 28–30.

Caroselli, Henry M. *Cult of the Mouse: Can We Stop Corporate Greed from Killing Innovation in America?*. Berkeley, CA: Ten Speed Press, 2004.

Christensen, Clayton M., and Michael E. Raynor. *The Innovator's Solution: Creating and Sustaining Successful Growth*. Boston: Harvard Business School Press, 2003.

Christensen, Clayon M., Scott D. Anthony, and Erik A. Roth. *Seeing What's Next: Using the Theories of Innovation to Predict Industry Change*. Boston: Harvard Business School Press, 2004.

Cialdini, Robert B. *Influence: The New Psychology of Modern Persuasion*. New York: Quill, 1993.

Cialdini, Robert B. *Influence: Science and Practice*. 4th ed. Needham Heights, MA: Allyn and Bacon, 2001.

Coens, Tom, and Mary Jenkins. *Abolishing Performance Appraisals: Why They Backfire and What to Do Instead*. San Francisco: Berrett-Koehler Publishers, Inc., 2000.

Cohen, Martin. *Smith's Wealth of Nations: A Beginner's Guide*. London: Hodder & Stoughton, 2001.

Collins, James C., and Jerry I. Porras. *Built to Last: Successful Habits of Visionary Companies*. New York: HarperBusiness, 1997.

Collins, James C. *Good to Great: Why Some Companies Make the Leap ... and Others Don't*. New York: HarperBusiness, 2001.

Conway, Susan, and Char Sligar *Unlocking Knowledge Assets: Knowledge Management Solutions from Microsoft*. Redmond, WA: Microsoft Press, 2002.

Covey, Stephen R. *The 7 Habits of Highly Effective People: Powerful Lessons in Personal Change*. New York: Fireside, 1989.

Covey, Stephen R. *The 8th Habit: From Effectiveness to Greatness*. New York: Free Press, 2004.

Cowen, Tyler, and David Parker. *Markets in the Firm: A Market-Process Approach to Management*. London: The Institute of Economic Affairs, 1997.

Coyle, Diane. *The Soulful Science: What Economists Really Do and Why It Matters*. Princeton, NJ: Princeton University Press, 2007.

Culp, Christopher L., and William A. Niskanen, eds. *Corporate Aftershock: The Public Policy Lessons from the Collapse of Enron and Other Major Corporations*. Hoboken, NJ: John Wiley & Sons, Inc., 2003.

Darling, Marilyn, Charles Parry, and Joseph Moore. "Learning in the Thick of It." *Harvard Business Review*. July-August 2005: 84–92.

Dauten, Dale. *The Gifted Boss: How to Find, Create, and Keep Great Employees*. New York: William Morrow and Company, Inc., 1999.

Davenport Thomas H., and Laurence Prusak. *Working Knowledge: How Organizations Manage What They Know*. Boston: Harvard Business School Press, 1998.

Davenport, Thomas H. *Thinking for a Living: How to Get Better Performance and Results from Knowledge Workers*. Boston: Harvard Business School Press, 2005.

Davenport, Thomas O. *Human Capital: What It Is and Why People Invest It*. San Francisco: Jossey-Bass Publishers, 1999.

DeLong, David W. *Lost Knowledge: Confronting the Threat of an Aging Workforce*. New York: Oxford University Press, 2004.

Deming, W. Edwards. *The New Economics: For Industry, Government, Education*, 2nd ed. Cambridge, MA: MIT Press, 1994.

Disney Institute. *Be Our Guest: Perfecting the Art of Customer Service*. New York: Disney Editions, 2001.

Dougherty, Peter J. *Who's Afraid of Adam Smith?: How the Market Got Its Soul!*. Hoboken, NJ: John Wiley & Sons, Inc., 2002.

Drucker, Peter F. *Toward the Next Economics and Other Essays*. New York: Harper & Row, Publishers, 1981.

Drucker, Peter F. What Is Business Ethics? *The Public Interest 63*, 1981.

Drucker, Peter F. *The Effective Executive*. New York: HarperBusiness, 1993.

Drucker, Peter F. *Adventures of a Bystander*. New Brunswick, NJ: Transaction Publishers, 1994.

Drucker, Peter F. *Management Challenges for the 21st Century*. New York: HarperCollins, 1999.

Drucker, Peter, F. *Managing in the Next Society*. New York: Truman Talley Books, 2002.

Drucker, Peter F. *Peter Drucker on the Profession of Management*. Boston: Harvard Business Review, 2003.

Drucker, Peter F. *A Functioning Society: Selections from Sixty-five Years of Writing on Community, Society, and Polity*. New Brunswick, NJ: Transaction Publishers, 2003.

Drucker, Peter F., with Joseph A. Maciariello. *The Daily Drucker: 366 Days of Insight and Motivation for Getting the Right Things Done*. New York: HarperBusiness, 2004.

Drucker, Peter F. and Joseph A. Maciariello. *The Effective Executive in Action*. New York: HarperCollins Publishers, 2006.

D'Souza, Dinesh. *The Virtue of Prosperity: Finding Values in an Age of Techno-Affluence*. New York: The Free Press, 2000.

Duffy, Jan. *Harvesting Experience: Reaping the Benefits of Knowledge*. Prairie Village, KS: ARMA International, 1999.

Ebenstein, Alan. *Hayek's Journey: The Mind of Friedrich Hayek*. New York: Palgrave Macmillan, 2003.

Eccles, Robert G., Robert H. Herz, E. Mary Keegan, and David M.H. Phillips. *The ValueReporting Revolution: Moving Beyond the Earnings Game*. Hoboken, NJ: John Wiley & Sons, Inc., 2001.

Edersheim, Elizabeth Haas. *The Definitive Drucker*. New York: McGraw-Hill, 2007.

Emerson, Ralph Waldo *Self-Reliance: The Wisdom of Ralph Waldo Emerson as Inspiration for Daily Living*. New York: Bell Tower, 1991.

Fallon, Pat, and Fred Senn. *Juicing the Orange: How to Turn Creativity into a Powerful Business Advantage*. Boston: Harvard Business School Press, 2006.

Feulner, Edwin J., and Doug Wilson. *Getting America Right: The True Conservative Values Our Nation Needs Today*. New York: Crown Forum, 2006.

Flaherty, John E. *Peter Drucker: Shaping the Managerial Mind*. San Francisco: Jossey-Bass Publishers, 1999.

Florida, Richard. *The Rise of the Creative Class . . . and How It's Transforming Work, Leisure, Community and Everyday Life*. New York: Basic Books, 2002.

Florida, Richard. *The Flight of the Creative Class: The New Global Competition for Talent*. New York: HarperBusiness, 2005.

Foray, Dominique. *The Economics of Knowledge*. Cambridge, MA: MIT Press, 2004.

Ford, Henry, and Samuel Crowther. *My Life and Work*. Whitefish, MT: Kessinger Publishing, 1922.

Freiberg, Kevin, and Jackie Freiberg. *Nuts! Southwest Airline's Crazy Recipe for Business and Personal Success*. Austin, TX: Bard Press, 1996.

Freidheim, Cyrus. *The Trillion-Dollar Enterprise: How the Alliance Revolution Will Transform Global Business*. New York: Perseus Books, 1998.

Friedman, Milton. "The Social Responsibility of Business Is to Increase Its Profits." *The New York Times Magazine*. September 13, 1970.

Friedman, Milton and Rose. *Free to Choose: A Personal Statement*. New York: Harcourt Brace, 1980.

Fukuyama, Francis. *Trust: The Social Virtues and the Creation of Prosperity*. New York: Free Press, 1995.

Gandossy, Robert P., Elissa Tucker, and Nidhi Verma, eds. *Workforce Wake-Up Call: Your Workforce Is Changing, Are You?* Hoboken, NJ: John Wiley & Sons, Inc., 2006.

Gardner, Howard. *Changing Minds: The Art and Science of Changing Our Own and Other People's Minds*. Boston: Harvard Business School Press, 2004.

Garvin, David A. *Learning in Action: A Guide to Putting the Learning Organization to Work*. Boston: Harvard Business School Press, 2000.

Gilder, George. *Wealth and Poverty*. New York: Basic Books, Inc., 1981.

Gilder, George. *The Spirit of Enterprise*. New York: Simon & Schuster, 1984.

Gilder, George. *Men and Marriage*. Gretna, LA: Pelican Publishing Company, Inc., 1986.

Gilder, George. *Recapturing the Spirit of Enterprise: Updated for the 1990s*. San Francisco: ICS Press, 1992.

Gilder, George. *Wealth and Poverty: A New Edition of the Classic*. San Francisco: ICS Press, 1993.

Gilder-technology-report, The Gilder Friday Letter, Friday, December 13, 2002.

Gilder, Joshua. Web page: www.newmysteryreader.com/joshua_gilder.htm, undated, accessed December 27, 2006.

Gladwell, Malcolm. *The Tipping Point: How Little Things Can Make a Big Difference*. Boston: Little, Brown and Company, 2000.

Gladwell, Malcolm. *Blink: The Power of Thinking without Thinking*. New York: Little, Brown and Company, 2005.

Gregory, John Milton. *The Seven Laws of Teaching*. Grand Rapids, MI: Baker Books, 1995.

Gustafsson, Anders, and Michael D. Johnson. *Competing in a Service Economy: How to Create a Competitive Advantage through Service Development and Innovation*. San Francisco: Jossey-Bass, 2003.

Hahn, Robert W., and Paul C. Tetlock, eds. *Information Markets: A New Way of Making Decisions*. Washington, DC: AEI-Brookings Joint Center for Regulatory Studies, 2006.

Hamel, Gary. "The Why, What, and How of Management Innovation." *Harvard Business Review*, February 2006: 72–84.

Hamilton, Roger. *Your Life, Your Legacy: An Entrepreneur Guide to Finding Your Flow*. Pre-launch E-Book Edition, 2006.

Handy, Charles. *Myself and Other More Important Matters*. London: William Heinemann, 2006.

Harrison, Suzanne S., and Patrick H. Sullivan Sr. *Einstein in the Boardroom: Moving beyond Intellectual Capital to I-Stuff*. Hoboken, NJ: John Wiley & Sons, Inc., 2006.

Hayek, Friedrich A. "The Use of Knowledge in Society." *American Economic Review* 35, September 1945: 519–530.

Hayek, Friedrich A. *Individualism and Economic Order*. Chicago: University of Chicago Press, 1948.

Hazlitt, Henry. *Economics In One Lesson*. New York: Crown Publishers, Inc., 1979.

Herrnstein, Richard J., and Charles Murray. *The Bell Curve: Intelligence and Class Structure in American Life*. New York: Free Press, 1994.

Hoopes, James. *False Prophets: The Gurus Who Created Modern Management and Why Their Ideas Are Bad for Business Today*. Cambridge, MA: Perseus Publishing, 2003.

Horibe, Frances. *Managing Knowledge Workers: New Skills and Attitudes to Unlock the Intellectual Capital in Your Organization*. Ontario, Canada: John Wiley & Sons Canada Limited, 1999.

Howey, Richard S. *The Rise of the Marginal Utility School*, 1870–1889. New York: Columbia University Press [Morningside Edition], 1989.

Howkins, John. *The Creative Economy: How People Make Money from Ideas*. England: Penguin Books, 2001.

Huber, Peter W., and Mark P. Mills. *The Bottomless Well: The Twilight of Fuel, the Virtue of Waste, and Why We Will Never Run Out of Energy*. New York: Basic Books, 2005.

Imagineers, The. *The Imagineering Way: Ideas to Ignite Your Creativity*. New York: Disney Editions, 2003.

Jensen, Daniel L., ed. *Challenge and Achievement in Accounting During the Twentieth Century: A Conference Celebrating the Fiftieth Anniversary of the Accounting Hall of Fame*. Columbus, OH: Ohio State University, 2002.

Johnson, H. Thomas. "Reflections of a Recovering Management Accountant." Society for Organizational Learning Initiative, First Research Forum, January 14-16, 1998. Accessed on September 24, 2005 at:www. solonline.org/repository/download/johnson.html?item_id = 443237.

Johnson, H. Thomas, and Anders Bröms. *Profit Beyond Measure: Extraordinary Results through Attention to Work and People*. New York: Free Press, 2000.

Johnson, Paul. *A History of the American People*. New York: HarperCollins, 1997.

Johnson, Paul. *Creators: From Chaucer and Dürer to Picasso and Disney*. New York: HarperCollins, 2006.

Kay, John. *Foundations of Corporate Success: How Business Strategies Add Value*. New York: Oxford University Press, 1995.

Kay, John. *Culture and Prosperity: The Truth about Markets—Why Some Nations Are Rich but Most Remain Poor*. New York: HarperBusiness, 2004.

Kay, John. *Everlasting Light Bulbs: How Economics Illuminates the World*. London: Erasmus Press, 2004.

Kay, John. *The Hare & the Tortoise: An Informal Guide to Business Strategy*. London:Erasmus Press, 2006.

Keen, Steve. *Debunking Economics: The Naked Emperor of the Social Sciences*. Annandale, Australia: Pluto Press, 2002.

Kehrer, Daniel. *Doing Business Boldly*. New York: Time Books, 1989.

Kessler, Sheila. *Measuring and Managing Customer Satisfaction: Going for the Gold*. Milwaukee: ASQC Quality Press, 1996.

Khalsa, Mahan. *Let's Get Real or Let's Not Play: The Demise of Dysfunctional Selling and the Advent of Helping Clients Succeed*. Salt Lake City, Utah: White Water Press, 1999.

King, Thomas A. *More Than a Numbers Game: A Brief History of Accounting*. Hoboken, NJ: John Wiley & Sons, Inc., 2006.

Klein, David A. *The Strategic Management of Intellectual Capital*. Woburn, MA: Butterworth-Heinemann, 1998.

Koch, Richard. *The Natural Laws of Business: How to Harness the Power of Evolution, Physics, and Economics to Achieve Business Success*. New York: Doubleday, 2001.

Koch, Richard. *The 80/20 Individual: How to Accomplish More by Doing Less—the Nine Essentials of 80/20 Success at Work*. New York: Currency Doubleday, 2003.

Kuhn, Thomas S. *The Structure of Scientific Revolutions*, 3rd ed. Chicago, IL: The University of Chicago Press, 1996.

Lapin, Rabbi Daniel. *Thou Shall Prosper: Ten Commandments for Making Money*. Hoboken, NJ: John Wiley & Sons, Inc., 2002.

Layard, Richard. *Happiness: Lessons from a New Science*. London: Allen Lane, 2005.

Lev, Baruch. *Intangibles: Management, Measurement, and Reporting*. Washington, DC: Brookings Institution Press, 2001.

Liebowitz, Jay. *Building Organizational Intelligence: A Knowledge Management Primer*. Boca Raton, FL: CRC Press LLC, 2000.

Low, Jonathan, and Pam Cohen Kalafut. *Invisible Advantage: How Intangibles Are Driving Business Performance*. Cambridge, MA: Perseus Publishing, 2002.

Machlup, Fritz. *The Production and Distribution of Knowledge in the United States*. Princeton, NJ: Princeton University Press, 1962.

Marcus, Stanley. *Minding the Store: A Memoir*. Denton, Texas: University of North Texas Press, 1997 Facsimile Edition [Original Publication, 1974].

Marshall, Alfred. *Principles of Economics*. Amherst, NY: Prometheus Books, 1997.

Marx, Karl, and Frederick Engels. *The Communist Manifesto*. London: Verso, 1998 (modern edition; originally published 1848).

Marx, Karl. *Value, Price and Profit*. New York: International Publishers, 1995 (paperback edition; originally published 1865).

Maxwell, John C. *There's No Such Thing as Business Ethics*. New York: Warner Books, 2003.

May, Matthew E. *The Elegant Solution: Toyota's Formula for Mastering Innovation*. New York: Free Press, 2007.

McCloskey, Deirdre. *How to Be Human—though an Economist*. Ann Arbor, MI: University of Michigan Press, 2000.

Menger, Carl. *Principles of Economics*, transl. James Dingwall and Bert F. Hoselitz. New York: New York University Press, 1976 [1871].

Micklethwait, John, and Adrian Wooldridge. *The Witch Doctors: Making Sense of the Management Gurus*. New York: Times Books, 1996.

Miniter, Richard. *The Myth of Market Share: Why Market Share Is the Fool's Gold of Business*. New York: Crown Business, 2002.

Mintzberg, Henry. *Mintzberg on Management: Inside Our Strange World of Organizations*. New York: Free Press, 1989.

Mintzberg, Henry. *Managers Not MBAs: A Hard Look at the Soft Practice of Managing and Management Development*. San Francisco: Berrett-Koehler Publishers, Inc., 2004.

Mokyr, Joel. *The Gifts of Athena: Historical Origins of the Knowledge Economy*. Princeton, NJ: Princeton University Press, 2002.

Morris, Edmund. *Dutch: A Memoir of Ronald Reagan*. New York: Random House, 1999.

Mourkogiannis, Nikos. *Purpose: The Starting Point of Great Companies*. New York: Palgrave Macmillan, 2006.

Murray, Charles. *Human Accomplishment: The Pursuit of Excellence in the Arts and Sciences, 800 B.C. to 1950*. New York: HarperCollins, 2003.

Neuhaus, Richard John. *Doing Well and Doing Good: The Challenge to the Christian Capitalist*. New York: Doubleday, 1992.

Niskanen, William A., Editor. *After Enron: Lessons for Public Policy*. Lanham, MD: Rowman & Littlefield Publishers, Inc., 2005.

Nonaka, Ikujiro and Hirotaka Takeuchi. *The Knowledge-Creating Company: How Japanese Companies Create the Dynamics of Innovation*. New York: Oxford University Press, 1995.

North, Douglass C. *Understanding the Process of Economic Change*. Princeton, NJ: Princeton University Press, 2005.

Novak, Michael. *The Catholic Ethic and the Spirit of Capitalism*. New York: Free Press, 1993.

Novak, Michael. *Business as a Calling: Work and the Examined Life*. New York: Free Press, 1996.

Novak, Michael. *The Universal Hunger for Liberty: Why the Clash of Civilizations Is Not Inevitable*. New York: Basic Books, 2004.

Novak, Michael, and Brian C. Anderson, eds. *On Cultivating Liberty: Reflections on Moral Ecology*. Lanham, MD: Rowman & Littlefield Publishers, Inc., 1999.

O'Kelly, Eugene. *Chasing Daylight: How My Forthcoming Death Transformed My Life*. New York: McGraw-Hill, 2006.

O'Rourke, P.J. *On The Wealth of Nations*. New York: Atlantic Monthly Press, 2007.

O'Shea, James, and Charles Madigan. *Dangerous Company: Management Consultants and the Businesses They Save and Ruin*. New York: Free Press, 1998.

Pacioli, Fra Luca. *Particularis de Computis et Scripturis, 1494, A Contemporary Interpretation by Jeremy Cripps*. Seattle, WA: Pacioli Society, Seattle University, 1995.

Paine, Thomas. *Rights of Man and Common Sense*. New York: Alfred A. Knopf, Inc., 1994.

Parkinson, C. Northcote. *Left Luggage: A Caustic History of British Socialism from Marx to Wilson*. Boston, MA: Houghton Mifflin Company, 1967.

Paul, Annie Murphy. *The Cult of Personality Testing: How Personality Tests Are Leading Us to Miseducate Our Children, Mismanage Our Companies, and Misunderstand Ourselves*. New York: Free Press, 2004.

Penrose, Edith. *The Theory of the Growth of the Firm*, 3rd ed. Oxford: Oxford University Press, 1995.

Peppers, Don, and Martha Rogers, PhD. *Return on Customer: A Revolutionary Way to Measure and Strengthen Your Business*. New York: Currency, 2005.

Perazzo, John. *The Myths That Divide Us: How Lies Have Poisoned American Race Relations*. Briarcliff Manor, NY: World Studies Books, 1999.

Peters, Tom. *Re-Imagine!: Business Excellence in a Disruptive Age*. London: Dorling Kindersley Limited, 2003.

Pfeffer, Jeffrey. *The Human Equation: Building Profits by Putting People First*. Boston: Harvard Business School Press, 1998.

Pfeffer, Jeffrey and Robert I. Sutton. *The Knowing-Doing Gap: How Smart Companies Turn Knowledge into Action*. Boston: Harvard Business School Press, 2000.

Pfeffer, Jeffrey, and Robert I. Sutton. *Hard Facts, Dangerous Half-Truths and Total Nonsense: Profiting from Evidence-Based Management*. Boston: Harvard Business School Press, 2006.

Pink, Daniel H. *A Whole New Mind: Why Right-Brainers Will Rule the Future*. New York: Riverhead Books, 2006.

Polanyi, Michael. *Knowing and Being*. Chicago: University of Chicago Press, 1974.

Poole, Jr., Robert W. and Virginia I. Postrel. *Free Minds and Free Markets: Twenty-Five Years of Reason*. San Francisco: Pacific Research Institute for Public Policy, 1993.

Postrel, Virginia. *The Future and Its Enemies: The Growing Conflict over Creativity, Enterprise, and Progress*. New York: Free Press, 1998.

Prusak, Laurence, and Dan Cohen. "How to Invest in Social Capital." *Harvard Business Review*, June 2001: 86–93.

Reagan, Ronald. *Speaking My Mind: Selected Speeches*. New York: Simon & Schuster, 1989.

Reagan, Ronald. *An American Life: The Autobiography*. New York: Simon & Schuster, 1990.

Roberts, Russell. *The Choice: A Fable of Free Trade and Protectionism*. Upper Saddle River, NJ: Prentice Hall, 2001.

Roos, Göran, Stephen Pike, and Lisa Fernström. *Managing Intellectual Capital in Practice*. Burlington, MA: Butterworth-Heinemann, 2005.

Rosenzweig, Phil. *The Halo Effect . . . and the Eight Other Business Delusions That Deceive Managers*. New York: Free Press, 2007.

Sanford, Linda S., with Dave Taylor. *Let Go to Grow: Escaping the Commodity Trap*. Upper Saddle River, NJ: Prentice Hall PTR, 2006.

Schumpeter, Joseph A. *Capitalism, Socialism, and Democracy*. New York: Harper & Row, 1950.

Schumpeter, Joseph A. *Ten Great Economists From Marx to Keynes*. New York: Oxford University Press, 1951.

Seabright, Paul. *The Company of Strangers: A Natural History of Economic Life*. Princeton, NJ: Princeton University Press, 2004.

Semler, Ricardo. *Maverick: The Success Story Behind the World's Most Unusual Workplace*. New York: Warner Books, 1993.

Semler, Ricardo. *The Seven-Day Weekend: A Better Way to Work in the 21st Century*. London: Arrow Books, 2003.

Senge, Peter, C. Otto Scharmer, Joseph Jaworski, and Betty Sue Flowers. *Presence: An Exploration of Profound Change in People, Organizations, and Society*. New York: Currency, 2005.

Sertoglu, Cem, and Anne Berkowitch. "Cultivating Ex-Employees." *Harvard Business Review*, June 2002: 20–21.

Skousen, Mark. *The Making of Modern Economics: The Lives and Ideas of the Great Thinkers*. Armonk, NY: M. E. Sharpe, 2001.

Smith, Adam. *An Inquiry into the Nature and Causes of the Wealth of Nations*. Introduction by Ludwig von Mises. Washington, DC: Regnery Publishing, Inc., 1998.

Smith, Adam. *The Theory of Moral Sentiments*. Amherst, NY: Prometheus Books, 2000.

Sowell, Thomas. *A Conflict of Visions: Ideological Origins of Political Struggles*. New York: William Morrow and Company, 1987.

Sowell, Thomas. *The Vision of the Anointed: Self-Congratulation as a Basis for Social Policy*. New York: Basic Books, 1995.

Sowell, Thomas. *Knowledge and Decisions*. New York: Basic Books, Inc., 1996.

Sowell, Thomas. *Barbarians inside the Gates and Other Controversial Essays*. Stanford, CA: Hoover Institution Press, 1999.

Sowell, Thomas. *Basic Economics: A Citizen's Guide to the Economy*. New York: Basic Books, 2000.

Sowell, Thomas. *Applied Economics: Thinking Beyond Stage One*. New York: Basic Books, 2004.

Sowell, Thomas. *Basic Economics: A Citizen's Guide to the Economy, Revised and Expanded Edition*. New York: Basic Books, 2004.

Sowell, Thomas. *Basic Economics: A Common Sense Guide to the Economy*, 3rd ed. New York: Basic Books, 2007.

Stewart, Thomas A. *Intellectual Capital: The New Wealth of Organizations*. New York: Currency, 1997.

Stewart, Thomas A. *The Wealth of Knowledge: Intellectual Capital and the Twenty-First Century Organization*. New York: Currency, 2001.

Sullivan, Gordon R., and Michael V. Harper. *Hope Is Not a Method: What Business Leaders Can Learn from America's Army*. New York: Broadway Books, 1996.

Sveiby, Karl Erik. *The New Organizational Wealth: Managing and Measuring Knowledge-Based Assets*. San Francisco, CA: Berrett-Koehler Publishers, Inc., 1997.

Taylor, Frederick Winslow. *The Principles of Scientific Management*. New York: W. W. Norton & Company, 1967.

Taylor, William C. and Polly LaBarre. *Mavericks and Work: Why the Most Original Minds in Business Win*. New York: William Morrow, 2006.

Tedlow, Richard S. *Giants of Enterprise: Seven Business Innovators and the Empires They Built*. New York: Harper Business, 2001.

The Economist. "The Brains Business: A Survey of Higher Education." September 10, 2005.

The Economist. "The Ageing Workforce: Turning Boomers into Boomerangs." February 18, 2006.

The Economist. "The Battle for Brainpower: A Survey of Talent." October 7, 2006.

Toffler, Alvin, and Heidi Toffler. *Revolutionary Wealth.* New York: Alfred A. Knopf, 2006.

Torvalds, Linus, and David Diamond. *Just for Fun: The Story of an Accidental Revolutionary.* New York: HarperBusiness, 2001.

Turchi, Peter. *Maps of the Imagination: The Writer as Cartographer.* San Antonio, TX: Trinity University Press, 2004.

Vance, Mike, and Diane Deacon. *Think Out of the Box.* Franklin Lakes, NJ: Career Press, 1995.

Warsh, David. *Knowledge and the Wealth of Nations: A Story of Economic Discovery.* New York: W. W. Norton & Company, 2006.

Watson, Robert A., and Ben Brown. *The Most Effective Organization in the U.S.: Leadership Secrets of the Salvation Army.* New York: Crown Business, 2001.

Wattenberg, Ben J. *Fewer: How the New Demography of Depopulation Will Shape Our Future.* Chicago: Ivan R. Dee, 2004.

Wetherbe, James C. *The World On Time: The 11 Management Principles That Made FedEx an Overnight Sensation.* Santa Monica, CA: Knowledge Exchange, 1996.

Wheelan, Charles. *Naked Economics: Undressing the Dismal Science.* New York: W. W. Norton & Company, Inc., 2002.

Wheen, Francis. *Idiot Proof: Deluded Celebrities, Irrational Power Brokers, Media Morons, and the Erosion of Common Sense.* New York: PublicAffairs, 2004.

Whyte, David. *Crossing the Unknown Sea: Work as a Pilgrimage of Identity.* New York: Riverhead Books, 2001.

Wight, Jonathan B. *Saving Adam Smith: A Tale of Wealth, Transformation, and Virtue.* Upper Saddle River, NJ: Prentice-Hall, Inc., 2002.

Will, George. *Suddenly: The American Idea Abroad and at Home 1986–1990.* New York: Free Press, 1992.

Williams, Tim. *Take a Stand for Your Brand: Building a Great Agency Brand from the Inside Out.* Chicago: Copy Workshop, 2006.

Young, S. David. *The Rule of Experts: Occupational Licensing in America.* Washington, DC: Cato Institute, 1987.

Young, Jeffrey S., and William L. Simon. *iCon: Steve Jobs, the Greatest Second Act in the History of Business.* Hoboken, NJ: John Wiley & Sons, Inc., 2005.

Younkins, Edward W. *Three in One: Essays on Democratic Capitalism, 1976–2000, Michael Novak.* New York: Rowman & Littlefield Publishers, Inc., 2001.

Yutang, Lin. *The Importance of Living.* New York: Quill, 1998 edition.

SUGGESTED READING

Books, not which afford us a cowering enjoyment, but in which each
thought is of unusual daring; such as an idle man cannot read, and a
timid one would not be entertained by, which even make us
dangerous to existing institutions—such call I good books.
—*H. D. Thoreau: A Week on the Concord and Merrimack Rivers,*
1849

Arranging blind dates and recommending books are quite similar
trials. Not only does everyone have different reading preferences,
either activity can waste an enormous amount of time if it does
not lead to a more desirous future. I offer the following suggested
reading list knowing full well the risks, because I am fairly certain
the books reviewed will enhance your intellectual capital, and
may even be the catalyst to your seeing the world differently.
All of the books are included in the Bibliography, hence subtitle,
publisher, and copyright date are omitted here.

Mark Allen, PhD, ed., *The Corporate University Handbook*. An excellent
overview of the corporate university movement, including lots of ideas
and case studies of successful universities. Allen makes it clear that
corporate universities are more than merely training grounds, but the
connective tissue of organizations linking learning to strategy. One of
the most important lessons from this book is the corporate university
should report to the CEO, not the traditional HR department, if it is to
have an impact on the culture.

Chris Anderson, *The Long Tail*. The digital age, like the knowledge age,
makes matter more and more insignificant; it also does the same to
shelf space. This has important ramifications for retailers who have
traditionally been dependent on superstars, hits, and most popular items
for the majority of their profits. In a world where you can get your first
choice, we do not need 500 TV channels, only one—specifically, the
one you want, when you want it. The long tail will make businesses
reevaluate the traditional 80/20 rule, as customers will demand exactly
what they want—and be able to get it.

Ronald J. Baker, *Professional's Guide to Value Pricing*, 6th ed. The author's first book, written specifically for accountants, lawyers, and other professional knowledge firms. It challenges the pricing-by-the-hour paradigm (a form of cost-plus pricing) and offers alternatives for professionals to get out from under the artificial ceiling imposed—on themselves—by the billable hour, while offering alternatives to maintaining timesheets.

Ronald J. Baker and Paul Dunn, *The Firm of the Future*. This book explores the old and new practice equations for leveraging intellectual capital in today's knowledge economy. Topics discussed include intellectual capital, customer selection, pricing, key performance indicators, leadership, and issues facing the professions.

Ronald J. Baker, *Pricing on Purpose*. The first book in the Intellectual Capitalism Series, it discusses the old and new business equations, the labor versus subjective theories of value, cost-plus pricing's epitaph, price-led costing, what and how people buy, the value proposition, price discrimination, Baker's Law, ethics of pricing, antitrust law, the concept of a chief value officer, and an extensive bibliography and suggested reading list.

Ronald J. Baker, *Measure What Matters to Customers*. The second book in the Intellectual Capitalism Series, it deals with "effectiveness" in the new business equation, discussing why it is more important than "efficiency" in knowledge firms. In an example of *knowledge creep*, it also introduces the crucial difference between a key *performance* indicator and a key *predictive* indicator, while challenging the famous McKinsey maxim of "what you can measure you can manage" by suggesting we cannot change our weight by weighing ourselves. Other topics include: constructing a theory, developing KPIs for your company, increasing knowledge worker effectiveness, managing by results versus managing by means, the moral hazards of measurements, an extensive bibliography, and suggested reading list.

Frederic Bastiat, *Economic Sophisms*. If you enjoyed the essay in Chapter 1, "The Right Hand and the Left," this book contains much more of Bastiat's brilliance. Austrian economist Joseph Schumpeter—famous for his "perennial gale of creative destruction" metaphor—said Bastiat was "the most brilliant economic journalist who ever lived." Read this book, and his others, to find out why. You can also access Bastiat's books at the Library of Economics and Liberty, at www.econlib.org.

Gary S. Becker, *Human Capital*, 2nd ed. This is Becker's classic study of human capital; although quite academic and mathematical, there are insights to be gleaned for all readers. His *Accounting for Tastes* is more accessible, although still quite theoretical, presenting a coherent explanation for how individuals develop tastes, which has implications for leveraging social capital. *The Economics of Life*, written with his historian wife, Guity Nashat Becker, is a compilation of his monthly columns for *BusinessWeek*, examining a wide range of topics through the lens of economic theory and arriving at counterintuitive conclusions, which is Becker's specialty. He was awarded the Nobel Prize for economics in 1992.

Eric D. Beinhocker, *The Origin of Wealth*. A senior adviser to McKinsey & Company, Beinhocker has assembled a well-researched journey through the economics of wealth, though it is too rambling in places. His assertion that "economics in the future may be able to make prescriptive recommendations about business and public policy with a level of scientific authority that it has not had before" illustrates the amount of faith he is putting into the "Complexity Economics Revolution" he documents. Being a free market proponent, I took exception to nearly all of his political and economic positions, but still found the book well worth reading.

Peter L. Bernstein, *Against the Gods*. A fantastic book, very well written. Bernstein takes us on a historical crossing of man's increasing capacity to deal with risk, all the while understanding how important risk is to increasing a society's standard of living. Highly recommended.

Peter Block, *The Answer to How Is Yes*. This is a splendid book, detailing the importance of starting with *why* questions rather than *how* questions when confronted with any change. Anyone involved in changing people's minds needs to read this illuminating and lucid book. For more information on Peter Block, visit www.designedlearning.com.

Warren T. Brookes, *The Economy in Mind*. I read this book the year it was published, 1982, and it was the inspiration—along with the books by George Gilder discussed below—for the book you are now holding. Brookes was an economics columnist for the *Boston Herald-American*, with the ability to discuss complex economic issues with clarity and great insight. This was the book cited by President Reagan in his speech at Moscow State University (reproduced in Chapter 3). It is only available used, but worth finding for its historical contribution to the intellectual capital economy.

Clayton M. Christensen et al., *The Innovator's Solution* and *Seeing What's Next*. Christensen is one of the few management thinkers who understands the importance of utilizing theory in the embryonic discipline of management science, and these two books are excellent examples of the usefulness of positing, testing, falsifying, and advancing theories in business. With more thinkers like Christensen, the discipline of management might someday reach parity with economics in the understanding of human behavior.

Robert B. Cialdini, *Influence*, 4th ed. Containing many examples from marketing and advertising, this absolutely fascinating discussion of human behavior is entertaining and informative.

Tom Coens and Mary Jenkins, *Abolishing Performance Appraisals*. This book forever altered my worldview regarding the uselessness and destructiveness of the annual performance appraisal process. The authors do a wonderful job dispelling every conventional myth about why this archaic method is still necessary. The fact is, it's not, even for legal reasons (Coens should know, he's a former labor attorney). After reading this book, I was even more convinced of the effectiveness of utilizing After Action Reviews. I strongly suggest you read this book to see what conclusions you reach about a practice that is increasingly irrelevant in organizations comprised of knowledge workers.

Stephen R. Covey, *The 8th Habit*. In this follow-up to his classic *The 7 Habits of Highly Effective People*, Covey provides a framework I believe is relevant to knowledge workers, even if a bit dense and convoluted. Though I remain unconvinced by some of his arguments, such as his "5 ages of civilization"—from hunter/gatherer, agricultural, industrial, information/knowledge worker, to wisdom—which makes it sound as if there was no wisdom prior to modern times (what about Aristotle, Adam Smith, etc.?), Covey does a superb job focusing on doing the right things (effectiveness) rather than doing things right (efficiency). He also calls on existing leaders to begin treating their people like the knowledge workers they are, in order to achieve greatness.

Christopher L. Culp and William A. Niskanen, eds., *Corporate Aftershock*; and William A. Niskanen, ed., *After Enron*. Without doubt, these are the best books written so far on why Enron happened and the public policy implications for this and other accounting scandals. One of the editors, William Niskanen, is a former acting chairman of President Reagan's Council of Economic advisers and has been chairman of the Cato Institute since 1985. Both books dissect the failures leading up to Enron, from its board (which complied with all elements of the Sarbanes-Oxley Act) to internal and external auditors, attorneys, bankers, credit rating agencies, stock analysts, the business press, and, most egregious, the Securities and Exchange Commission—the watchdog that didn't bark. The latter book especially is the only one I've read that offers meaningful ideas on accounting and auditing reforms, such as the innovative idea of having the stock exchanges select which accounting standards its listed companies should be required to follow, as well as paying the auditors itself in order to remove the ultimate conflict that exists between auditors and their clients—the fact that they are being paid by the very companies they are hired to audit. This would force competition into the promulgation of accounting standards as different exchanges would select different standards, a salutary idea. Both books are very deep, grounded in solid economic theory, and, unfortunately—but not surprisingly—I've never seen anyone in the mainstream accounting press mention any of the ideas they contain. For true accounting and auditing reform, we must look to the think tanks, not the universities, government, or the regulatory sector. These books prove, beyond doubt, that think tanks are the modern-day "idea brokers" in the arena of public policy and have definitively eclipsed the universities as the ultimate intellectual institutions.

Dale Dauten, *The Gifted Boss*. Another book that will challenge you on many different levels, helping any company with what it needs to do to attract and inspire great people.

Thomas H. Davenport, *Thinking for a Living*; and Thomas H. Davenport and Laurence Prusak, *Working Knowledge*. We are going to need more books like this, and more thinkers like Davenport and Prusak, if we are going to keep alive Peter Drucker's legacy of increasing the effectiveness of knowledge workers. The fact that there are so many disagreements over the definition of a knowledge worker, their optimal working environment, and how to manage them, among other points of contention, vivifies how much work is left to be done.

David W. DeLong, *Lost Knowledge*. An excellent examination of how, in the coming years, companies stand to lose an enormous amount of knowledge as workers retire, providing many examples of how organizations can capture some of this at-risk knowledge. DeLong thinks the distinction between explicit and tacit is too general to be useful, so he provides four categories instead—implicit rule-based knowledge, implicit know-how, tacit knowledge, and deep tacit knowledge. I think these are a distinction without a difference, so I stayed with the simpler tacit/explicit definitions in deference to Occam's razor.

Peter F. Drucker. Drucker is one of the truly serious thinkers the management consultant industry can point to with justifiable pride. Read anything and everything by Drucker; for aficionados, his autobiography, *Adventures of a Bystander*, is essential. Even though Drucker passed away November 11, 2005, at age 95, it does not mark the beginning of the end, but the end of the beginning, since he has left such a rich legacy. It is too bad the Nobel Prize is not given posthumously, since he certainly deserved one. Along with the economics profession, Drucker alone is responsible for introducing—and being among the first to recognize—the knowledge worker and economy to the business world. For excellent one-book summaries of his life's work, see *The World According to Peter Drucker*, by Jack Beaty; *Peter Drucker: Shaping the Managerial Mind*, by John E. Flaherty; and *The Definitive Drucker*, by Elizabeth Haas Edersheim.

Richard Florida, *The Rise of the Creative Class*; and *The Flight of the Creative Class*. Florida is another thinker contributing to the knowledge worker topic, though he labels it the creative class. While I have serious doubts about some of his proposals with respect to government "investing" in furthering creativity, his books are thought-provoking expositions of this important sector of the workforce, providing a global perspective on the coming competition for this type of talent.

Milton Friedman and Rose Friedman, *Free to Choose*; and "The Social Responsibility of Business Is to Increase Its Profits." Milton and Rose Friedman are each eminent economists, with this book and article being among their classics, and a must-read for anyone who wants an understanding of how free markets work. Milton passed away November 16, 2006, but his ideas live on. You can watch his *Free to Choose* PBS series (the original from the 1980s as well as the updated version from the 1990s, at www.ideachannel.tv).

Francis Fukuyama, *Trust*. Like Peter Bernstein's historical tour of risk, Fukuyama does the same for trust, a virtue he believes is an economic factor of production. Well written and highly recommended, especially if you have an affinity for history. Combine trust with Adam Smith's "invisible hand," and you have the "invisible handshake," the moral and ethical foundation of free markets.

David A. Garvin, *Learning in Action*. An excellent book for creating a learning organization. Garvin makes clear that "intelligence gathering is aimed at the present; experiential learning is aimed at the past; and experimentation is aimed at the future"—present, past, and future—and how to put it all together effectively. Includes many examples, along with Garvin's lively writing, a rarity, especially compared to other books on this topic.

George Gilder, *Recapturing the Spirit of Enterprise* and *Wealth and Poverty*. In my opinion, Gilder is the best writer and thinker on economics, sociology, technology, and entrepreneurship that you will find. I discovered his work, *Wealth and Poverty*, in 1981, and it forever altered my vision of the way the world works (thanks dad!). His thinking greatly influenced the Reagan administration, and was echoed in Reagan's Moscow State University speech. These two books are his classics, but he has written many others. If you read only two books from this entire list, read anything by Gilder—twice. Gilder is a senior fellow at Seattle's Discovery Institute (www.discovery.org); he blogs at http://blog.gildertech.com.

Robert W. Hahn and Paul C. Tetlock, eds., *Information Markets*. This book is from the American Enterprise Institute and the Brookings Institute Joint Center for Regulatory Studies, two think tanks that have teamed up to study alternatives to regulatory policy. This book is a compendium of essays on information markets, as discussed in Chapter 14 on accounting model reform. The book explains how these markets can be constructed and maintained to reduce bias, demonstrating just how much we have learned about the usefulness of these markets. Some of the more popular information markets are examined, such as the Iowa Election Markets (www.biz.uiowa.edu/iem), which has an excellent track record in predicting political campaigns, as well as other uses for which this innovative tool could be used, such as weather forecasts, economic indicators, international relationships, and terrorism, to name just a few. For a list of active event markets and more information visit www.aei-brookings.org/policyfutures.

Charles Handy, *Myself and Other More Important Matters*. Charles Handy is the United Kingdom's Peter Drucker. This is his autobiography, not only splendidly written but parts of it are deep and profound. I particularly enjoyed his "portfolio life" metaphor for today's knowledge worker along with his idea of studying a theatrical program to understand how knowledge workers should not be managed, merely directed. A fantastic read from an innovative management thinker.

Suzanne S. Harrison and Patrick H. Sullivan Sr., *Einstein in the Boardroom*. This book contains many resources and examples of companies successfully leveraging their "I-Stuff," an unfortunate, trivial moniker, which is all right since the authors don't much care for it either. The authors are attempting to expand the concept of intellectual capital beyond the boundaries of legal definitions (intellectual property), while also subscribing to "if you can't measure it, you can't manage it," which is nonsense on stilts, as I pointed out in *Measure What Matters to Customers*.

That said, the book is still quite valuable, and has a good discussion of how the accounting profession is trying to reform its model, even though it does not reach the same conclusions about the obsolescence of the accounting model because it is not a theory, as I explain in Chapter 14.

H. Thomas Johnson, "Reflections of a Recovering Management Accountant"; and *Profit Beyond Measure*. The first is an excellent paper Johnson delivered that especially resonated with me since I, too, consider myself a recovering accountant. The second is the book that is Johnson's study of the legendary Toyota (and Scania) production process, all done without a standard cost accounting system, as discussed in the first two books of the Intellectual Capitalism Series. I believe both of these works are seminal, and will further the debate between managing by results versus managing by means, the former approach being embodied by the Balance Scorecard, while the latter is more akin to the Toyota Production System.

John Kay, *Foundations of Corporate Success*; *Culture and Prosperity*; *Everlasting Light Bulbs*; and *The Hare & the Tortoise*. Kay is one of Britain's leading economists, currently a visiting professor at the London School of Economics. He's quite adept at explaining economic theory and how it applies to real-life business situations. The first two books are not easy reads, but worth the effort to understand how economic theory and business really are complements, not to mention how nations create wealth. The latter two books are compilations of articles that contain maximum wisdom in a minimum of words. You can learn more about Kay at www.johnkay.com.

Rabbi Daniel Lapin, *Thou Shall Prosper*. No matter which religious faith you maintain, or even if you don't have one, everyone needs a rabbi ("teacher" in Hebrew). I'm proud to say Daniel Lapin is my rabbi, especially after listening to his radio show, and certainly after reading this book. Rabbi Lapin is the founder and director of Toward Tradition (www.towardtradition.org). This is an incredibly important work, offering a learned, cogent, entertaining, and exceptionally well-written moral defense of capitalism. That's no small feat, since capitalism works better in practice than it sounds in theory. Lapin sincerely hopes you want to make more money, since "if you are living on a park bench, panhandling passersby and feeling quite content with your life, you are unlikely to be motivated to do anything for me." There is so much wisdom in this book, it is impossible for me to do it justice in a short review. It is one of the best books I've read on this topic in years, establishing Lapin as a serious contributor along with Gilder, Novak, Hayek, and the other writers mentioned herein. Well done, Rabbi Lapin. I'm proud to have you as my rabbi (and I'm not even Jewish).

Richard Layard, *Happiness*. Layard is an economist and, since 2000, a member of the House of Lords, who does not believe that happiness correlates to income. If you want to explore economists' attempts to measure happiness and innovative public policy proposals for promoting it, this is an excellent resource. While I have severe misgivings of some of Layard's policy prescriptions—they will strike lovers of liberty as redolent of the nanny state—his writing is cogent, learned, and informative.

Matthew May, *The Elegant Solution*. If you want to delve into the secrets of Toyota's incredible success, this is the book. May is senior adviser to the University of Toyota, so he is well qualified to take you on an insider's journey through the DNA of this incredible company. Highly recommended.

John Micklethwait and Adrian Wooldridge, *The Witch Doctors*. This piercing work—by two editors from *The Economist*—gave voice to the back-lash against the $100 billion-plus profession known as "consulting." Although the authors bestow far too much power on the consultants in altering the course of life, referring to them as "the unacknowledged legislators of mankind," their four defects of the "witch doctors" of our age are fatally accurate. The profession has yet to refute success-fully the charges against it, so eloquently laid out in this book. For all those who have suffered through many a poorly written business book, Micklethwait and Wooldridge offer a refreshing alternative.

Richard Miniter, *The Myth of Market Share*. This little book makes a simple, but important, claim: Companies that pursue market share rather than profits hurt shareholders. A great read, which also provides the historical context for the term *market share*.

Henry Mintzberg, *Mintzberg on Management* and *Managers Not MBAs*. Mintzberg is Cleghorn professor of management studies at McGill University in Montreal, Canada. If you ever thought our business education—especially the MBA—is dysfunctional, you will find Mintz-berg's work compelling. The second work is especially relevant, and Mintzberg, like Peter Drucker and Clayton Christensen, is another man-agement thinker who understands the importance of theory.

Joel Mokyr, *The Gifts of Athena*. Mokyr is a professor of arts and sciences, and economics and history, at Northwestern University; as you would expect, this book is highly academic. While it is not meant to be an explanation of how knowledge is leveraged to create wealth, it does explain the historical origins of the knowledge economy, which, of course, is not a new phenomenon. For those craving a more thorough history of this fascinating topic, this is an excellent book.

Nikos Mourkogiannis, *Purpose*. My VeraSage colleague, Tim Williams, has enhanced my knowledge of the importance of purpose in business. Mourkogiannis has done the same. I especially like how he discusses purpose as more important than strategy, and how business is really about ideas and worldviews, not merely competitive positioning. An excellent book, highly recommended.

Charles Murray, *Human Accomplishment*. Murray, a senior fellow at the American Enterprise Institute, studied outstanding human accomplish-ment from 800 B.C. to 1950, and concludes that we stand on the shoul-ders of 4,002 individuals who invented, created, or otherwise innovated all human progress in the sciences (including technology), philosophy, music, visual arts, and literature. What is astonishing about these 4,002 individuals is the mean age at the time of their contribution was 40. This book proves there is, indeed, such a thing as a free lunch. A good companion read is Benjamin Jones, "Age and Great Invention." Available at http://www.kellogg.northwestern.edu/faculty/jones-ben/htm/Research.htm.

Richard John Neuhaus, *Doing Well and Doing Good*. An excellent book, exploring the moral foundations of work, enterprise, and profits, as well as the late Pope John Paul's encyclical of May 1, 1991, *Centesimus Annus(The Hundredth Year)* as discussed in Chapter 15. Neuhaus is a theologian and editor of the religious magazine *First Things*.

Michael Novak, *The Catholic Ethic and the Spirit of Capitalism*; *Business as a Calling*; *On Cultivating Liberty*; and *The Universal Hunger for Liberty*. Four exceptional books from one of the most thoughtful and gifted writers of our times, also a theologian and senior fellow at the American Enterprise Institute. Novak makes a profound argument for why business is a serious moral enterprise. Required reading for anyone interested in morality, ethics, and enterprise. For more information on Novak, visit www.michaelnovak.net.

Eugene O'Kelly, *Chasing Daylight*. This may seem like a peculiar book to suggest, but I found it profound. I knew the author; he was a partner in the same office I was at Peat, Marwick, Mitchell (now KPMG) in the mid-1980s. In the last week of May 2005, at the age of 53, he was told he had three months to live. When he consulted another specialist on how long he had, the doctor replied: "You're not a statistic." What is fascinating is how O'Kelly, who went on to become CEO of KPMG, the international accounting firm and one of the Big Four, changed his perspective on evaluating people from competency, proficiency, and quality, to the *energy* that someone puts into a task. He admits he could have limited his office schedule, spent more time with his family, and probably have been *more* focused and creative at work, and gotten more done. In other words, he confused being busy with being effective. This is especially relevant to increasing the effectiveness of knowledge workers, and I hope we have the wisdom to learn from it—and practice it—without having to wait for a fatal diagnosis.

P. J. O'Rourke, *On the Wealth of Nations*. O'Rourke is the Cato Institute's Mencken research fellow and a gifted humorist. This is P. J.'s attempt to explain Adam Smith's *The Wealth of Nations* so the rest of us don't have to read it ourselves. An excellent summary of Smith's ideology, along with a valuable alphabetized quote dictionary from Smith's writings, and pithy statements, such as this one: "Incidentally, if the labor theory of value were true, certain children would be less worthless than they are." Highly recommended.

Annie Murphy Paul, *The Cult of Personality Testing*. A devastating critique of the personality testing industry that I found compelling, based on solid evidence and scholarly research. If you have ever taken a personality test, you know they have a tendency to reinforce what we already know about ourselves. But as Paul points out, *labeling* our personalities is not the same as *understanding* them, let alone predicting our behavior based on them. A very interesting read, especially the historical origins of some of the most famous of the test's creators—a real hodgepodge of eccentrics.

Jeffrey Pfeffer, *The Human Equation*; *The Knowing-Doing Gap*; *Hard Facts, Dangerous Half-Truths and Total Nonsense*. Pfeffer is another management thinker who understands the importance of theory, whose books contain excellent examples, including much wisdom along the way.

Daniel H. Pink, *A Whole New Mind*. Pink's general thesis is the creative and intuitive right-centered brain is going to become more dominant than the left-centered brain in the knowledge economy. He says the six senses on which knowledge worker success depends are design, story, symphony, empathy, play, and meaning. Of course, there is not much new here, and some of Pink's ideas are irritatingly simplistic. Nevertheless, it is a useful book to further our understanding of how knowledge workers differ from industrial and service workers.

Göran Roos, Stephen Pike, and Lisa Fernström, *Managing Intellectual Capital in Practice*. For those who want a very comprehensive survey of managing intellectual capital, this book qualifies. It also brings an international perspective to the topic, with many case studies of companies from around the world. One novel fact I gleaned from this erudite book was that the Balanced Scorecard idea originated in France in the 1960s as the *Tableau de Bord*, such as with the book *Des Ratios au Tableau de Bord*, by P. Lauzel and A. Cibert. If part of your job entails managing intellectual capital, this book should be in your library.

Phil Rosenzweig, *The Halo Effect*. In the spirit of *The Witch Doctors*, reviewed above, this book takes a shot across the bow of the pabulum that emanates from the faddish management consultancy industry. Rosenzweig is fearless, attacking *Built to Last*, *Good to Great*, and other books he claims may tell good stories but have little empirical evidence to support their conclusions. If you are an avid reader of business books or the business press in general, this book is essential reading to increase your sensitivity to nonsensical conclusions drawn based on looking at financial performance alone. Rosenzweig has written a valuable contribution that will help management thinkers understand the difference between a process and a result—if they heed his advice. In the meantime, I urge you to read this incredibly important book.

Paul Seabright, *The Company of Strangers*. This book is outstanding. Why is it that our ancestors, thousands of years ago, roamed around in small bands highly suspicious of any strangers they encountered, but now we walk out our front doors and disappear into a city of 10 million strangers? This seismic change has happened in a historically relative short period of time. We are so dependent on complete strangers for our everyday sustenance, and in some cases our very existence, we no longer are even cognizant of it—a situation that would baffle our ancestors. Seabright is an economist who has that rare talent of also being an engaging writer. If you want to deepen your understanding of the salutary effects of Adam Smith's invisible hand, while enjoying a great historical journey, I highly recommend this book.

Ricardo Semler, *Maverick* and *The Seven-Day Weekend*. Since I implored you in Chapter 15 to read these books, I won't add anything else here, except to reiterate a strong desire that you suspend everything you think you know about running an organization and read these two books, especially the latter. Please. The present owes it to the future.

Adam Smith, *The Theory of Moral Sentiments* (1759) and *An Inquiry into the Nature and Causes of the Wealth of Nations* (1776). These are Smith's major books, which are the basis for the classical economic view of markets. Smith is wrongly attributed with saying—or making the case that—greed is good; he never said or implied any such thing. He believed in a system of natural liberty, operating under the guidance of an "invisible hand." For an excellent summary of Smith's thinking, in the genre of an academic novel, see *Saving Adam Smith*, by Jonathan B. Wight, a well-written, innovative work of economic history. The Liberty Fund has an excellent electronic library, the Library of Economics and Liberty, containing each of Smith's works (and many other classics), which you can search by topic, keyword, phrase, and so forth, at www.econlib.org. Also, visit www.adamsmith.org.

Thomas Sowell. Since Thomas Sowell is one of the nation's leading economic writers and scholastic thinkers, *all* of his books are worth reading. One reviewer wrote that reading Thomas Sowell was like chewing on nails, since his work is so powerfully logical, not to mention that Sowell is fearless in reaching conclusions that are not politically correct, or at all intuitive. Friedrich Hayek in a 1985 interview said of Sowell: "He's a genius." Sowell's *Knowledge and Decisions* would be the most directly relevant to intellectual capital—it was inspired by the paper Hayek wrote in 1945, "The Use of Knowledge in Society"—and Sowell considers it his finest book. For those interested in exploring the topic of Chapter 14 (knowledge versus beliefs) in greater depth, his *A Conflict of Visions* is just exceptional. How can people of good intentions hold two opposite beliefs of the world? As Sowell writes, "Conflicts of interests dominate the short run, but conflicts of visions dominate history." A book that, again, will change how you view the world, or at the least help you understand how others do. Sowell is the Rose and Milton Friedman senior fellow on public policy at the Hoover Institution, Stanford University. You can learn more about Thomas Sowell at www.tsowell.com.

Thomas A. Stewart, *Intellectual Capital* and *The Wealth of Knowledge*. Probably the two best books written on intellectual capital, since Stewart is such an excellent writer on what can be a very dry topic. He's now editor of *Harvard Business Review*, but began his passionate study of intellectual capital as a *Fortune* writer. Required reading.

Gordon R. Sullivan, *Hope Is Not a Method*. Sullivan was chief of staff of the Army from 1991 to 1995, and was largely responsible for disseminating the After Action Review throughout the entire ranks to increase effectiveness and learning. It is unusual to read a business book by a military leader, but well worth it, since he peppers his topics with fascinating military historical stories. Highly recommended.

Karl Erik Sveiby, *The New Organizational Wealth*. Sveiby, one of the leading thinkers in the intellectual capital movement, was the first (in 1989) to propose the framework of separating intellectual capital into its three components of human, structural, and social. This work is a profound, yet very accessible and easily written, exploration of the importance of intellectual capital. Highly recommended. You can learn more about Sveiby at www.sveiby.com.

William C. Taylor and Polly LaBarre, *Mavericks and Work*. Written by editors at *Fast Company*, this is a breezy book packed with many examples of some of the most progressive companies, especially relevant to knowledge workers. It also contains many resources you will want to explore in greater depth.

Richard S. Tedlow, *Giants of Enterprise*. Fred Smith, founder of FedEx, said in an interview with *USA Today*, "There are only about six business books worth reading. For enduring lessons, read history." If that is true, then Richard Tedlow is one of the business historians who can bring those lessons to life. This work is a fascinating historical account of the lives of Andrew Carnegie, George Eastman, Henry Ford, Thomas J. Watson Sr., Charles Revson, Sam Walton, and Robert Noyce. A great read from a great writer.

Alvin Toffler and Heidi Toffler, *Revolutionary Wealth*. You are probably familiar with the Tofflers from *Future Shock* and other best-sellers they have written over the decades. As usual, Toffler makes you think about the world around you in new ways, pointing out interesting trends along the way. This book, though long, is an excellent survey of how wealth is now created in the knowledge economy.

Linus Torvalds and David Diamond, *Just for Fun*. Linus, of course, is the creator of the open source (not free!) Linux operating system. Reading this book restores one's faith in the free marketplace, where people get together to change the world the rest of us live in. Linus comes across as just your average techno-nerd, but as with most geniuses, he had a burning desire to achieve something great. He explains why humans do the things they do based on three instincts: survival; your place in the social order; and entertainment. I would add liberty to that list, but there can be no doubt his list has some wisdom. This is a great book, a better story, and an illustration of how knowledge is a nonrival asset that can be used by many people at the same time without diminishing it, creating untold wealth in the process. Despite Bill Gates's and Microsoft's protestations to the contrary, the open source movement is far more consistent with capitalism—since it is a bottom-up revolution—than the traditional proprietary, closed-looped R&D labs of yesterday.

David Warsh, *Knowledge and the Wealth of Nations*. The epigraph to Warsh's book says it all: "The construction of a model, or of any theory for that matter (or the writing of a novel, a short story or a play) consists of snatching from the enormous and complex mass of facts called reality a few simple, easily-managed key points which, when put together in some cunning way, become for certain purposes a substitute for reality itself" (Evsey Domar, *Essays in the Theory of Economic Growth*). This is the story of "new growth theory" in economics, led by Paul Romer, whom we met in Chapter 7. An excellent survey of this exciting new field, and highly recommended for those who want to enhance their economic education of the power of ideas and knowledge to better the world.

Robert A. Watson and Ben Brown, *The Most Effective Organization in the U.S.* Peter Drucker said, "The Salvation Army is by far the most effective organization in the U.S. No one even comes close to it with respect to clarity of mission, ability to innovate, measurable results, dedication, and putting money to maximum use." This book, by the former national commander and 44-year veteran, is the story of how it earned Drucker's admiration. There are untold lessons in this book for inspiring knowledge workers to be their best. As Drucker taught us so well, the nonprofit sector has an enormous amount to teach the for-profit sector about purpose, dedication, and meaning. Everyone needs to read this exceptional book.

Ben J. Wattenberg, *Fewer*. Demography may not be destiny, but it is still important to understand how it will affect all of our futures. No one does this with greater ease than Ben Wattenberg, a senior fellow at the American Enterprise Institute. Smashing the conventional wisdom of a rising and unsustainable world population, Wattenberg proves—utilizing and interpreting the United Nation's population statistics, recognized to be the best in the world—the population is actually shrinking. What are the ramifications of this? Well, we don't know for sure because we don't have a model for it. But Wattenberg's commentary seems sane and reasoned, and worthwhile reading for anyone interested in the future landscape of the world. To access the United Nations' population statistics, visit www.unpopulation.org.

David Whyte. *Crossing the Unknown Sea*. Another unusual book to include, especially since Whyte describes himself as a corporate poet. Yet what he has to say about work is especially relevant to knowledge workers, hence I believe worth reading. He is also a terrific writer.

Lin Yutang. *The Importance of Living*. If you enjoyed reading the quote from Yutang in the first part of Chapter 15, you will thoroughly enjoy this classic, a far cry from the self-help books so ubiquitous today. Superbly written and an enchanting read.

ADDITIONAL RESOURCES

To make it easier for you to find additional online resources on topics not already specifically cited in the book, this list is sorted by chapter (though not all chapters have additional resources). For the books cited in each chapter, see the bibliography and the suggested reading list for more information. An easily accessible starting source for all topics can usually be found by searching on www.wikipedia.org, which also contains links and additional resources.

Chapter 1: Mind over Materialism
For more information on Adam Smith, visit www.adamsmith.org.
For Smith's and Frederic Bastiat's books online, visit the Library of Economics and Liberty at www.econlib.org.
Chapter 2: Mind Over Marxism
More information on Karl Marx, including his writings, is available at www.marxists.org.
For those interested in the marginalist revolution, including modern-day Austrian economists who are carrying on the tradition, visit www.marginalrevolution.com.
Chapter 3: The Economy in Mind
For a copy of Ronald Reagan's speech at Moscow State University, visit www.reagan.utexas.edu/archives/speeches/1988/053188b.htm.
For more information on Ronald Reagan, visit his presidential library web site, at www.reaganlibrary.com/welcome.asp.
For information on all presidential libraries, visit http://archives.gov/presidential-libraries/index.html.
Chapter 4: A Flawed Theory—The Old Business Equation; and Chapter 5: A Better Theory—The New Business Equation
VeraSage Institute, the author's think tank, is dedicated to promoting the new business equation, especially in professional knowledge firms, at www.verasage.com.
Karl Sveiby, who proposed the three types of intellectual capital—human, structural, and social—can be found at www.sveiby.com.
Chapter 6: The Scarcest Resource of All

Thomas Sowell can be found at www.tsowell.com.

For information on Friedrich Hayek, visit www.hayekcenter.org/friedrich-hayek/hayek.html.

Chapter 7: Ideas Have Consequences

Economist Paul Romer's selected writings can be found at www.stanford.edu/promer/index.html.

Charles Murray can be found at www.aei.org/scholars/scholarID.43/scholar.asp.

Chapter 9: Human Capitalism

Nobel Prize–winning economist Gary S. Becker's home page is http://home.uchicago.edu/gbecker .

Becker blogs, along with Judge Richard Posner, at www.becker-posner-blog.com.

Many countries now recognize the importance of the knowledge economy with iniatitives meant to attract knowledge workers and organizations, such as:

The Scottish National Intellectual Assets Centre (the IA Centre), www.ia-centre.org.uk

Arabian Knowledge Economy Association, www.akea-me.com/akea.asp

IDA Ireland, www.idaireland.com

EDB Singapore, www.sedb.com

Chapter 11: Developing and Inspiring Knowledge Workers

For more information on Frederick Winslow Taylor, with links to his writings, see http://en.wikipedia.org/wiki/Frederick_Winslow_Taylor.

For more on Frank Gilbreth, see: http://gilbrethnetwork.tripod.com/front.html.

To download a copy of Henry Ford's autobiography, *My Life and Work*, see www.gutenberg.org/etext/7213.

Chapter 12: Structural Capital: If Only We Knew What We Know

For Ben Wattenberg, visit www.aei.org/scholars/scholarID.59,filter.all/scholar.asp.

For the United Nations' population statistics, see www.unpopulation.org.

Visit the U.S. Library of Congress's American Folklife Center, at www.storycorps.net.

For Paul O'Byrne and Paul Kennedy, of O'Byrne & Kennedy in Great Britain, visit www.obk.co.uk.

For information on After Action Reviews from the U.S. Army, see http://call.army.mil.

Chapter 13: Social Capital: No Man Is an Island

For more information on U.K. consultancy Interbrand that values the world's leading brands, visit www.interbrand.com.

For more information on Rabbi Daniel Lapin, see www.towardtradition.org.

For the author's series, "Earning My Mouse Ears," Parts 1–3, visit www.verasage.com.

For more information on O'Byrne & Kennedy's GOBS MBA programs, visit www.obk.co.uk.

For the Josephson Institute on Ethics, see www.josephsoninstitute.com.

For an excellent example of the open source movement applied to an application other than software, visit http://librivox.org, where you can download amateur recordings of books in the public domain.

Chapter 14: Knowledge versus Beliefs

For more information on George Gilder, see www.discovery.org, www. gildertech.com, and his blog, http://blog.gildertech.com.

For the Enhanced Business Reporting Consortium, visit www.ebr360.org.

For the New Paradigm Initiative, see http://npi.valuemeasurement.net.

For more information on information markets, visit The American Enterprise Institute–Brookings Institution Joint Center, at www.aei-brookings.org/ policyfutures, which contains an active list of information markets, research, articles, links to software for building them, and other information.

For the Hollywood Stock exchange, using pretend money, see www.hsx.com.

Chapter 15: Purpose

See the World Database on Happiness, at http://www2.eur.nl/fsw/research/ veenhoven/Pub1980s/84-wdh.htm.

For Richard Layard's web site, with information and research on the science of happiness, see http://cep.lse.ac.uk/layard.

A great web site for budding entrepreneurs, a partnership between Walt Disney Company and the charitable Ewing Marion Kauffman Foundation, is www.hotshotbusiness.com.

See Virginia Postrel's blog at www.dynamist.com/weblog.

See George Gilder's speech to the Vatican, June 1, 1997, "The Soul of Silicon," one of the most profound pieces of writing on the morality of markets, at www.discovery.org/scripts/viewDB/index.php?command = view&id = 230.

For Pope John Paul II's 1991 encyclical *Centesimus Annus* ("The Hundredth Year") wherin the Pope writes about the morality of profits, see www.vatican.va/edocs/ENG0214/_INDEX.HTM.

For the Heritage Foundation's Index of Economic Freedom, visit www. heritage.org/index.

The Economic Freedom Network's web site can be found at www. freetheworld.com.

INDEX

Absorptive capacity, 174
Accountability of knowledge workers, 130, 156, 161, 165
Accounting principles
  goodwill, 273
  human capital, 108, 109
  and knowledge assets, 103
  origin of, 270, 271
  reform, 277–283
  relevance of, 66, 268–277, 279
  tangible and intangible assets, 103
  trade deficits and surpluses, 8
  and valuing intellectual capital, 48, 49
After Action Review (AAR), 121, 171, 202–211
Alliances, 221, 230–232
Alumni as part of social capital, 221, 233, 234
Amazon.com, 223, 226, 245
American Airlines, 49, 199, 200
Ash, Mary Kay, 220
"Ash heap of history," 32, 45, 55
Autarky, 3
Authentication process, 76, 77, 82, 91, 115, 266

Baker's Law, 61, 182, 223
Balance of trade, 3, 6–13
Balanced Scorecard, 275, 276
Barter economy, 3, 6
Bastiat, Frédéric, 9, 13, 21
Becker, Gary S., 107, 108, 173, 174, 189, 218, 219, 258
Before Action Review (BAR), 208, 211
Behavior, 15, 219, 220, 286
Beliefs, 169, 260, 261, 266, 267, 299
Benchmarking, 59, 84, 266
Bill and Melinda Gates Foundation, 288

Blogs, 180, 193, 194, 210, 212, 226, 268
Böhm-Bawerk's Law, 70
Brands, 80, 221, 224, 225
Brin, Sergey, 135, 272
Bullion as wealth, 1, 2, 5, 6
Business equation
  new business equation, 59–69, 72, 301
  traditional model of enterprise, 52–57, 72
Business organizations as interdependent system, 64, 65
Business purpose, 55, 65–67, 222, 285

Capacity, 53
Capital, origin of term, 110, 111
Capital goods (producer goods), 24
Capitalism, 16, 17, 45, 66, 91, 94, 144, 213, 214, 266
Carnegie, Andrew, 109, 146, 187, 287, 288
Change, 26, 27, 60, 64, 266, 267, 296, 297. *See also* Creative destruction
Chief knowledge officer (CKO), 118, 119
Chrysalis metaphor, 35, 44, 45
Classical model of competition, 15, 16
Coca-Cola, 67, 104, 122, 201, 224, 225, 271
Coincident indicators, 274
Communism, 13, 19, 20, 32, 44, 45, 216, 217
Communities of practice (CoPs), 192–199
Competition, 15, 16, 262, 263
Competitive advantage, 56, 137
Concierge Service Model, 254–257
Conscience, 15, 16
Consultants, 85, 89, 143, 266
Consumer goods, 23

Consumerism, 66
Consumers as determiner of value, 22
Corporate social responsibility, 230
Corporate universities, 174, 221, 236–243
Correlation and causation, 86
Cost of production theory of value, 18
Cost-plus pricing, 52, 53, 55, 267, 299
Creative destruction, 31, 45, 91, 92, 264–265, 296
Creativity, 31, 45, 97
Culture, 217, 221, 251
Customers. *See also* Social capital
  Baker's Law, 61, 182, 223
  and business purpose, 65, 66
  creating value for, 65, 67, 129
  creating wealth for, 55, 65, 154
  customer relations and employee relations, 141
  as part of social capital, 221–224
  selecting, 61

Danish Financial Statement Act, 278, 279
Data, 81, 82
"Deathbed test," 300, 301
Decision making, 80, 86, 87, 155, 226
Demographics, 188–190
Discretionary effort, 141
Disney. *See* Walt Disney Company
Disney, Walt, 2, 54, 104, 162, 237, 290, 291, 294, 301
Disney Institute, 180
Disney University, 237, 239, 290
Double-entry bookkeeping, 3, 110, 270, 274
Drucker, Peter, 30, 54, 64–66, 71, 73, 82, 93, 99, 101, 103, 111, 117, 125, 127, 132, 133, 139, 143, 148, 151–153, 164, 166, 174, 222, 237, 246, 252, 262, 268, 269, 273, 290

Economic growth, 52, 92–97, 114, 115, 264
Economic rewards, 132
Economic self-sufficiency, 3

Education, 30, 95, 111–117, 173–177, 221, 236–243
Effectiveness
  versus efficiency, 62, 63, 68, 155, 156, 212
  improving, 59
  IQ as predictor of, 168
  knowledge workers, framework for, 151–156
  and removal of tasks, 165, 166
  and Scientific Management, 144, 145
Efficacious, 68
Efficiency, 53, 54, 62, 68, 123, 149, 150, 154–156, 212, 267
Emotional intelligence, 168
Emotions, 62, 63, 134, 135, 155
Enhanced Business Reporting Model, 278
Entrepreneurs, 95, 264, 267, 269, 282, 291
Epistemology, 75, 77
Ethical capital, 221, 251–254
Ethical egoism, 215, 216
Ethnography, 158, 159
European Union (EU), 114, 116, 117
Executives, 132
External stakeholders, 221, 229, 230

Faith in the future, 36, 40, 45, 261, 262, 283, 284
Falsification principle, 47, 83, 86, 87, 90, 91, 301
FedEx, 53, 100, 140, 141, 173, 183, 228, 290, 291
Financial statements as lagging indicators, 274
Ford, Henry, 5, 145, 146, 264, 266
Franklin, Benjamin, 125, 301
Free trade, 7, 8
Friedman, Milton, 70, 82, 90, 217, 230, 283

Gates, Bill, 44, 54, 95, 114, 130, 246, 288, 290
General Electric (GE), 56, 174, 237

General Motors, 163, 228

Generally accepted accounting principles (GAAP), 48, 49, 270, 271, 280, 282

Germ theory, 88, 266

G.I. Bill of Rights, 30, 111, 112

Gilbreth, Frank, 146–148

Gilder, George, 1, 264, 268, 296

Gold. *See* Bullion as wealth

Goldcorp Challenge, 249, 250

Goodwill, 273

Google, 48, 49, 100, 135, 171, 226, 245, 246, 272, 273

Gorbachev, Mikahil, 27, 29, 32, 45

Gresham's law, 61

Growth opportunities, 131

Hansei, 208

Happiness, 286–287

Hayek, Friedrich A., 76, 78, 79, 81, 90

Heuristics, 80

Hewlett Packard, 50, 229, 290, 293

"Higher order" goods, 24

Hiring choices, 134, 182–184

Human capital. *See also* Knowledge workers

as category of intellectual capital, 50, 61, 62

competition for, 117

defined, 218

development of as social process, 216

and education. *See* Education

and emotions, 62, 63, 123, 155

and human traits, 123

importance of, 109, 110

and intellectual capital, 48

"Karl Marx's revenge," 122

and meaning of capital, 110, 111

meaningful work, need for, 122, 123

measuring, 112–117

negative, 51, 182–184

origin of term, 107, 108

ownership of, 104

and performance capacity of organization, 122

as source of wealth, 31, 46, 108

and spirit of enterprise, 115, 116

theory of, 108

and treatment of people, 122

Human spirit, 48, 49, 123, 134

Ideas, 75–77, 82, 91–97

Identity statements, 274

Imagineering, 97, 104, 105

"Impartial Spectator," 16

Industrial Age, 29, 30

Industrial Revolution, 29, 30, 44, 114, 122, 123

Industry associations, 221, 232, 233

Information, 80–82

Information age, 80, 81

Information Era, 44

Information markets, 281, 282

Innocentive, 247

Innovation, 69, 94, 96–97, 99, 172, 264, 276

Inputs and outputs, 146, 148–150, 153, 159, 171, 175, 182

Intangible assets, 49, 103, 104

Intellectual capital economy, 45

Intellectual capital (IC). *See also* Human capital; Social capital; Structural capital

characteristics of, 99–104

components of, 49–51, 61

and dealing with people, 134, 135

defining, 104, 105

and destruction of wealth, 259

economy, 44

and future value creation, 278

individual development of, 295, 296

and intellectual property, 103

leveraging, 48, 51, 199–201, 212

negative, 51, 52, 260

ownership of, 104

and problems with GAAP, 270–272

as source of wealth, 44, 48–50, 301

and tangible and intangible assets, 104

as theory, 279

Intellectual property, 103

Intelligence quotient (IQ), 168, 169

Interdependent nature of business, 64, 65
Intrinsic rewards, 131, 135, 136
Invention, 102
"Invisible hand," 16, 17
Ireland, 116–117

Jefferson, Thomas, 92, 102, 172
Jobs, 130, 131
Jobs, Steve, 49, 95, 114, 115, 160, 184,
    244
Johnson & Johnson, 253, 292
Joint venture partners and alliances as
    part of social capital, 221, 230–232
Judgment, 151, 152, 155, 161

Keynes, John Maynard, 17, 19, 20, 26,
    253
Knowledge, 75–80
  authentication process, 82
  and bad ideas, 60
  and beliefs, 260, 261, 266, 267
  capturing, 121
  characteristics of, 82, 102
  and creation of value, 104
  data and information distinguished, 81,
    82
  explicit, 117–122, 197–199
  and formal education, 114
  and human capital, 109
  ideas compared, 75, 76, 91
  importance of, 100, 101
  leveraging, 50
  loss of, 187–191
  as nonrival asset, 50, 101–102
  purpose of, 82
  sharing, 50
  specific knowledge, 76, 77, 105
  tacit, 80, 82, 91, 117–122, 192
  transfer of, 82, 120, 121, 192–199,
    211, 212. See also After Action
    Review (AAR)
  types of, 101
  validating, criteria for, 86, 87
  velocity versus viscosity of, 195, 196
  as a verb, 100–104

Knowledge balance sheet, 279
Knowledge bank, 197–199
Knowledge companies, 50, 51, 161–166
Knowledge creep, 90
Knowledge economy, 44, 99–101
Knowledge industry, 30, 31
Knowledge management (KM), 104, 118,
    119, 121, 122, 195–197
Knowledge society, 111
Knowledge theory, 50
Knowledge work, 30, 123, 150
Knowledge workers, 30, 101, 109, 111,
    119
  accountability of, 130, 156, 161, 165
  and accounting, 125, 126
  as assets, resources, or inventory, 125,
    126, 184
  attracting, 133–137, 139, 160, 179,
    180, 185
  autonomy, 159–161
  and continuing education, 173–177
  and customer relations, 141
  effectiveness, framework for, 151–156
  emotions, 62, 63, 134, 135, 155
  and employer/employee relationship,
    131–133
  firing, 182–184
  as human capital investors, 123, 126,
    134–136, 185
  and human traits, 122, 123, 184
  loyalty, 165, 179
  and management style, 157–161
  and number of jobs, 156
  as owners of company's means of
    production, 122
  personality testing and performance
    appraisals, 166–173
  and productivity, 148–154, 157, 159,
    185
  professionals as, 157, 158
  putting workers first, 140, 141
  and removal of tasks, 165, 166
  retaining talent, 139, 140
  strengths and weaknesses, 164, 165
  and trust, 141, 142
  value of, 130–133, 136
  as volunteers, 126, 130
  and work-life balance, 178–182

Labor, specialization and division of, 3–5, 101

Labor theory of value, 17–21, 24–27, 55

Labor unions, 70, 221, 234–236

Lagging indicators, 274, 279

Lapin, Rabbi Daniel, 123, 168, 169, 225, 261

Law of comparative advantage, 18

Law of diminishing marginal utility, 21

Law of diminishing returns, 18

Law of imputation, 23, 24

Leading indicators, 210, 274

Learning, importance of, 50. *See also* Education

Lenin, Vladimir Ilyich, 143, 144

Linux operating system, 44, 245, 246, 249

Loyalty, 131, 132, 141, 165, 179, 180, 292

Management
  innovations, 96, 97
  micromanagement, 161
  origin of term, 143
  research, 84
  theory, 89
  and treatment of knowledge workers, 157–160, 164–166

Manager, use of term, 132, 133

Marginal utility, 24

Marginalist Revolution, 22–27, 55, 101

Market share, 55, 56, 223

Marketing, attracting human capital investors, 134, 135

Marketing concept, 65

Marx, Karl, 15–17, 19–22, 24, 29, 31, 45, 55, 122

Mary Kay Cosmetics, 220, 226, 293

Materialism, 1–13, 27, 31

MBNA, 227, 228

McDonald's, 174, 210, 211, 231

McKinsey Global Institute, 242, 243, 293

Menger, Carl, 22–24, 101

Mentoring, coaching, and shadowing
  and development of individual intellectual capital, 295, 296
  as means of knowledge transfer, 192, 193

Mercantilism, 1–3, 5, 6, 27, 48

Meta-inventions, 95

Metcalfe's Law, 258

Microsoft, 48, 49, 51, 207, 246, 291

Mill, John Stuart, 22, 90, 139, 286

Money, 2, 6, 48, 109

Morris, Daniel D. (Dan), 124, 157, 159, 160, 178, 180, 182, 254–256, 268

Myelin Repair Foundation, 248, 249

Napster, 244, 245

National Aeronautics and Space Administration (NASA), 187, 188

Natural resources, 1–2, 20, 92

New growth theory, 93–96, .97

New Paradigm Initiative (NPI), 278

New United Motor Manufacturing Inc., 163

NineSigma, 247, 248

Nonprofit sector, 126, 127, 140

Nonrival assets, 50, 92, 96, 101, 102, 258

Nordstrom, 154, 161, 172, 237, 289

O'Byrne, Paul, 177, 197–199, 208, 240, 268, 273

Open source and mass collaboration as part of social capital, 221, 244–251

Opportunity
  and loyalty, 131
  and work-life balance, 180–182

Opportunity cost, 24

Pareto Principle, 295

Pepsi, 67, 201

Performance appraisals, 166, 169–173

Personality tests, 166–169, 173

Peter Principle, 170

Physical assets. *See* Tangible assets

Physical fallacy, 1, 45, 46, 92, 93, 100

Pixar, 160, 239

Popper, Karl, 47, 83, 301

Population statistics, 188–190

Portfolio life concept, 178

Potty test, 113, 216

Poverty, 2
Prediction, 262, 273, 274, 279, 281, 282
Procter & Gamble (P&G), 56, 246, 247
Production, 8, 69
Productivity
    and "clean desk" requirement, 158
    inputs and outputs, 146, 148–150, 153,
        159, 171, 175, 182
    and learning, 175, 176
    measurement, 152, 153, 157
    and Scientific Management Revolution,
        143–151
Profit centers, 65, 66
Profitability
    economic profit, 77
    epistemological profit, 77
    and human spirit, 293, 294
    and market share, 55
    and new business theory, 60, 61
    profits from investment in human
        capital, 109
    and risk, 296, 297
    source of profits, 69–72
Promotions, 172, 173
Pronoun test, 129, 130
Psychological egoism, 215, 216
Purpose, 286–295

Reagan, Ronald, 27, 32, 33, 44, 45, 52,
    73, 81
    remarks at Moscow State University,
        34–43, 81
Recognition of accomplishments, 131,
    132, 171
Referral sources and networks as part of
    social capital, 221, 226–228
Reputation as part of social capital, 221,
    224, 225
Revenue and traditional business
    equation, 53, 55
Ricardo, David, 18–20, 22, 24
Risk
    categories, 71
    costs and benefits, 70, 71
    importance of, 264, 265
    and intangibles, 51

management, 263
    responses to, 69, 70
    reward for risk-taking, 172
    as source of profits, 69, 71, 72,
        262–268
    uncertainty distinguished, 262
Rival assets, 92
Romer, Paul, 93–95, 97, 99

Salvation Army, 127–129, 140, 292
Sarbanes-Oxley Act of 2002 (SOX), 280,
    281
Scalability, 49
Scarcity, 2, 19
Scientific Management Revolution,
    142–148
Scientific method, 87–89
Search costs, 82
Selection bias, 86
Self-interest, 15
Service Economy, 30
Service worker, 30, 147
Shareholder value, 67
Shareholders as part of social capital,
    221, 229, 230
Singapore, 117
Singapore Airlines, 176
Smith, Adam, 2–5, 7, 8, 15–18, 22, 29,
    48, 67, 92, 100, 101, 108, 114, 142,
    146, 150, 214, 215
Smith, Fred, 53, 54, 100, 123, 141, 290
Social capital
    as category of intellectual capital, 50,
        62
    Concierge Service Model, 254–257
    and culture, 217
    defined, 214
    elements of, 221, 258
    importance of, 213–217
    and individual preferences, 218–220
    leveraging, 221–254
    negative, 51, 52
    ownership of, 104
    and self-education, 113
Social proof principle, 219, 220
"Socially necessary labour," 21, 22

Society, stages of, 29
Solow, Robert, 94, 95, 149
Solow model of economic growth, 94, 95
Southwest Airlines, 56, 133, 134, 176, 290
Soviet Union, 45, 51, 52
Sowell, Thomas, 8, 9, 26, 75–77, 81, 83, 91–93, 105, 109, 114, 115, 264
Specialization of labor. See Labor, specialization and division of
Storytelling, 192
"Stradivarius secret," 187
Strengths and weaknesses, 164, 165, 170–172, 183
Structural capital
    as category of intellectual capital, 50, 62
    economics of, 190–192
    leveraging intellectual capital, 199–201, 212
    and loss of knowledge, 187–190
    negative, 51
    ownership of, 104
    and transfer of knowledge. See Knowledge
Subjective theory of value, 22, 25, 26, 44
Subjective well-being, 25, 286
Success, 287, 288
Sun Microsystems, 244, 246
Suppliers as part of social capital, 221, 228, 229
Supply and demand, 274, 275

Tacit knowledge. See Knowledge
Tacit workers, 156
Tangible assets, 1, 48, 49, 103, 104, 108
Taylor, Frederick Winslow, 142–148, 155, 156
"The Right Hand and the Left," 9–13, 21
Theories, 56, 57, 59, 68
    construction of, 83
    diffusion of, 88
    disproving, 83–86, 90
    as essential part of education, 85, 86
    and practical knowledge, 47, 48
    and predictions, 47, 262, 273, 274, 279

and scientific method, 88–90
    supply and demand, 274, 275
    and use of knowledge, 82
3M, 174, 290
Time-and-motion studies, 142, 146–148, 150, 155, 184
Time sheets, 160, 161
Toffler, Alvin, 29, 86, 102, 113, 216, 295
Toffler, Heidi, 29, 102
Torvalds, Linus, 44, 245, 246
Torvalds, Nil, 43, 44
Toyota, 162, 163, 173, 174, 208, 238
Trade deficits, 6–13
Training, 177
Transfer of knowledge, 82, 120, 121, 192–199, 211, 212. See also After Action Review (AAR)
Trust, 16, 17, 141, 142, 159, 161, 170, 185
Turnover, 180

Uncertainty, 70, 71, 262–268
Unions, 70, 221, 234–236
U.S. Army, After Action Reviews. See After Action Review (AAR)
Utility, 25

Value, theories of
    cost of production theory, 18
    labor theory, 17–21, 24–27, 55
    marginalism, 23–27
    subjective theory, 22, 25, 26, 44
    and utility, 25
Vendors as part of social capital, 221, 228, 229
VeraSage Institute, 124, 157, 160, 177, 178, 180, 197, 210, 254, 256
Vocation, 288–295
Voluntary labor, 113
Volunteers, 287

Wages, 109, 111, 132, 172
Wal-Mart, 56, 231, 293

Walt Disney Company, 2, 97, 100, 160,
    162, 173, 174, 289, 291, 293
War analogy, 67
Wealth
  defined, 3
  and human capital, 31, 46, 108
  intellectual capital as source of, 44,
    48–50, 301
  and knowledge economy, 100

and money, 2, 6, 48, 109
systems, 29
and tangible assets, 1, 48, 49
Wikipedia, 249
Work environment, 158, 159
Work-life balance, 178–182

Zero-sum trade, 2, 3, 7, 8, 67